Both In One Trench:
Saddam's Secret Terror Documents

ISBN: 1-4196-7866-3

ISBN-13: 9781419678660

Visit www.booksurge.com to order additional copies.

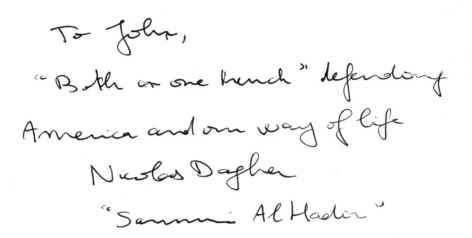

To John,

"Both in one trench" defending
America and our way of life
Nicolas Dagher
"Sammmi Al Hadin"

Both In One Trench:

Saddam's Secret
Terror Documents

Ray Robison

For our families, for the brave men and women who served and their families, especially those who gave their lives in lonely, far away places to allow others to enjoy the blessings of liberty. God bless America's warriors and their loved ones.

Special thanks to our agent Don Gastworth. Also thanks to those whose work encouraged us to keep digging for the truth: Roger Simon, Christopher Hitchens, Stephen Hayes, and the editors and talent of Fox News Channel and Fox News.com, American Thinker, and Pajamas Media.

The only thing necessary for the triumph of evil is for good men to do nothing.
—Edmund Burke

Note: Because this book is the product of a grass roots effort with limited resources the authors have not been able to provide a professionally edited manuscript at this time. It is our hope that sales of this book will allow us to increase the quality so that the best version possible will be available to the public in the future. If the reader feels a need to write us about a grammatical error please wait until after we go to editing as any errors should be caught in the editing process.

CONTENTS

"There's no question that Saddam Hussein had al-Qaeda ties."

President George Bush

Remarks by the President After Meeting with Members of the Congressional Conference Committee on Energy Legislation.

Office of the Press Secretary

September 17, 2003

www.whitehouse.gov

"The evidence now shows clearly that Saddam did not want to work with Osama bin Laden at all, much less give him weapons of mass destruction."

Former Vice President Al Gore

Saddam's al-Qaeda Connection

The Weekly Standard, Stephen F. Hayes

September 1, 2003, Volume 008, Issue 48

"Credible information indicates that Iraq and al-Qaeda have discussed safe haven and reciprocal non-aggression... Baghdad's links to terrorists will increase."

Former C.I.A. Director George Tenet

The Unknown: The C.I.A. and the Pentagon take another look at Al Qaeda and Iraq.

The New Yorker, Jeffrey Goldberg

Issue of February 10, 2003

"I believe that the 9/11 report, the early evidence, is that they're going to indicate that we didn't have the kind of terrorists links that this administration was asserting. I think that's a very, very serious finding."

Sen. John Kerry

Al Qaeda-Hussein Link Is Dismissed

Washington Post, Walter Pincus and Dana Milbank

June 17, 2004

[Saddam Hussein] "had long-established ties with al Qaeda."

Vice President Cheney

Al Qaeda-Hussein Link Is Dismissed

Washington Post, Walter Pincus and Dana Milbank

June 17, 2004

"There is evidence of exaggeration"

[of Iraq-al Qaeda links]

Sen. Carl Levin,

Saddam's al Qaeda Connection

The Weekly Standard, Stephen F. Hayes

09/01/2003, Volume 008, Issue 48

INTRODUCTION

THE CHARGES AND countercharges surrounding the Iraq War are widely known. The American left through a mostly sympathetic media has persisted in the claim that the Bush Administration led the United States of America into an unnecessary war. They claim that Saddam had no stockpiles of Weapons of Mass Destruction (WMD), nothing to do with Islamic terrorism, and thus was not a threat to the United States. In their estimation the war against Saddam was a distraction from the Global War on Terror—a concept that they also mock while relegating Islamic terrorism to an issue of law enforcement with little or no military component.

They argue that Saddam was constrained to only subjugating 25 million people to horrendous brutality while acting as a destabilizing force in the Middle East and was not worth fighting. The Democrat position is weak enough without the revelations contained here. But with this work based on documents captured in Iraq and Afghanistan and supporting media reports it can be shown that the Democrat position is a fiction from beginning to end. The documents reveal that the Saddam regime was complicit in supporting the *global Islamic jihad movement* as a whole and specifically the Taliban and al Qaeda. As such, it was a major threat to the United States and Iraq was—under Saddam and after—a frontline in the war on terror.

Democratic leaders have tried to de-legitimize the Iraq War for years. Their strategy has been somewhat successful. Since December 2003, CBS News has conducted a regular poll that includes the following question: "Looking back, do you think the United States did the right thing in taking military action against Iraq, or should the U.S. have stayed out?" Responses supporting the war in Iraq dropped from an initial sixty-three percent to forty-four percent in two and a half years. Since then, support for the Iraq war has declined even further. This decline in public approval was mirrored by a growing distrust of the Bush Administration.

The American public has been subjected to a nonstop cacophony of Democratic leaders and pundits in the media claiming the Saddam regime did not pose a genuine threat to the United States. This claim is somewhat supported by the fact that no significant WMD stocks were found in Iraq (some WMD was found but not that much). There is still reason to question at what point the regime divested itself of its WMD but Saddam didn't have it as of the start of Operation Iraqi Freedom on March 19th, 2003 as far as we can tell. Thus, the Democrats claim that the Iraq war was superfluous.

President Bush and other administration officials spoke of intelligence failures. For left-wing activists the mantra soon became, "Bush Lied, People Died." The more widespread criticism holds that the Bush administration was mistaken if not actually incompetent in its assessment of pre-war intelligence.

The reasons for war in Iraq are of paramount political and historical importance. The rest of the world may judge the United States by its' actions in Iraq for years to come. Now, for the first time, a new voice has arisen to contribute to the debate over the war against the Saddam Hussein regime. That voice comes from

Iraq's past and tells us what was happening in Iraq under Saddam. That voice is heard in the Saddam regime's internal documentation and it tells the story about the dictator's intent to expand his global sphere of influence by supporting Islamic terrorism. The voice also tells us that Saddam habitually refused to comply with his obligations under UN resolutions up until the end. Finally, the voice gives us a glimpse into Saddam's methods of manipulation to secure his power.

In 2005 a few hundred out of millions of documents that were captured in Iraq were made available to the public by the U.S. government. These documents may change the way some of the public perceives the war against Saddam Hussein and his regime. This collection of memorandums, audio tapes and video tapes provides evidence that the Saddam regime more closely resembled the image portrayed by President Bush than that portrayed by his detractors.

The rush to judgment regarding pre-war intelligence was based on a massive information gap which is now bit by bit being filled in. While there is no doubt that much of the prewar analysis concerning WMD was in error (a common risk of intelligence exploitation) the evidence provided here supports the prewar assessment that Saddam was a threat to the United States predominately because of his support to the *global Islamic jihad movement* as embodied by the Taliban and al-Qaeda.

The documents that were captured in Iraq and Afghanistan and kept from the American public in a U.S. intelligence database for years must now become part of the national (and international) debate over the wisdom and necessity of the Iraq War. They must also contribute to determining how the history of Saddam Hussein, the Iraq War and President George W. Bush will be written.

In the period leading up to the U.S. invasion of Iraq, there was widespread concern—if not a general consensus—that Iraq had failed to meet its proscribed obligations under UN resolutions to destroy its pre-Gulf War WMD stockpiles. Secretary of State Colin Powell delivered a lengthy presentation to the United Nations (UN) concerning Saddam Hussein's failure to turn over tons of WMD precursor materials. Many intelligence agencies abroad and even some UN officials strongly believed that Saddam was hiding older chemical or biological weapons that he agreed to destroy in order to end the Gulf War. Although less the subject of Bush Administration statements than is portrayed by the media the development of new large-scale military production programs including nuclear weapons was discussed.

Shortly after the toppling of the Saddam regime, the U.S. government began a program to exploit captured Iraqi documentation. The effort was led by the Iraq Survey Group (ISG—created for this purpose and others) and supported by the Defense Intelligence Agency (DIA), Federal Bureau of Investigation (FBI), Central Intelligence Agency (CIA), and the National Security Agency (NSA). The primary mission of this multi-agency effort was the search for WMD, to investigate regime links to and thereby gain intelligence on terrorists, and search for Lieutenant Commander Scott Speicher missing in action since the Gulf War.

The Iraqi insurgency began in earnest a few months after the toppling of the Saddam regime, causing intelligence officials to divert resources from exploiting historical records to support the fight. Thus while analysis of the Saddam documents was ongoing the level of effort was reduced even though the amount of captured documentation was voluminous. And while the effort was ongoing new documentation, such as jihadist propaganda stemming from the strengthening insurgency, required an even further diversion of effort. Even without an insurgency it would have taken years to analyze the tens of thousands of video and audio tapes and millions of documents that required translation.

Yet within months of the overthrow of Saddam the U.S. government began turning out report after report that made determinations regarding Saddam's pre-war activities. These reports noted U.S. intelligence mistakes. Consequently the media reported a steady stream of intelligence failures. Democratic leaders and numerous pundits claimed the Bush Administration had knowingly falsified the perception of the pre-war intelligence—and some even claimed it falsified the intelligence itself—to engender support for the war.

Some leftwing and even a few rightwing commentators began to claim President Bush "cherry-picked the intelligence." Those government reports and subsequently much of the public concluded that Saddam had no WMD and did not support Islamic terrorism thus was incapable of supplying WMD to Islamic terrorists a main concern of the administration. Lost somewhere in the discussion was the fact that the attacks of 9/11 were executed without WMD. Therefore, state sponsors of terrorism—along with the terrorists themselves—are a true danger regardless of whether those states possess WMD.

In 2004, a few notable investigative journalists began to request the release of documentation captured from Iraq. Among them were Roger Simon of the blog alliance known as *Pajamas Media* and Stephen Hayes of the conservative journal *The Weekly Standard* who perhaps led the charge to urge release of Saddam's documentation. Upon returning from Qatar where I spent a year working with the Iraq Survey Group (ISG) I first read Hayes' work and was astounded at his grasp of the situation. He quite accurately depicted the situation as millions of documents and limited resources. Hayes and others (including myself who joined the effort after completing my work with the ISG) called on the U.S. government to make the documents available to the general public for historical analysis.

My reason for urging the public release of the documents was simple. I saw video after video of atrocities committed by the Ba'athists. I read gists—summaries of the English translations of the original Arabic documents—and knew that the entire story of the Saddam regime wasn't getting out to the public. History may determine that Saddam Hussein had not retained significant WMD stockpiles but such is not the whole story of Saddam and Iraq.

The real story of Saddam Hussein is hidden in those documents. Saddam and his cronies had every reason to lie and keep secret their support to Islamic terrorism. But the authors of this book have reviewed Ba'athist documentation and found it contradictory to the claims of Democratic Party leadership, some high profile intelligence experts and Saddam Hussein.

The authors of this book have provided document translation and analysis to link several distinct documents that strongly parallel each other in content that in some cases is not available from other sources (a strong indicator of the genuineness of the documents). The authors have done their utmost to examine the validity of the documents and consider counter arguments to conclusions that are drawn here. The authors make findings but also suggest theories to answer questions raised by some of the records. Some of the theories are highly unconventional and are proposed as potential avenues for further investigation. After all, they are theories and are not final conclusions. The authors distinguish between the two, conclusion and theory in the writing because critics will invariably and inevitably take theory out of context and purport it to be a claim that has been made by the authors.

Of course document validity is crucial. Having worked with such documents while with ISG definitely gives one of this book's authors the perspective to make some determinations about the physical appearance of these documents. But we did not rely on that alone. We researched media and government sources for conflicting or supporting evidence.

Document forging activity in Iraq was played up by some media organizations in a cynical attempt to throw doubt on all the documentation while the real story of document forgery is rather (no pun intended) insignificant and isolated. Most of the fake documents were easily identified and weeded out by government analysts. And being as Iraq was a closed society in absolute tumult following the overthrow of Saddam it seems likely that most people just had more important concerns than rushing out to the wreckage of a government office in order to plant forged documents. Furthermore, it is unlikely that many Iraqi citizens had the expertise to forge the internal documents of a closed government that did not make its correspondence available to the public—a necessity because a potential forger would at the very least have to know what such a document should look like. In the end it will be up to the reader to determine for himself or herself as to whether or not the information provided here should be believed or even if it adds to the understanding of the cause for war.

The following pages will provide evidence to support this work's conclusions about the Saddam regime. Those conclusions can be summarized as follows:

1. The Saddam regime supported Islamic terrorists the same as it supported other 'secular' terrorists. The key to understanding this issue is the logical distinction between working with Islamic extremists to achieve mutual objectives outside of Iraq versus having them exist uncontrolled inside Iraq. Saddam's regime was "open for business" to leaders from al-Qaeda, Egyptian Islamic Jihad, the Taliban, Hamas, Afghani warlords and other Islamic extremist organizations. A singular instance or two of the Saddam regime meeting with Islamic terrorist leaders could possibly be discounted in the overall scheme of things. However, document after document indicates that Saddam's strategy was to support Islamic terrorists to achieve mutual objectives. His embrace of Islamic extremists at odds with his supposedly secular regime was a survival technique.

2. Documents provide strong evidence that Saddam was the instigator and ultimately behind the Battle of Mogadishu in 1993. They also provide evidence to suspect that Saddam was complicit in the Millennium Plot as executed by al Qaeda against the United States. Furthermore, documents reveal what may be foreknowledge by Saddam of the American anthrax attack that occurred within days of 9/11.

3. Saddam was in material breach of UN resolutions. The authorization from Congress for the use of force in Iraq was based largely on the failure of the Saddam regime to comply with its obligations under agreement to the UN. This fact is salient: the Saddam regime was

in a state of noncompliance. But while WMD a significant part of the argument before the war it was never the sole justification despite cynical attempts by historical revisionists to portray it as the only justification provided by the Bush Administration.

4. Saddam corrupted mightily. He used unwitting dupes to spread his propaganda. His intelligence agencies claimed to have sources all over the world in sensitive organizations including the UN and the American media.

5. There are indications of activities in Iraq that we cannot make full determination on at this time but which raise interesting questions. Even though we cannot make conclusions we will pass the relevant information to the reader who may draw his or her own conclusions. For instance, a report by a respected journalist about a claim of an Iraqi underground nuclear test that happened in the late 1980's appears to have sparked concern within the Saddam regime. The internal memorandum shows active steps to conceal evidence related to the story.

6. For the sake of history we make the startling revelation that during President Bush's 2006 State of the Union Address a former spy for Saddam Hussein sat with the First Lady, Laura Bush. It should be noted that it was practically impossible to know this and at the time the man was a leader of the Afghan reform movement that supported the overthrow of the Taliban. There are many reasons why an Afghani might have been on Saddam's payroll; this alone does not automatically

imply hostile intent against the U.S. Indeed, subsequent to the overthrow of the Taliban the man has been fully supportive of the U.S. Nevertheless, according to Saddam's documentation the man is specifically named as being on his intelligence service's payroll.

Each chapter in the body of this book will focus on a document or set of related documents. An impression of the original Arabic document is provided when available along with an English translation. It must be noted that since the writing of this book began some of the electronic copies of original Saddam regime documents have been removed from public viewing. Although these documents were originally posted on a Department of Defense website for public research the government has since shut down the site and the original may no longer be available for reproduction here.

The *New York Times* reported just before the 2006 Congressional elections that members of the International Atomic Energy Agency complained about some of Saddam's nuclear documents posted at the website. Apparently they contained sensitive nuclear information. The website was shut down to keep this information out of the wrong hands. At the time of this writing it is not clear whether the site will reopen, but it appears unlikely given the Democratic Party's control of Congress. When the original is no longer available to the authors we will post the translation that was made prior to the shut-down of the website. We will also provide the administrative number that identifies the document should the U.S. government reopen the website at a later date or should a researcher desire to obtain those manuscripts through a Freedom of Information Act request.

It is a great irony that although *The New York Times* has ridiculed the work of private researchers on this matter, questioned the validity of the documents, and reported that there was nothing new in these documents, it subsequently expressed concern about Saddam's nuclear documents. It is humorous that *The New York Times* unintentionally validated these documents and proved that they are a source of new and interesting information after all. The Saddam regime failed to comply with the UN mandates to turn over all WMD related documentation because nuclear weapons designs were discovered amid Saddam's documents that were posted on the government website. *The New York Times'* article makes no mention of the fact that the very existence of these captured documents provides further evidence that Saddam was in material breach of his obligation under United Nations resolutions. The *Times* somehow failed to mention in its own reporting that it had just substantiated the Bush Administration's argument that Iraq had failed to comply with UN resolutions regarding WMD.

It is also worth noting that although *The New York Times* has systematically called for the release of America's classified information and taken it upon itself to release classified U.S. intelligence it has consistently sought to befuddle attempts to delve into Saddam's secrets. One has to wonder about the motivation of an American news organization that cares more about keeping Saddam's secrets than our own. In addition, it should be noted that the same reporters who wrote an article to embarrass the Bush Administration over the incidental release of Saddam's prohibited nuclear documentation—which was ultimately a process error by an analyst—has failed to report on many of the documents included here. They had the same access as the authors of this book and apparently only lacked the motivation to discover and report Saddam's secrets.

This work will examine related news and government reports for context to see how the documents expand our knowledge. It should be noted that this book is not intended to be a compendium of every bit of evidence in the public domain related to a specific subject, but rather it is a review of Saddam regime (and some al-Qaeda) documentation and relevant media reporting. The most exciting part of this book is that much of the documentation is self-evident with a little background research. The reader will find documents that counter everything the media (with the exception of *Fox News Channel*, *The Weekly Standard*, *The American Thinker*, *The Cyber News Service*, *The American Spectator*, *Pajamas Media* and a few other sources such as radio pundit Rush Limbaugh) has told the public—or that demonstrate what the Democratic leadership via the sympathetic media has failed to tell the American people. The reader will see not only the difference, but may begin to re-evaluate the stranglehold the professional media has on information in the public domain and how that information is presented through the lens of a journalist's or news organization's own bias.

— *Ray Robison*

CHAPTER 1:
THE RELEVANCY OF SADDAM'S SUPPORT OF ISLAMIC TERRORISM

ONE OF THE primary justifications given by the Bush administration and congressional supporters for the invasion of Iraq and removal of the Saddam regime was the regime's support to terrorism. The president and his supporters claimed that Saddam Hussein supported terrorism and was thus a legitimate target in the Global War on Terror. The congressional document that authorized the war in Iraq specifically outlined the multiple reasons to go to war. The words *terrorism* or *terrorists* are included sixteen times in the justifications portion of the authorization. By comparison, the word *weapon(s)* in reference to weapons of mass destruction—chemical, biological, or nuclear— is used fifteen times. The authorization shows that terrorism was at least as important to the case against the Saddam regime as WMD. The paragraphs of the justification that refer to terrorism are presented below:

> *Whereas members of al Qaida, an organization bearing responsibility for attacks on the United States, its citizens, and interests, including the attacks that occurred on September 11, 2001, are known to be in Iraq;*
>
> *Whereas Iraq continues to aid and harbor other interna-*

tional terrorist organizations, including organizations that threaten the lives and safety of American citizens;

Whereas the attacks on the United States of September 11, 2001 underscored the gravity of the threat posed by the acquisition of weapons of mass destruction by international terrorist organizations;

Whereas Iraq's demonstrated capability and willingness to use weapons of mass destruction, the risk that the current Iraqi regime will either employ those weapons to launch a surprise attack against the United States or its Armed Forces or provide them to international terrorists who would do so, and the extreme magnitude of harm that would result to the United States and its citizens from such an attack, combine to justify action by the United States to defend itself;

Whereas the United States is determined to prosecute the war on terrorism and Iraq's ongoing support for international terrorist groups combined with its development of weapons of mass destruction in direct violation of its obligations under the 1991 cease-fire and other United Nations Security Council resolutions make clear that it is in the national security interests of the United States and in furtherance of the war on terrorism that all relevant United Nations Security Council resolutions be enforced, including through the use of force if necessary;

Whereas Congress has taken steps to pursue vigorously the war on terrorism through the provision of authorities and funding requested by the President to take the necessary actions against international terrorists and terrorist organizations, including those nations, organizations or persons who planned, authorized, committed or aided the terrorist attacks

that occurred on September 11, 2001 or harbored such per-
sons or organizations;

Whereas the President and Congress are determined to con-
tinue to take all appropriate actions against international
terrorists and terrorist organizations, including those nations,
organizations or persons who planned, authorized, commit-
ted or aided the terrorist attacks that occurred on September
11, 2001, or harbored such persons or organizations;

Whereas the President has authority under the Constitu-
tion to take action in order to deter and prevent acts of in-
ternational terrorism against the United States, as Congress
recognized in the joint resolution on Authorization for Use of
Military Force (Public Law 107-40);

This legislation, entitled the *Joint Resolution to Authorize the Use of United States Armed Forces Against Iraq* was passed by Congress and signed by the president in October of 2002. It was approved by a near unanimous Republican vote in the House and Senate. Forty-three percent of Congressional Democrats voted in favor of this authorization for war.

At the time of the debate over the authorization legislation leading Democrats were supportive of the resolution because, as they stated, Saddam supported terrorism. Senator Hillary Clinton said on the Floor of the Senate "He [Saddam Hussein] has also given aid, comfort, and sanctuary to terrorists, including al-Qaeda members."

Senator John Kerry, in a speech from the Senate floor, made the case that the Bush Administration and the previous Clinton Administration had been too lax with the Saddam regime. Kerry connected Iraq's support of terrorism to 9/11:

Later in the year, [1998] Congress enacted legislation declaring Iraq in material, unacceptable breach of its disarmament obligations and urging the President to take appropriate action to bring Iraq into compliance. In fact, had we done so, President Bush could well have taken his office, backed by our sense of urgency about holding Saddam Hussein accountable and, with an international United Nations, backed a multilateral stamp of approval record on a clear demand for the disarmament of Saddam Hussein's Iraq. We could have had that and we would not be here debating this today. But the administration missed an opportunity 2 years ago and particularly a year ago after September 11th. They regrettably, and even clumsily, complicated their own case. The events of September 11th created new understanding of the terrorist threat and the degree to which every nation is vulnerable. That understanding enabled the administration to form a broad and impressive coalition against terrorism. Had the administration tried then to capitalize on this unity of spirit to build a coalition to disarm Iraq, we would not be here in the pressing days before an election, late in this year, debating this now. The administration's decision to engage on this issue now, rather than a year ago or earlier, and the manner in which it has engaged, has politicized and complicated the national debate and raised questions about the credibility of their case.

According to the October of 2002 words of Senator Kerry, President Bush waited a year too long to build a coalition to disarm Iraq because of its state support for terrorism. Yet two years later,

September of 2004, John Kerry had this to say about Iraq and
terrorism:

> *We owe it to the American people to have a real debate
> about the choices President Bush has made, and the choices
> I would make and have made, to fight and win the war on
> terror.*
>
> *That means that we must have a great and honest debate
> on Iraq. The president claims it is the centerpiece of his war on
> terror. In fact, Iraq was a profound diversion from that war
> and the battle against our greatest enemy.*

The words 'diversion' and 'distraction' now pepper the statements
of many Democratic leaders such as Howard Dean, Nancy Pelosi
and John Edwards in their discussion of the war in Iraq and its
relationship to the *Global War on Terror.*

How did we come to this division of opinion about whether
or not Saddam Hussein supported terrorism? How is it that a
U.S. Senator can take a president to task for not moving against
Iraq's sponsorship of terrorism related to 9/11 and then a few
years later claim that such action was a distraction from fighting
terrorism?

Without trying to specifically delve into the motivations of a
U.S. Senator who was the Democratic nominee for president at
the time he disassociated Iraq from the war on terror, what were
the stated reasons for this change of course as outlined by the
Democratic leadership? Part of the answer can be found in the
distinction between al-Qaeda, Islamic terrorism, and the general
concept of terrorism. As the war in Iraq dragged on (and indeed
a few voices from before the war), the Democratic opposition be-

gan to distinguish between Saddam's general support to terrorism and support of al Qaeda.

The argument of many Democratic leaders became that even though it is clear Saddam supported terrorism his support did not include al Qaeda or those responsible for the 9/11 attacks. Even further, the argument has become that Saddam had no inclination to support *Islamic-based* terrorism what so ever. And since the greatest terroristic threat to the United States is posed by Islamic terrorists, or those Muslims who find justification for their actions in the Quran rather than political ideology, Saddam could be disassociated from their attacks against the United States. Thus they argued Saddam was not a part of the *Global War on Terror.* In other words Iraq is the wrong war because Saddam supported the wrong terrorists.

The ramifications of this distinction as argued by the Democratic opposition ranges from accusations that the president "cherry-picked" the intelligence, suppressed intelligence that was counter to his argument and even lied about the relationship of Saddam Hussein to Islamic terrorism.

The Democratic leadership and the media have subsequently seized upon a slew of U.S. government reports to substantiate this differentiation (many of these reports are of their own making). Although U.S. government reports over the past decade show a clear and overwhelming pattern of support to terrorism by the Saddam regime those reports deal mainly with *secular terrorists* or terrorists who happen to be Muslims but claim to be motivated by politics instead of religion. The theory here is that these groups are focused on various governments in the Middle East and thus are not a threat to the United States. Their political based violence is limited by geographical boundaries versus theocratic ones. In contrast the religious terrorist considers the whole world a battlefield. An Islamic terrorist will kill Christians wherever they may be found and thus poses a threat to the United States. The Islamic terrorist wants a clash of civilizations and posses a threat to the world.

We are supposed to ignore the fact that these same Arabic 'nationalistic' anti-government movements tend to have Islamic characteristics and tend to spawn other movements that become international and threaten the U.S. such as how the Muslim Brotherhood spawned the Egyptian Islamic Jihad, the National Islamic Front in Sudan and Hamas. Nevertheless, Democratic leadership made a distinction and their argument is based upon this distinction.

Reports from the Senate Select Committee on Intelligence and the 9/11 Commission indicated that there was contact and attempted collaboration between al-Qaeda and the Saddam regime, but there was no conclusive evidence of an operational relationship. The reports say that they may have talked about working together, but there is no solid evidence that they did. Given that there are indications of attempted collaboration if we want to find the truth we must ask questions. Does the evidence lead us to believe that these contacts led to an operational relationship? Given what we know is it reasonable to suspect they would work together? Did Saddam support Islamic terrorists? Was his regime a legitimate target in the *Global War on Terror*? This is the gray area that entangles the political and rhetorical arguments that surround the war in Iraq.

In response to these questions, certain political, diplomatic and intelligence professionals have stated that the Saddam regime would not work with Islamic terrorists because they were a threat to his regime and because the two sides were ideologically opposed. Thus not only is there no solid evidence that Saddam worked with them they also say he couldn't work with them because they were his enemy.

If the very possibility of an operational relationship between the Saddam regime and Islamic terrorists can be precluded then there is no reason to believe Saddam would support al- Qaeda. Such a case would be a sound refutation of the Bush Administration and Iraq war supporters. In practice this argument has become so convoluted that actual evidence has become secondary to the rhetorical argument made by the Democratic congressional leadership. Actual evidence of Saddam's support to Islamic terrorism is dismissed because 'he wouldn't have supported Islamic terrorism because of the ideological separation between his Ba'athist regime and Islamic terrorism.' Thus, no evidence can be accurate, authentic or real enough to overcome the rhetorical argument.

It is this aspect of the political debate that these documents illuminate. It is here that these documents matter. The evidence provided here shows that the Democratic leadership and the cooperative elements of the media have clearly overreached with their extended argument. This argument began by bashing the Bush Administration for not moving against Iraq because of terrorism and then made the leap of calling Iraq a distraction from the *Global War on Terror.*

These documents provide evidence of a clear and consistent trend of support from Islamic terror groups to the Saddam regime and reciprocation by the regime. While the Senate Intelligence Committee was writing reports which quoted from Saddam Hussein's own words as evidence that he would not work with Islamic terrorists, private citizens were translating documents that show the true nature of this relationship. Whereas Democratic leadership in the Senate expects the American public to take Saddam Hussein at his word to back their rhetorical arguments, researchers are looking at the real record of Saddam's government—the regime's own records. The captured documents provide a substantially different view to that of the Senate Intelligence Committee and it is a devastating indictment of that committee. Clearly, national security has been overcome by political posturing within the Senate and as such threatens the very citizenry it is charged with protecting.

The Senate Intelligence Committee had this to say in its Phase II report on prewar intelligence concerning Iraq:

> *Conclusion 1: Postwar findings indicate that the Central Intelligence Agency's (CIA) assessment that the relationship between Iraq and al-Qa'ida resembled "two independent actors trying to exploit each other," accurately characterized bin Ladin's actions, but not those of Saddam Hussein. Postwar findings indicate that Saddam Hussein was distrustful of al-Qa'ida and viewed Islamic extremists as a threat to his regime, refusing all requests from al-Qa'ida to provide material or operational support.*

The documents included here will show this finding by the Senate Intelligence Committee to be nothing other than absurd. If anything, Saddam was chasing a recalcitrant Usama bin Laden who was surrounded by other jihad leaders who had a relationship to Saddam.

> *Conclusion 2: Postwar findings have identified only one*
> *meeting between representatives of al-Qa'ida and Saddam*
> *Hussein's regime reported in prewar intelligence assessments.*
> *Postwar findings have identified two occasions, not reported*
> *prior to the war, in which Saddam Hussein rebuffed meeting*
> *requests from an al-Qa'ida operative. The Intelligence Com-*
> *munity has not found any other evidence of meetings between*
> *al-Qa'ida and Iraq. (Ibid)*

Whereas the Senate Intelligence Committee makes or rather fails to make distinctions to mislead the public about the true nature of the Saddam regime, this book gives the reader the raw evidence. The fact is that the Saddam regime was in consistent contact and provided support to al-Qaeda through third party affiliates and subordinate commanders. Usama bin Laden might not have been a contact for Saddam but he didn't need to be. The Senate Intelligence Committee relies on the fact that al-Qaeda was not al-Qaeda as it is now known to make its' conclusions. But there is strong evidence that Saddam worked repeatedly with the Egyptian Islamic Jihad which would join with bin Laden's followers to become the al Qaeda we know today. Therefore, the committee finds no evidence of an al Qaeda relationship even though al Qaeda's 'number two man' as he is commonly known, Ayman al Zawahiri had an operational relationship with the Saddam regime. It is a distressing display of misdirection for such an esteemed committee. This work will analyze a set of documents in the public domain that were not considered by the Senate Intelligence Committee that provide compelling evidence that Saddam worked directly with al-Qaeda.

Conclusion 9: While document exploitation continues, additional reviews of documents recovered in Iraq are unlikely to provide information that would contradict the Committee's findings or conclusions. (Ibid)

This book provides a wealth of information not previously in the public domain.

The Senate Intelligence Committee has concluded that Saddam viewed Islamic extremists as a threat to his regime. The plain truth is that the Intelligence Committee was correct in that Saddam had reason to fear Islamic extremists, but it failed to realize that the fear of Islamic extremism is exactly what spurred Saddam to support Islamic terrorists.

It is not too different from the position taken by the Saudi government which supported Usama bin Laden before 9/11. Usama was supported in order to placate him and keep him busy outside of Saudi Arabia.

It is the exact same technique that Saddam used to protect his regime. By supporting Islamic extremists in their terroristic activities he ensured they would leave his regime alone. It is popular for Democratic pundits to claim that there were no al Qaeda terrorists in Iraq before we got there. This raises the question: If these Islamic terrorists hated him so much, where was Iraq's 9/11? Why did they not attack Iraq? These documents make the answer obvious—because they were getting more from Saddam than they would have had they attacked him.

CHAPTER 2:
WHAT THE DOCUMENTS REVEAL
ABOUT SADDAM'S SUPPORT OF
ISLAMIC TERRORISM

MEN IDENTIFIED BY codename in secret documents met to make international deals at various locations in the heart of Saddam Hussein's seat of power in Baghdad. We don't know exactly what all the terms of the agreements were, but we know the men committed to mutual cooperation. They found common ground amid expressions of sympathy and Muslim identity and professed animosity against the common enemy—the United States of America. In one of the meetings an Iraqi official, the Director of the Iraqi Intelligence Service (IIS), spoke with a man known in Pakistan as the *Father of the Taliban,* Maulana Fazlur Rahman (Maulana is a religious title). The IIS Director described the relationship between the Ba'athist government of Saddam Hussein and the Taliban in Afghanistan by stating "We already believe that there are no points of disagreement between us and the Taliban because we are both in one trench facing the world's oppression."

Saddam's senior intelligence official had just informed the *Father of the Taliban* that Iraq would help the Taliban against its' enemies. It was November of 1999. Usama bin Laden was already known to be in Afghanistan conducting operations against the United States under the protection of the Taliban and President Clinton was putting pressure on the Taliban to kick him out or hand him over. The Taliban refused under the pretense of a lack of evidence against him.

Bin Laden had fought to a small degree alongside the mujahideen or Islamic resistance fighters to oust the Soviet Army from Afghanistan in the 8o's but he mostly funded and recruited them. He was a competitor to the United States for influence with the mujahideen not a client of the U.S. as many leftists have inaccurately painted him. At the same time, Saddam Hussein was courting mujahideen commanders in Afghanistan. A quick look at a map of the region shows why Saddam was concerned about influence in Afghanistan. It is located on the opposite side of Iran from Iraq and as an ally to Saddam would place Iran in a vice.

Usama bin Laden returned to Afghanistan several years later where he worked under the protection of the Taliban to train al Qaeda forces for the jihad against America and to plot those attacks. In those years the two organizations became intertwined, distinct as the U.S. State Department and U.S. Department of Defense are distinct, but with a common interest and authority. Their authority they believed was the Quran, and their interest was jihad against the west. Some of their leaders, such as Fazlur Rahman Khalil (different from Maulana Fazlur Rahman) were considered both al-Qaeda and Taliban and were responsible for duties that involved both organizations.

According to some reports, Mulla Mohammad Omar, the leader of the Taliban had a bond of kinship to Usama bin Laden through intermarriage of the two families. Other reports claim that UBL built

Mulla Omar a palatial estate in Afghanistan. It is said that Mulla Omar refused to even meet with people who were not Muslim.

Usama bin Laden had relocated to Afghanistan near Kandahar from Sudan just before the Taliban took control of the region. Consequently, al-Qaeda and the Taliban rose up together in Afghanistan the same as they fell together in 2001. Mulla Omar was the man who had set the stage for Usama bin Laden to kill thousands of Americans and destroy the World Trade Center in 2001. It is worth remembering that the war in Afghanistan was and is just as much against the Taliban as it is against al-Qaeda. Many people try to put too fine a distinction on who was responsible for the 9/11 attacks. Both al-Qaeda and the Taliban are culpable. The evidence will show they are not alone.

In November of 1999, Mulla Omar sent his personal representative and Defense Minister to Saddam asking for assistance. According to the record of the event, the Saddam regime agreed to provide that vital support to a desperate Taliban regime. The representative was Maulana Fazlur Rahman. The Defense Minister of the Taliban, Abdul Razaq who has also been cited as its' Interior Minister is listed as being in at least one of the meetings with Iraqi officials. As part of the entourage it is likely he attended the other meeting revealed here as well.

An agent of Saddam's intelligence service was present to transcribe the meetings in Arabic. His spy tradecraft was a little sloppy at times and perhaps he never considered that his records would someday lead to a revealing look at Saddam's ties to international Islamic jihad. This man, whose name is believed to be Khaled Abd El Majid acted as a liaison between Saddam's government and jihad groups in Pakistan and Afghanistan including al-Qaeda and the Taliban. He moved between Iraq and Pakistan as evidenced by entries in a notebook he kept that was bought in Pakistan. He coordinated meetings between the Saddam regime and Islamic terrorists.

The Iraqi agent used codenames to conceal the identity of some of the meeting participants. However, he made errors. In later writings he provided clues as to who these men are and in some cases provided direct writing as to who is associated with what codename. It seems as though he carelessly put the encryption key for the notebook inside the notebook itself. In a least one instance he used codenames to protect the identities of the men in these meetings but he listed the date of the meeting. Then in another part of the book he listed visitors by name and the date they visited allowing a simple crosslink of date-name to date-codename thus providing a legend. It is fortunate that his sloppy tradecraft provided yet another key to cracking Saddam's secret support to the *global Islamic jihad movement.*

He scribbled tantalizing clues from meetings with terrorists including references to a request for Saddam to fund "centers" in Baghdad or Tajikistan. Although the Iraqi Intelligence Service (IIS) agent did not record what these centers were for specifically the man in the meeting had previously been identified by the State Department as a prolific Islamic terrorism training camp operator with camps in Tajikistan. His name is Gulbuddin Hekmatyar, currently one of the world's most wanted men. He trained the Islamic jihad fighters that went to al Qaeda and most likely Hezb'Allah in Lebanon even though he was fighting the Taliban to take control of Afghanistan himself.

Hekmatyar has subsequently released a video tape pledging his allegiance to Usama bin Laden. Before then he was in Baghdad asking Saddam for money for terror camps. Even before that he was an Afghani warlord supported by the CIA in the operation to oust the Soviet Army from Afghanistan since his men were committed Islamists who would fight the godless communists to the death.

But that is the *realpolitik* of Islamic jihad. Yesterday's friends are today's enemies who might become useful in the future against another common foe. Life for the jihadist is not always about ideology. Hekmatyar would later side with a communist to fight the Taliban. Sometimes ideology is about a means to an end, namely power. Sometimes it is about reaching compromises to ensure survival. It was the same for the Saddam regime with its tenuous hold on power in Iraq and greater concern for internal dissension than American intervention. This more than anything is what placed Saddam and the Taliban "both in one trench." They needed each other as the enemies within and without were adding up. Debates about secular socialist movements versus Islamic extremism often lose relevance when shear survival is at stake.

The IIS agent logged the effective range of a Stinger surface-to-air missile in the conversation with Hekmatyar. He noted that Hekmatyar said "they will bring them in through Iran or Northern Iraq." It was not specifically stated what they will bring, but the context provides strong evidence that he wanted to smuggle Islamic jihadists into Iraq from Afghanistan for a training camp.

The IIS agent noted meetings that he arranged between the Saddam regime and other nefarious men. One of these men is a well known *global Islamic jihad movement* supporter and close associate of Usama bin Laden. Fazlur Rahman Khalil specialized in recruiting the men from Pakistani Islamic schools or madrassas to join al-Qaeda and the Taliban. It is possible that his terrorist recruits trained at Hekmatyar's camps. As a Muslim cleric, he signed an Islamic edict or *fatwa* providing Usama bin Laden with religious authority to prosecute his war against the United States. The *fatwa* issued in 1998 was cosigned by Khalil, who is also a leader of one of several smaller Islamic jihad centric political parties in Pakistan. Khalil's group is a subgroup to Maulana Fazlur Rahman's terror-supporting, Pakistani groups. A leader of yet another subgroup to the Maulana's group also signed the *fatwa* placing its theocratic legitimacy ultimately at the hands of the Maulana.

The Federation of American Scientists has provided a translation of the 1998 *fatwa* at its website. The authors of this book have added bold for reference. (http://www.fas.org/irp/world/para/docs/980223-fatwa.htm)

Jihad Against Jews and Crusaders
World Islamic Front Statement

23 February 1998

Shaykh Usamah Bin-Muhammad Bin-Ladin

Ayman al-Zawahiri, amir of the Jihad Group in Egypt

Abu-Yasir Rifa'i Ahmad Taha, Egyptian Islamic Group

Shaykh Mir Hamzah, secretary of the Jamiat-ul-Ulema-e-Pakistan

Fazlur Rahman, amir of the Jihad Movement in Bangladesh

Praise be to Allah, who revealed the Book, controls the clouds, defeats factionalism, and says in His Book: „But when the forbidden months are past, then fight and slay the pagans wherever ye find them, seize them, beleaguer them, and lie in wait for them in every stratagem (of war)"; and peace be upon our Prophet, Muhammad Bin-'Abdallah, who said: I have been sent with the sword between my hands to ensure that no one but Allah is worshipped, Allah who put my livelihood under the shadow of my spear and who inflicts humiliation and scorn on those who disobey my orders.

The Arabian Peninsula has never — since Allah made it flat, created its desert, and encircled it with seas — been stormed by any forces like the crusader armies spreading in it like locusts, eating its riches and wiping out its plantations. All this is happening at a time in which nations are attacking Muslims like people fighting over a plate of food. In the light of the grave situation and the lack of support, we and you are obliged to discuss current events, and we should all agree on how to settle the matter.

No one argues today about three facts that are known to everyone; we will list them, in order to remind everyone:

First, for over seven years the United States has been occupying the lands of Islam in the holiest of places, the Arabian Peninsula, plundering its riches, dictating to its rulers, humiliating its people, terrorizing its neighbors, and turning its bases in the Peninsula into a spearhead through which to fight the neighboring Muslim peoples.

If some people have in the past argued about the fact of the occupation, all the people of the Peninsula have now acknowledged it. The best proof of this is the Americans' continuing aggression against the Iraqi people using the Peninsula as a staging post, even though all its rulers are against their territories being used to that end, but they are helpless.

Second, despite the great devastation inflicted on the Iraqi people by the crusader-Zionist alliance, and despite the huge number of those killed, which has exceeded 1 million... despite all this, the Americans are once against trying to repeat the horrific massacres, **as though they are not content with the protracted blockade imposed after the ferocious war** or the fragmentation and devastation.

So here they come to annihilate what is left of this people and to humiliate their Muslim neighbors.

Third, if the Americans' aims behind these wars are religious and economic, the aim is also to serve the Jews' petty state and divert attention from its occupation of Jerusalem and murder of Muslims there. The best proof of this is their eagerness to destroy Iraq, the strongest neighboring Arab state, and their endeavor to fragment all the states of the region such as Iraq, Saudi Arabia, Egypt, and Sudan into paper statelets and through their disunion and weakness to guarantee Israel's survival and the continuation of the brutal crusade occupation of the Peninsula.

All these crimes and sins committed by the Americans are a clear declaration of war on Allah, his messenger, and Muslims. And ulema have throughout Islamic history unanimously agreed that the jihad is an individual duty if the enemy destroys the Muslim countries. This was revealed by Imam Bin-Qadamah in "Al-Mughni," Imam al-Kisa'i in "Al-Bada'i," al-Qurtubi in his interpretation, and the shaykh of al-Islam in his books, where he said: "As for the fighting to repulse [an enemy], it is aimed at defending sanctity and religion, and it is a duty as agreed [by the ulema]. Nothing is more sacred than belief except repulsing an enemy who is attacking religion and life."

On that basis, and in compliance with Allah's order, we issue the following fatwa to all Muslims:

The ruling to kill the Americans and their allies — civilians and military — is an individual duty for every Muslim who can do it in any country in which it is possible to do it, in order to liberate the al-Aqsa Mosque and the holy mosque [Mecca] from their grip, and in order for their armies to move out of all the lands of Islam, defeated and unable to threaten any Muslim. This is in accordance with the words of Almighty Allah, "and fight the pagans all together as they fight you all together," and "fight them until there is no more tumult or oppression, and there prevail justice and faith in Allah."

This is in addition to the words of Almighty Allah: "And why should ye not fight in the cause of Allah and of those who, being weak, are ill-treated (and oppressed)? — women and children, whose cry is: 'Our Lord, rescue us from this town, whose people are oppressors; and raise for us from thee one who will help!'"

We — with Allah's help — call on every Muslim who believes in Allah and wishes to be rewarded to comply with Allah's order to kill the Americans and plunder their money wherever and whenever they find it. We also call on Muslim ulema, leaders, youths, and soldiers to launch the raid on Satan's U.S. troops and the devil's supporters allying with them, and to displace those who are behind them so that they may learn a lesson.

Almighty Allah said: "O ye who believe, give your response to Allah and His Apostle, when He calleth you to that which will give you life. And know that Allah cometh between a man and his heart, and that it is He to whom ye shall all be gathered."

Almighty Allah also says: "O ye who believe, what is the matter with you, that when ye are asked to go forth in the cause of Allah, ye cling so heavily to the earth! Do ye prefer the life of this world to the hereafter? But little is the comfort of this life, as compared with the hereafter. Unless ye go forth, He will punish you with a grievous penalty, and put others in your place; but Him ye would not harm in the least. For Allah hath power over all things."

Almighty Allah also says: "So lose no heart, nor fall into despair. For ye must gain mastery if ye are true in faith."

Despite the fact that this *fatwa* is signed "Fazlur Rahman," it is not believed to be Maulana Fazlur Rahman. Most experts claim it is Fazlur Rahman Khalil who left off the Khalil when he signed. Experts agree it is Khalil because of the reference to Bangladesh where Khalil is known to operate as opposed to Maulana Fazlur Rahman who does not operate in Bangladesh. To make it a little more confusing, Fazlur Rahman Khalil is also referred to as a Maulana because he is an Islamic cleric as well. This work will abstain from that convention for clarity. But be forewarned, there are many references that have mixed up the two men which is easy to do. It takes considerable research to identify the distinguishing characteristics of each. In Fact, the authors have reason to suspect that many experts are in error and that this signature is Maulana Fazlur Rahman. But both arguments have validity and until either of these men make clear who is the signatory the authors will go with the consensus opinion for now.

In either case, both men, the Maulana and Khalil were providing public, religious justification to Usama bin Laden and al-Qaeda for Islamic jihad against America. The edict lists three provocations to jihad:

- U.S. presence in Saudi Arabia.
- *U.S. support of UN sanctions on Iraq and the Gulf War itself.*
- U.S. support of Israel.

These documents show that the same men behind the Bin Laden declaration of war against the U.S. were meeting with the Saddam regime in Baghdad a year after. This actually makes sense. Why wouldn't these terrorists want to capitalize on the *fatwa* and gain Saddam's support if they didn't already have it? Although our knowledge of the event lacks specificity the fact that such a meeting took place flies in the face of conventional theory that Saddam was ideologically opposed to involvement with al Qaeda. It is unlikely Khalil or the Maulana would visit Baghdad without some sort of material reciprocation or to phrase it more specifically, Iraqi support to there Islamic jihad movement.

Khalil and Hekmatyar were involved with the day-to-day operational aspects of supporting the jihad. Hekmatyar is still on the run at the time of this writing (as far as we know publicly) Khalil was beaten into a coma in March of 2006 just hours after a translation of this notebook was released publicly at www.rayrobison.com and www.pajamasmedia.com. While these men are important they are not the lynchpins of the *global Islamic jihad movement*. That dishonor goes to men like Usama bin Laden, Ayman al Zawahiri, Mulla Omar, and Maulana Fazlur Rahman.

Maulana Fazlur Rahman is not a hands-on terrorist who plants bombs or makes suicide vests. He is much worse; a politician and diplomat working at the highest levels to make international deals for the terrorists. He is the ambassador for the *global Islamic jihad movement* centered in Pakistan and Afghanistan who stands out as one of the most dangerous men on the planet because of his political proximity to Pakistan's nuclear arsenal and because of his strong support from the Pakistani jihadists of the North-West Frontier Province. Men like the Maulana are the archetypal terrorists fighting for prestige, money, and power while the pawns die for Islam.

Just recently Rahman was considered a strong candidate for Prime Minister of Pakistan. He leads a number of Islamic jihad-centric political parties in Pakistan. Maulana Fazlur Rahman hates the west; he despises anything that does not abide by the strictest Islamic codes (with one curious exception that will be discussed later). He leads Islamic jihad fighters and supporters under the guise of political factions. The Maulana was personal friends with Saddam Hussein, Moammar Kadafi of Libya, and Mulla Mohammad Omar, leader of the Taliban. He is an official in the Pakistani government akin to a senior U.S. Senator. And it seems he is involved in every bad news story that comes out of Pakistan such as the recent murderous furor over Danish cartoons about the Prophet Mohammed. He is not followed by the American media. He should be.

Rahman is a leader of the Deobandi Muslim sect which is a Pakistani version of the Sufi sect in Saudi Arabia that instigated the *global Islamic jihad movement* (along with the Wahhabis or Salafi in Saudi Arabia). This movements support of terrorism culminated in the 9/11 attacks. High-ranking al-Qaeda leaders who plotted and supported 9/11 were captured in Pakistan while under the protection of members of the Maulana's political party. He is currently in the news (at the time of this writing) for fighting attempts in Pakistan to revise horribly unfair rape laws. A Muslim woman in Pakistan must produce four witnesses to a rape. If she cannot she pays the legal penalty for a false allegation. The Maulana is fighting to protect that law.

Maulana Fazlur Rahman provided material support to al Qaeda and the Taliban before and after 9/11. He was a coconspirator in the 9/11 attacks even if only in a support role. His men smuggled the leadership of al Qaeda out of Afghanistan. This same man was meeting with the Saddam regime to negotiate not only the support of the Taliban, but also the support of the radical Islamists of the North-West Frontier Province who would soon assist the 9/11 plotters. This is one link of several that this book will show between Saddam and the same people who attacked the United States.

It is disingenuous to argue that al Qaeda orchestrated the 9/11 attacks independently. It had the support of the Taliban, other supposedly unaffiliated of freelance terrorists (some argue their affiliation was in fact with Saddam—an interesting theory that is supported by this evidence), Pakistani accomplices, and many others all playing separate roles within the *global Islamic jihad movement*. All three of the men meeting in Baghdad—Rahman, Khalil, and Hekmatyar—are major leaders of the *global Islamic jihad movement*.

It is beyond coincidence that they all came to Iraq with no reasonable expectations of support from Saddam. If Saddam was disposed to deny their requests, why would they come to Baghdad? Wouldn't word spread within the *global Islamic jihad movement* to not bother with Saddam if he provided nothing? Why did they trust him enough to expose themselves to the Ba'athists by coming to Baghdad if he was an enemy? Instead, they appear to be practically streaming in with hat in hand, so to speak.

Why would Saddam even invite them if he had nothing to offer or no plans to deliver assistance? The argument has been made that Saddam invited these men to Baghdad to "keep tabs" or gather intelligence on them. While this argument deserves consideration it fails upon further scrutiny. In several instances these terrorists who pledged support to Saddam actually followed through on the pledges as verified in unwitting media reports. The Maulana Fazlur Rahman was often quoted before the Iraq War as lending support to Saddam Hussein directly instead of in the more subtle fashion of Usama bin Laden who declared war for the sake of the Iraqi people. Why was the Maulana still supporting him publicly in 2003 if Saddam had made agreements with the Maulana in 1999 with no intention to follow through?

A letter captured in Afghanistan written by an al-Qaeda leader confirms that Maulana Fazlur Rahman was a personal friend of Saddam Hussein. This appears to be a pretty well kept secret as there are very few public reference to the relationship before these documents were captured and revealed. The al-Qaeda document also reveals that another al-Qaeda leader, Ayman al Zawahiri had been to Iraq. Another Saddam regime document corroborates that information which was not publicly known before.

To find a singular fact in one secret Iraqi document that appears only in another secret al-Qaeda document provides nice validation *from both parties involved,* the Saddam regime and the Islamic terrorists. The a-Qaeda letter was used in a study of al-Qaeda at West Point's Combating Terrorism Center which lends great weight to its' authenticity. The fact that the Iraqi documents provide corroborating secret information speaks volumes about their authenticity. It is by linking information between the documents that their true nature can be determined.

Further evidence of the relationship between the Saddam regime and the Maulana can be found in another document that was written before the IIS agent's notebook and the al Qaeda letter but which was not made public until after the al-Qaeda letter and IIS agent's notebook were written. That memo was in a group of documents reported on by the Cyber News Service (CNS) in 2004. CNS stated that it received the documents from an Iraqi Survey Group (ISG) official. The lack of any way to authenticate that they even came from Iraq caused most observers to dismiss them. While the authors of this book agree that the consensus was a valid one under the circumstances, the authors have found solid reason to believe those documents released by CNS were authentic Iraqi documents. We thus include them within the scope of this work.

One of the CNS News memorandums is a brief from the early 90's that lists and describes the Iraqi Intelligence Service's contacts with Islamic terrorist groups that might be willing to attack

American forces in Somalia. Saddam was essentially looking for a hit man to kill U.S. troops. That document mentions the Pakistani political group JUP led at the time by the Maulana Fazlur Rahman who is mentioned by name in the document. It states that Rahman is a close associate of the IIS and ready to cooperate with any mission.

Thus there are three documents that reference the relationship between Maulana Fazlur Rahman, the *Father of the Taliban* and the Saddam regime. One is an IIS memo from 1993, before the Taliban was created, another is an IIS notebook from 1999 and the other is an al-Qaeda letter from 2002. Outside of these documents, there is almost no media reference to this relationship. This makes a strong argument that all three documents are authentic.

The 1993 memorandum released by CNS also mentions that the IIS worked with Gulbuddin Hekmatyar. This is one more relationship that was corroborated by the IIS agent's notebook and almost nowhere else. If the CNS documents are fakes as some have claimed the forger had a staggering amount of prescience to know the same things would show up in a validated IIS document released by the U.S. government.

And when we find evidence to substantiate one of those CNS documents, it increases the likelihood that they are all genuine documents from Iraq. Because if someone working for ISG had access to one authentic document to leak it to CNS then they likely had access to others. It makes no sense that they would release one authentic document and dilute its impact with other fake documents. This is the most reasonable determination the authors can make through deduction and examination until the U.S. government responds to a Freedom of Information Act request and hopefully validates or invalidates the CNS documents.

Another document provides evidence that the Palestinian Islamic terror group Hamas had an authorized presence in Iraq as well as an official liaison. It demonstrates that even though the regime might have been opposed to Islamic terrorists running loose in Iraq the regime certainly didn't mind hosting Islamic terrorists under controlled conditions.

An *Insurgency Plan* document provides evidence that the current insurgency in Iraq was pre-planned and that the plan involved regime officials working closely with Islamic elements. There is a suggestive statement that may indicate that Muqtada al Sadr might be involved in the insurgency as part of pre-coordination with Saddam regime elements, an allegation also made by the Iraqi government. As unconventional as the notion may seem to western minds there is corroborating evidence in the public domain.

Other documents provide evidence that the Saddam regime asked for and reciprocated support from an Islamic fundamentalist group in Algeria, the FIS which counted many Afghan mujahideen veterans among its members. The evidence shows that Saddam made payments to an Afghani mujahideen commander. Although he is rather moderate for a mujahideen commander this record demonstrates that Saddam thought Afghanistan was very important to his regime's security. Documents presented here show dialogue with al Qaeda, the NIF in the Sudan, and Egyptian Islamic terror groups.

But so far, none of this really tells us why the secular Saddam regime would work with Islamic terrorists. One can make reasonable guesses as to why: revenge for the Gulf War, deniability by using terrorists instead of Iraqi forces, to placate a foe and turn his enemies on each other, but these papers don't usually specify the 'why'. Interestingly enough these are much the same reasons the CIA supported the Islamic jihad against the Soviets in Afghanistan at the direction of President Jimmy Carter. How much easier is it to imagine Saddam would work with Islamic militants if Noble-Peace Prize winner Jimmy Carter did the same?

In one document the motivation is clear and simple. Saddam ordered the IIS to work with Islamists to "hunt the Americans". But there are other clues as to the conditions that made this confluence of Ba'athists and jihadists possible. The clues point to one ultimate finding.

CHAPTER 3:
WHY SADDAM SUPPORTED ISLAMIC TERRORISTS

FOR THE BA'ATHISTS in Iraq their ideology was a survival tool and not a suicide pact.

Saddam resisted the surge of Islamic fanaticism that engulfed many Muslim nations following the defeat of the Soviets in Afghanistan and battles with the Russians in Chechnya and the Serbians in Bosnia and Kosovo. He pursued and persecuted Islamic extremists in Iraq. But there came a time when he began to look the other way in regards to Islamic fundamentalism, when it infected his senior council. His senior military officers were tied to Islamic extremists in Iraq.

The UN sanctions against Saddam unintentionally drove cash-poor Iraqi officials into a collaborative relationship with Islamic extremists in smuggling oil as part of the corruption of the oil-for-food program. The Ba'athists had the oil. The Islamic extremists who already lived under the radar of Arab regimes that sought them out had the ability to smuggle the oil and needed the funds to spread their theology.

Saddam would ultimately come to portray himself as a Muslim more than as a secularist. Among the videos captured in Iraq is a scene of Saddam on an Islamic prayer rug in a Mosque. It is tempting to view it as a pure propaganda event and there may be truth to that assumption. However, by the same principle, Saddam's perception of the usefulness of the image of a devout Muslim and cultivation of that image to mainstream Islam could be applied to the concept of his support to Islamic extremists from whom he desired mutual support and security. Saddam needed to cooperate with the extremists because the extremists had come to Iraq and were *important to his government.*

The evidence of the close association between Saddam's leadership and Islamic extremists became apparent in the post-Saddam era when former Ba'athists fueled and led the insurgency in cooperation with Islamic extremists, or foreign fighters, who streamed into Iraq before the war. Some commentators such as Iraq expert Dr. Laurie Mylroie, journalists Christopher Hitchens and Mark Echeinlaub, and author Sam Pender argued that there must have been a pre-existing relationship, but direct evidence was lacking in the public domain, until now.

A document has been discovered in the repository that is nothing less than the insurgency plans for Iraq should Saddam fall. It provided eleven directives for the Ba'athist officials to follow. Four of the directives are discussed here:

- Recruit reliable sources and direct them to the mosques.
- Join with the Islamic Hawza `Alemiya in Najaf. [Translator's comment: The Hawza is an Islamic religious teaching institution.]
- Associate with the national and Islamic groups and parties.
- Develop relationships with those returning from abroad.

Three out of eleven crucial directives involve Islamic institutions or individuals. One could be interpreted as a cryptic instruction to work with Islamic foreign fighters who were already known to be in Iraq at the time this memorandum was written. This is compelling evidence of prewar coordination between the Ba'athists and Islamic extremists who would indeed fight together against the coalition forces.

The Saddam regime's documentation provides clues as to how this could happen. One of Saddam's men, Izzat Ibrahim al-Douri the former Vice President of Saddam's revolutionary council is still on the loose at the time of this writing. Some reports say that he died of Leukemia in 2005. However the BBC reported in a January of 2007 article entitled Saddam aide is New Baath Leader that the Iraqi Ba'ath party remnants believed to be in Syria had just declared him their leader. He is a devout Muslim who presented Saddam with a copy of the Quran written with Saddam's own blood. The existence of such a Quran has been reported as a curiosity in the western media but not from whence it came. A bizarre ceremony is noted in a captured daily planner for al-Douri. A government provided translation released at the Foreign Military Studies Office, the Department of Defense website where the documents were formerly available, states:

> Pages 151-155 contain a meeting minute between the vice-president Izzat Ibrahim and the Iraqi President Saddam Hussein, dated 23 Sep 2000, the vice president hands Saddam a Holy Quran written in Saddam's blood, the meeting only contains intensive complements.

The reference comes from a document numbered BIAP-2003-00003100-HT. *HT* means it is a government provided translation as opposed to having been translated by our in-house translator, whom we will call Sammi to protect his identity.

It certainly is an odd juxtaposition to imagine the secular madman Saddam giving of his blood for a Quran. This incident raises an interesting question. Was the Ba'athist party a truly secular governing party? It appears that such is not the case.

A well regarded military research website called Global Security.org has a fascinating description of Izzat Ibrahim al-Douri. The website provides information derived from government and media reports:

> Izzat [Ezzet] Ibrahim al-Douri, former vice president of Saddam's revolutionary council, was believed to be behind some attacks against coalition forces and Iraqis. He is the "King of Clubs" No. 6 on the coalition's most-wanted list. Following the capture of Saddam Hussein he became the most wanted man in Iraq.

(http://www.globalsecurity.org/military/world/iraq/al-douri. htm)

Al-Douri was a leader of the insurgency after Saddam was captured. He was the leader of the JM:

> Jaysh Muhammad (JM) is an anti-Coalition group with both politically motivated and religiously motivated elements. The politically motivated members are Ba'athist, pro-Saddam elements who tend to be of the Sufi religious soca. The Sufi enjoyed special status during the Ba'ath Regime and hold Izzat al-Duri, the ex-vice-president, in exceptionally high esteem. They were members of intelligence, security, and police forces from the previous regime. [Ibid]

A major insurgency group (the insurgency is ultimately a combination of many sometimes competing elements vying for control) is a combination of Islamic extremists and Ba'athist leaders. This

Global Security report is supported by the *Insurgency Plan* document, which also illustrates pre-war coordination between Islamic fighters and the supposedly secular Ba'athists. It is worth noting that the regime support came from a Sufi sect of Islam, according to Global Security.org. Although Sufi is distinct from Sunni, it is more closely related to Sunni than to Shi'a Islam. Often Sufi and Sunni are combined into a Sufi-Sunni theology which happens to also be practiced by the Egyptian Islamic Jihad and al-Qaeda. (http://www.semp.us/biots/biot_299.html).

To reiterate, Saddam was dependent on his leaders for internal political support and security. A religious group that backed his supposedly secular regime and thus gaining Saddam's deference was the Sufi/Sunni, an Islamic sect. Al Qaeda leaders, Usama bin Laden and Ayman al Zawahiri and many of the Deobandi adherents of Maulana Fazlur Rahman in Pakistan and the Taliban in Afghanistan are also Sufi/Sunnis. In addition, these groups also contain a Salafi or Wahhabi strand of Islamic adherents. Although there seems to be some strife between these two branches of Sunni Islam, they are much closer to each other than disparate. Immediately, it becomes obvious that this shared theocracy could have been a uniting influence.

Many members of the Ba'athist security apparatus maintained a common religious affiliation, Sufi/Sunni. This notion is completely at odds with the image of the Saddam regime as promoted by the mainstream American media. It differs from a truly secular regime, for example a Soviet style government promoting atheism. The Ba'athists were not really the secular atheists they pretended to be in order to curry favor with European socialists and the former Soviet Union. Such reasoning finds precedent in the Palestinian Authority. The PA has long characterized itself as a political secular movement but any serious examination shows Islamic extremism to be central to their actions. It is nothing more than a political façade to make Islamic extremism more palatable and thus leftist westerners more sympathetic.

The Ba'athists also used the claim of secular-socialism as a justification to crack down on competing sects. They portrayed sectarian warfare against the Shi'ites as suppression of religious extremists by a secular-socialist government, a tactic that shockingly worked with European socialists. Bizarrely, this openly sectarian warfare, Ba'athist Iraqi Sunni against Iraqi Shi'ites has often been misidentified as evidence of the secular nature of the Saddam regime. It is often used in comparisons to the current sectarian violence to demonstrate how well the Iraqis got along under a strong central socialist government before the U.S. action.

The fact is that the regime did not persecute Iraqis because they were religious or Muslims but because they weren't the right kind of Muslims. It is easy to see how an observer who does not know the particulars might mistake the suppression of Shi'ites in Iraq as evidence of a secular-socialist government trying to stamp out Islamic extremists. This is the true genesis of the 'Saddam hated Islamic extremists' myth. Saddam did not want to rule as an Islamic extremist because such governing would lead to more power for the Imams. But in all other ways he was happy to use Islam in the same way he used everything else, as a blunt force weapon.

In 1993 the regime embarked on the Return to Faith Campaign (al-Hamlah al-Imaniyyah), under the direction of Izzat Ibrahim al-Douri. The Ministry of Endowments and Religious Affairs monitored places of worship, appointed the clergy, approved the building and repair of all places of worship, and approved the publication of all religious literature. The

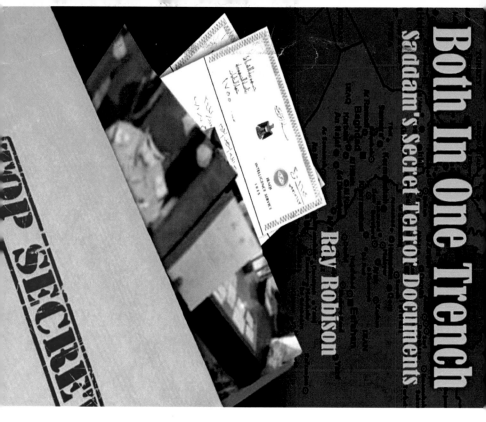

Both In One Trench
Saddam's Secret Terror Documents

Ray Robison

Nicolas Dagher would personally like to invite you to the signing of his recently published book:

Both in One Trench
Saddam's Secret Terror Documents

The event will take place on Sunday July 13th from 1:30 to 4:30 PM at the Hard Bean Coffee & BookSellers.

36 Market Space, Annapolis, MD 21401

The only thing necessary for the triumph of evil is for good men to do nothing. -Edmund Burke

Imam (Faith) Campaign allowed Sunni mosques more freedom in practicing religious ceremonies and rites, which reduced substantially the opposition to the regime amongst Sunni Islamists.

Forces from the Intelligence Service (Mukhabarat), General Security (Amn al-Amm), the Military Bureau, Saddam's Commandos (Fedayeen Saddam), and the Ba'ath Party killed senior Shi'a clerics, desecrated Shi'a mosques and holy sites (particularly in the aftermath of the 1991 civil uprising), arrested tens of thousands of Shi'a, interfered with Shi'a religious education, prevented Shi'a adherents from performing their religious rites, and fired upon or arrested Shi'a who sought to take part in their religious processions. Security agents were reportedly stationed at all the major Shi'a mosques and shrines and searched, harassed, and arbitrarily arrested worshipers. (Ibid)

The secular Ba'athists did not suppress Islam in Iraq despite the notional secular-Islamic divide. To believe so is to misinterpret the suppression of one sect of Islam in favor of another sect as a rejection of all Islam among the Ba'athists in Iraq.

There are strong indications that the Saddam regime was often involved with Islamic extremists. The al Douri daily planner notes that the former Vice President of Saddam's Revolutionary Council met with an Islamic militant group leader Sheikh Abbas Madani in 1990. Madani led the Islamic Salvation Front (FIS) which sought to overthrow the government of Algeria by political and militant means and establish an Islamic state under Islamic holy law. While the group was more political than militant at the time of the meeting many of its members were veterans of the Afghani jihad against the Soviets likely to have fought alongside extremists such as Usama bin Laden. The FIS charter promoted *Sharia* or Islamic law. If you believe the western press version of the Saddam regime then it impossible to reconcile Ba'athist secularism with support for such extremism. However, if Saddam supported Islamic extremism so long as he could control and direct it than such alliances make perfect sense.

The FIS would later rally to support Saddam and pledged to send fighters to defend him during the Gulf War. This meeting and the support for an Islamic fundamentalist group by the Saddam regime is documented by terrorism researcher Thomas Joscelyn, who wrote for the *Weekly Standard* in a August 3rd, 2005 article entitled The Algerian Connection: Why did Saddam financially support an al Qaeda affiliate in Algeria?:

> The roots of Saddam's relationship with the GIA trace back to the 1991 Gulf War. The group's early history is particularly useful in understanding why Saddam would offer the GIA his support.
>
> As the war approached, Saddam sought and received support from a conspicuous group of Islamist radicals. Among them was the Sudanese leader Hassan al-Turabi and an Algerian Islamist named Abbas Madani, both of whom traveled to Baghdad in the months prior to the war and declared their support for Saddam.
>
> Madani was then the leader of Algeria's Islamic Salvation Front (the "FIS"), which was a consortium of four Islamist parties formed to obtain democratically-elected political power. Madani was somewhat more tempered in his support for Saddam than his cohort, Ali Benhadj, because he feared (correctly) that support for Saddam would end Saudi financial support for the FIS. Benhadj overcame Madani's reticence, however, and moved the FIS firmly into Saddam's camp. According to Gilles Keppel (**Jihad, The Trail of Political Islam**), Benhadj—who was accompanied by "a detachment of Afghan-garbed jihadists fresh from Peshawar"—took to the streets and "delivered a harangue in front of

the [Algerian] Ministry of Defense in which he demanded the formation of a corps of volunteers to join the forces of Saddam Hussein."

Writing in **Al Qaeda's Armies,** Middle East expert Jonathan Schanzer explains that as the Gulf War neared the "FIS became increasingly pro-Iraq and anti-U.S., as seen through their slogans, protests, and even training camps for volunteers to fight for Saddam Hussein's Iraq. The U.S. conflict with Iraq was a powerful symbol of FIS' soaring popularity."

The FIS was a precursor to the GIA which stands for Armed Islamic Group. It stands to reason that they did not offer support to Saddam's supposedly secular government for no reciprocation. This relationship provides yet another example of the Saddam regime working with Islamic extremists. Joscelyn also writes:

Bin Laden did not just finance the building of the GIA with money from his own pockets or his wealthy benefactors, however. He also received help from Saddam Hussein: At least one former CIA official has confirmed that some of the money bin Laden funneled to the GIA came from Saddam's Iraq. (Ibid)

Ahmed Ressam a former FIS-GIA member who later joined al Qaeda was arrested in 1999 for smuggling explosives into the U.S. near Seattle for the purpose of bombing the Los Angeles International Airport. This is one of many examples of support by the Saddam regime to those who would later work with or join al Qaeda. A reasonable assessment is that these interactions are an indicator of the Saddam regime's involvement and reliance upon Islamic terrorists to do its' bidding or to at least act in mutual interest.

Many of the supporting arguments used by those who deny cooperation between Saddam and Islamic terrorists are based more on misperception than on fact. Whether or not Saddam was sincere in his Islamic faith is irrelevant. What is relevant is that by even feigning piety he demonstrated that he recognized the need to garner support from Islamic fundamentalists. And once the secular barricade was lowered it is not so hard to reason that a brutal thug like Saddam would work with Islamic terrorists just as easily as he did secular terrorists.

To preface the next point there is no direct evidence presented here that proves Saddam Hussein worked directly with Usama bin Laden to conduct the 9/11 attacks. Saddam and Usama may have even hated each other. Even if this was the case it brings to mind the old saying "keep your friends close and your enemies closer." A historical comparison can be made by examining World War II. There is no doubt that Churchill and Stalin hated each other. However, the Nazis were a more threatening common enemy and Churchill along with Stalin set aside their differences long enough to defeat them. The mutual dislike between Saddam and Usama does not preclude Saddam's support to either al-Qaeda or Islamic terrorism.

It is beyond ludicrous that some pundits argue that if Saddam had no direct involvement in 9/11 or no direct relationship to Usama bin Laden then he is cleared of any culpability. Such an argument ignores that al-Qaeda is more than Usama bin Laden. Al-Qaeda is also made up of a large Egyptian Islamic Jihad (EIJ) contingent led by Ayman al Zawahiri (often called the number two man in al- Qaeda, which is a bit of a misnomer as it is more of a co-captaincy) who does appear to be tied to Saddam in these documents. There is also evidence that ties bin Laden to Saddam but to a much lesser extent.

The 9/11 attacks were not the sole responsibility of al-Qaeda but rather they were the result of the *global Islamic jihad movement* as embodied by the World Islamic Front, the umbrella group behind what is often mistakenly termed as the al Qaeda *fatwa*. This sometimes loose and sometimes strong association of various groups (who at times compete with each other for power) is more than al-Qaeda. Al-Qaeda is the centerpiece for jihad against the west but it is supported by many other groups that feed directly into their operations and funding. These groups include state sponsors who support the movement to spread Islam through violent intimidation. They are all a valid target as part of the *Global War on Terror* which included Saddam Hussein.

Many of these groups and states were told after 9/11 that either you are "with us or against us" by a president who would demand they stop supporting terrorists. Several of those nations realized that the 'jig is up' and chose to work with us. This hardnosed brand of foreign policy forced several governments to partner with the United States in the war on terror. Despite the fact that his detractors disdain his foreign policy and claim he won't work with other countries this action turned Libya and the U.A.E. at a minimum off the course of terror support and thus avoided war with the United States.

The Saddam regime was given the same choice as Iran and Syria. It was President Bush's declaration that helped to force Syria out of Lebanon. It was his tough stance that forced Iran to cooperate to a small extent in stopping terrorists; a cooperation from which they have both backslide as the U.S. has become entangled in and politically vulnerable because of Iraq. As even the most solid terror sponsors began to work with Washington to fight Islamic terrorism Saddam Hussein made no reconciliation and rebuffed all demands that he change his course of action.

This is critical to understand as a major reason behind the Iraq war. Saddam was the only national leader in the Middle East that failed to cooperate with Washington to at least some extent in the war on terror.

An example of how these documents can provide subtle nuances that dramatically shift our understanding of why Saddam supported the *global Islamic jihad movement* can be shown by re-examining expert testimony related to the subject of Saddam and terrorism. To clarify, the point of this review is not to challenge conclusions this expert stated, but rather it is to demonstrate how the documents enhance our understanding so we can re-evaluate conclusions that were made absent the information provided in these documents. Judith S. Yaphe, a CIA counterterrorism professional testified at the third public hearing of the *National Commission on Terrorist Attacks Upon the United States* also known as the 9-11 Commission. She made it clear that she is skeptical of a direct connection between Usama bin Laden and Saddam Hussein. However that is incidental to the point of Saddam's support to International terrorism:

> My testimony focuses on the role and actions of Iraq as a state sponsor of terrorism under the control of Saddam Husayn. Iraq under Saddam was a major state sponsor of international terrorism:
>
> Baghdad actively sponsored terrorist groups, providing safe haven, training, arms, and logistical support, requiring in exchange that the groups carry out operations ordered by Baghdad for Saddam's objectives. Terrorist groups were not permitted to have offices, recruitment, or training facilities or freely use territory under the regime's direct control without explicit permission from Saddam.

And that is at the heart of understanding the issue of why Saddam supported terrorism. The Saddam regime *was* threatened by Islamic extremists. This is a major part of the reason *why* Saddam's government supported them, mainly outside of Iraq, but even *inside Iraq under controlled conditions.*

The same condition existed in Saudi Arabia and is well documented. Steve Coll in his book *Ghost Wars* discussed how the House of Saud adopted the strategy of supporting Islamic extremists in operations external to Saudi Arabia in order to keep them out of the country:

> Prince Turki and other liberal princes found it easier to appease their domestic Islamic rivals by allowing them to proselytize and make mischief abroad than to confront and resolve these tensions at home.

Such appeasement by the Saudis came in the form of millions of dollars to Islamic fundamentalists involved in the Afghan jihad against the Soviets. What followed next is easily observable. The timeline is unmistakable and has strong implications.

The appeasement of these opposition groups in particular Usama bin Laden's by Saudi royalty occurred prior to the transition of the jihad to a focus against the United States. Bin Laden's rants against the House of Saud for allowing American troops on Saudi soil during the Gulf War ended this support. Although bin Laden was wealthy his individual finances came nowhere near that of an oil rich nation. Suddenly, Islamic jihad lost a major benefactor in Saudi Arabia—although to be sure private financing from Saudi Arabia made up some of that difference. It is important here to distinguish between the support of the Mujahideen provided by the United States versus that of Usama bin Laden.

The United States focused its' support channels to native Afghanis in Afghanistan and not the Arab al Qaeda elements. This support ended before the Taliban was created. Despite the claims that the U.S. supported bin Laden he was a competitor of the United States to woo Afghanis to his cause and not a client.

The Saddam regime which had worked with al Qaeda pre-cursor groups during the Gulf War saw the vacuum as American and Saudi money began to dry up in Afghanistan. At the same time it started to feel the influence of the Islamic jihad as an internal threat—thus the Return to Faith Campaign in 1993 to placate the Sufi/Sunni. Iraq was essentially isolated from any international support. Egypt and Saudi Arabia had both supported the American/UN action against Saddam. Saddam needed international support and internal political stability and influence with the Sufi/Sunni especially after the disastrous Kuwait invasion. That mistake had left his internal security apparatus and military weakened with new limitations under UN restriction as evidenced by the Shi'ite uprising following the Gulf War.

The Arab Islamic jihadists or mujahideen who had thrived on Saudi oil money in Afghanistan and Pakistan also now counted the same enemies (Egypt, Saudi Arabia, Israel and the U.S.A.) and shared a religious identification with the Ba'athists. Islamic jihad had a need for a new benefactor since they were mainly sponsored by Pakistan which is not an oil rich nation. It was the perfect confluence of need.

And it was after the mujahideen and Saddam found a need for mutual support that the jihad shifted away from the Russians (Saddam's perennial benefactor) to his enemy the United States (excepting of course the Chechnyan portion of the jihad which is as much a war for land as ideology). One does not need to be smacked over the head to get the implications.

With the inclusion of Saddam the *global Islamic jihad movement* shifted away from Saddam's friends and towards his enemies. As further evidence the jihad movement at that time began to use Iraq in its justifications for war against the United States. It is no coincidence. It is merely what should have been an obvious public manifestation of Saddam's hidden influence over the emerging Islamic jihad against the United States. As Judith Yaphe of the CIA noted Saddam used terrorism as a tool. Now the implications can be supported by direct evidence in these documents that was unavailable a short time ago in order to demonstrate that Saddam was closely tied to *Islamic terrorism* as well.

There is evidence that the Saddam regime hunted Islamic jihadists in its midst, but it is again a misinterpretation to think that this means he hunted all Islamic terrorists; he hunted those who worked against him and supported those who worked with him. And they could very well be the same individuals in different instances as these relationships changed. To return to Yaphe's testimony:

> Saddam used foreign terrorist groups as an instrument of foreign policy. Groups hosted by Saddam were denied protection if he wanted to improve relations with a neighboring country and encouraged to attack those Saddam wanted to pressure. If they refused Saddam's "requests," they were exiled from Iraq. (Ibid)

Saddam used terrorist groups as an instrument of foreign policy...to attack those Saddam wanted to pressure. That was also the motive for Saddam's support to *Islamic* terrorism. Yaphe's testimony continues:

Iraq under Saddam supported international terrorist organizations to bolster Iraq's revolutionary credentials, ensure his own role as Great Arab leader, and intimidate rival governments. In examining the history, methods, and patterns of behavior of Saddam Husayn in supporting international terrorism, some "truths" stand out. Beginning in the early 1970s, Saddam provided safe haven, training, arms, and other forms of assistance to Palestinian and Arab extremists. Baghdad hosted the Abu Nidal Organization (ANO), the Popular Front for the Liberation of Palestine (PFLP), the Democratic Front for the Liberation of Palestine (DFLP), and the Hawari faction of the PLO. In addition, Baghdad created the Arab Liberation Front (ALF) as its personal surrogate in the wars against Israel. Although the ALF conducted no terrorist operations, Saddam used it in the 1970s and resurrected it again in the current Palestinian intifada as a means to recruit Palestinians and, in 2001, to win praise for offering $25,000 to the family of each Palestinian "martyred" in an Israeli attack. Some examples of Iraqi support include:

• **Abu Nidal**. While enjoying safe haven in Iraq, the ANO conducted a number of terrorist attacks on Jewish and Israel targets in the 1970s and 1980s, including murders at synagogues and attacks on El Al airline passengers in Turkey, Austria, Belgium, and Italy, and the hijacking of a Pan Am airliner (Pan Am 73) in Karachi, in which 22 people (2 Americans) were murdered. ANO also attacked PLO representatives in Europe, murdered Jordanian diplomats, and attempted to assassinate Israel's ambassador in London. (This attack became the cause celebre for Israel's invasion of Lebanon in 1982.) When ANO leader Sabri al-Banna refused to conduct operations against the Syrian regime ordered by Iraq, he was cast out of the country, only to later be allowed back. He died in August 2002 in Baghdad from 4 gunshot wounds to the head, a suicide according to Iraqi security officials. I assume Saddam had decided to remove evidence of his links to one of the most notorious of international terrorists at a time when the United States was increasing pressure on him to reveal his WMD programs and was accusing him of sponsoring al-Qaida.

• **Abu Abbas.** Palestinian terrorist Mahmud Abbas, known as Abu Abbas, and his organization, the Palestine Liberation Front (PLF), enjoyed safe haven and support in Saddam's Iraq. Abu Abbas was responsible for the October 1985 hijacking of the Italian cruise ship Achille Lauro and the murder of Leon Klinghoffer, an elderly American confined to a wheelchair. In October 2000, following the outbreak of Israeli-Palestinian fighting, Abu Abbas announced from Baghdad that the PLF would resume attacks on Israel.

• **Others:** In the 1970s Saddam aided Palestinian radical factions that conducted terrorist operations on Israeli, Jewish, Western, and moderate Arab targets. In the 1980s, he sheltered the Kurdish anti-Turkish terrorist group, the Kurdish Workers Party (PKK) at the same time he allowed Ankara hot pursuit of PKK terrorists across its border. In the 1990s, he provided safe haven and supported attacks by the leftist anti-Iranian Mujahideen-e Khalq on targets inside Iran, including rocket attacks on government office buildings in Tehran. (Ibid)

While links to these groups are well known and most observers accept them as truth, some make a logical distinction that these are pro-Arab groups and such relations do not serve as evidence of support to Islamic terrorists. In that estimation, the fact that these groups are Islamic is more of a function of geography than motivation and Saddam would not support them otherwise. The authors of this book have examined that conclusion in light of the new evidence to see if it is a supportable hypothesis. The documents indicate that it makes no difference if they were pro-Arab groups with Islamic identity incidental to motivation, were non-terror centric groups that desired to inculcate Islamic law in their own countries, or were professional Islamic jihadists; Saddam supported them and they reciprocated.

Saddam used them as a tool to apply pressure to his enemies, which exemplified the strategy of *divide and conquer*. In order to pit enemies against each other, you may have to support one to influence the conflict. It is the exact same principle utilized by the United States under the presidency of devout Christian and Nobel Peace Prize winner Jimmy Carter. In 1979, Carter began support to Islamic extremists inside Afghanistan who were fighting the Soviet army. Despite the fact that the CIA cast a wary eye on some of the very people it assisted it was a means to an end. The degradation of Soviet prestige was possibly via these Afghani Islamic fighters if properly managed. Yet at the time some of these Islamic jihadists were seen as a possible threat because of their anti-American ideology. Despite this fact the aid continued as long as the threat could be managed and not be aimed at the U.S.; these Islamic radicals were not considered to be a direct threat to U.S. security.

So when it is argued that Saddam was ideologically incapable of working with Islamic radicals one has to determine how a Christian, peace-activist, American president would do so, yet Saddam would not. When put into that context, the argument that Saddam would not work with Islamic extremists appears somewhat ridiculous.

The Saddam regime's assistance to Islamic terrorists had nothing to do with being enemies or friends with individual leaders and everything to do with how Saddam Hussein could use them to achieve a goal. For Saddam, ideology was secondary to what someone could do for him. Saddam was a spectacular example of a thug who relied on street level cunning to survive. To continue with Yaphe:

> In my judgment, Saddam assessed Usama bin Ladin and al-Qaida as a threat rather than a potential partner to be exploited to attack the United States. Bin Ladin wanted to attack Iraq after it occupied Kuwait in 1990 rather than have the Saudi government depend on foreign military forces. Several captured al-Qaida operatives have said Usama refused to consider working for or with Saddam, according to press accounts. Saddam would have understood that after Usama had realized his ambition to remove U.S. forces from Arabia and eliminate the Al Sa'ud and other ruling families in the Gulf, that he would have been the next target. The threat would have appeared particularly risky to Saddam, given the modest indicators of a revival in personal piety and Islamist dress among Iraqi Sunnis in the last decade. He certainly suspected Saudi Arabia of encouraging Wahhabi pietism and practices among Iraq's Sunni Arabs and Bin Ladin's loyalists would have been suspect of similar anti-regime activities. (Ibid)

She writes, "The threat would have appeared particularly risky to Saddam, given the modest indicators of a revival in personal piety and Islamist dress among Iraqi Sunnis in the last decade." It was not a modest shift to Islam. It was a major shift toward cooperation with Islamic extremists to appease and use them.

Yaphe concludes that Saddam would have known Usama bin Laden would have come after him next if he dethroned the Saudi royalty. But why would he? Yaphe's reasoning fails to consider that Al-Qaeda is composed largely of the Egyptian Islamic Jihad (EIJ), whose *raison d'être* is the overthrow of the Egyptian government not Saddam Hussein. This is a motivating factor for Zawahiri's every attack. He wants to force western governments away from Egypt so he can take over just as Usama bin Laden wants to rule Saudi Arabia. In this, Saddam was a friend not a foe.

The Deobandi of Pakistan, an essential part of the jihad movement, were much more concerned with taking over in Pakistan. Algerian al Qaeda leaders were focused on taking over Algeria.

When you get right down to it, considering that Saddam was appeasing al Qaeda, its leaders had no real motivation to overthrow their fellow Sufi/Sunni Saddam regime at all in the short term. Did the 1998 *fatwa* that discussed Iraq demand the removal of Saddam? In fact, it made no such demand. It was a call to support the Iraqi people via measures that would have benefited the Saddam regime as well; an oversight or a calculation? In fact, Saddam would have been way down on the list perhaps just ahead of a conquest of Iran as an al Qaeda target. It is a great irony that leftists parrot the claim that "al Qaeda was not in Iraq before we got there" with no consideration of the fact that as Al Qaeda's enemy the U.S. has suffered sustained attacks by al Qaeda while Saddam suffered none. Yet they claim Saddam was an enemy to al Qaeda.

Yaphe's testimony before the 9-11 Commission makes a great point. The counterterrorism analyst points out that proof of the relationship should come from those involved in it:

> I find troubling the use of circumstantial evidence and the corresponding lack of credible evidence to jump to extraordinary conclusions on Iraqi support for al-Qaida. By credible, I mean reporting from sources with some record of credibility, from open sources or intelligence community clandestine sources; evidence of the signature of an attack to a known group, something tangible linking doer to deed to

sponsor. I worked in CIA's Counter Terrorist Center for 3 years and am all too painfully aware that information on terrorism does not come from librarians or patriots or other untarnished sources. It comes from people who do it themselves, who have an agenda or a grudge, or who enjoy watching fires put out. (Ibid)

Yaphe writes that any evidence of Saddam's support for al-Qaeda should come from the people who "do it themselves." Considering that the people who brokered and authorized these relationships with Islamic terrorists have every reason to lie the next best evidence is from their own records; just as any criminal investigation searches for relevant documentation. Now we have found those records and it destroys the notion that the Saddam regime was unwilling to work with any group that would help him.

So what would Saddam think of al Qaeda anyway? To answer this question the first thing a western thinker has to do is concede that western notions of Islamic radicalism are different than Middle Eastern notions. To Saddam Hussein an Islamic terrorist would not be someone who blew up American embassies but instead those that attacked his embassies. It is about perspective. If they did not confront him directly there was no moral issue with dealing with them—just as President Carter had no moral issue with supporting Islamic extremism in Afghanistan. And again one must ask, if al-Qaeda was such a threat to the Saddam regime where were the attacks when he was in power? Did al-Qaeda blow up his embassies? Did they kill his foreign diplomats?

We find evidence to support this line of reasoning in Arab media. According to Arab media reports from Iraq, Saddam knew Wahhabis (the extremist Islamic sect emanating from Saudi Arabia) were in Iraq and he originally hunted them. Ultimately, he realized that his senior leaders had become involved with them, and he was forced to compromise to keep the support of his senior leadership.

One document captured in Iraq is drafted on otherwise blank, white paper (it must be noted that another captured document instructs regime officials to write drafts on blank paper to be sent for typing) with the header *Presidency of the Republic, The President.* It contains a tantalizing lead in the investigation of Saddam's relationship with Islamic extremists. It simply states:

> Doctor Ahmad Al Kabissi gives lectures to the Wahhabis in Fallujah and then the Wahhabis have a karate class. —CMPC-2003-007859

This single note led to a fascinating article from the Arab media. Dr. Ahmad al Kabissi was included in a media report from Fallujah. A reporter, named Hazem al Amin wrote for *Dar al Hayat,* a news organization based in Lebanon. His article, entitled The Resistance In The "Sunni Triangle," is ostensibly about smuggling but reveals much more valuable information.

The author gives a description of what Fallujah was like before the war:

> It is the entrance of this district from Baghdad, and it is the most prosperous and religious city, not mention most loyal to the bath party. [sic]

How can this be? Is the epicenter of Saddam's support a religious hub for Iraq? Did no American reporter know this? Shouldn't that alone bring into question the soundness of the argument that the Ba'athists were dissociated from Islam? The author tells us that it has the largest number of Mosques per capita of any Iraqi city. The author writes about Fallujah in the post-Saddam era but prior to the large battle that took place there in 2004:

> In the markets of Fallujah, one could easily find former Iraqi officers left unemployed after the fall of the former regime. [Ibid]

Why was this the case? It was because Saddam gave land grants in Fallujah to his military officers and Ba'ath party officials. So naturally it had a high concentration of people invested in Saddam's dictatorship. This is not a condition unique to Fallujah; it was the same for Haditha and Ramadi two other flash points of the insurgency.

Military officers supported their Fallujah lifestyles by smuggling oil. In doing so, they worked with foreign peoples along tribal and ethnic affiliations. Some of these people were the Wahhabi Islamists:

> The district took advantage of its location, and the food for oil program. People used to smuggle goods in exchange for oil, and sell these good in exchange for cash. [sic] Most of these operations were held in the District of Anbar, where these operations prompted military and tribunal alliances. Many Officers had special privileges, and their own shares in these operations. Many of the tribes had historical connections with neighboring tribes in neighboring countries. These factors facilitated the conduct to these operations.
>
> On the other hand, the regime and it deteriorating institutions, disregarded these illegal operations and alliances in an attempt to persevere its remaining authority figure over this district, knowing that these deeds would not have been disregarded and these alliances se-

cured certain religious groups that began to emerge throughout the mosques in this that district, outside the scope of and understanding of Ba'athist Islam.

It is true that the regime went after these religious groups who infringed from neighboring countries, but these persecutions resulted only in imprisonment of its members for several months. These activists reminded protected by the tribe and their relatively close ties to prominent members of the security apparatus of the regime. And this regime (alliance system) will later on have a significant impact on the "resistance", for its methods of smuggling and ways of attaining money is very similar to the methods today's "resistant fighters" are using today to gather money and support for their fellow Arabs.

The strong religious incentives and environment, which was the product of exchange of ideas in the early ninety's of the past decade, is the major motive for these resistant fighters. One could feel that the resistance of Fallujah is a life style, people have been used to all along. These resistant fighter use the same roads that used previously to sway around the food for oil program and attain goods by slinking their boarders in their 4 wheel drives, and perhaps organizing certain trades and establishing new tribunal relations with other tribes in nearby areas. (Ibid)

This is a stunning revelation with some staggering implications that we found nowhere in the American media. To summarize, the author tells us:

- Saddam gave land grants to the Ba'athists in al Anbar province. (There are supporting media reports to this elsewhere.)

- Because of sanctions, the Saddam regime began oil smuggling operations to make money. It was conducted by the

Ba'athist officials in the Anbar province. (Oil-for-food corruption has been well documented, but it wasn't widely reported until after this late 2003 article. In other words, if Hazem was making this up, he was betting on a relatively unknown cause to explain the infiltration of Islamic extremists in Iraq.)

- The Ba'athists traded with men who were foreign Islamic extremists. Yet these men, who were already "under the radar," were the perfect trading partners for an illegal operation.

- As these Islamists smuggled out the oil they also infiltrated the province.

- And here is the key— these Ba'athists were linked by ethnic and religious identity to their extremist trading partners which was probably the initial reason for choosing them. Since these Ba'athists were protected by regime leaders, (for instance. al Douri, the Revolutionary Command Council Vice President who gave Saddam a blood Quran and who was known to be supremely favored by the Sufi/Sunnis of the Anbar province) it became impossible for Saddam to risk fighting the Islamic extremists. Because, like a vine, the Islamists had become entangled in the wallets and lifestyles of Saddam's regime.

Hazem al Amin tells us:

> A journalist from the city of Fallujah says that during the ninetey's [sic] the city witnessed the emergence of many Islamic militant groups the city had known before. Men with long beards started to appear. and certain groups started to buying TV sets and destroying them in one of the roads of the city. [Ibid]

This is witness testimony from a resident to the rise of the Wahhabi in Fallujah under the Saddam regime. The regime first tried to stop it:

> The Iraqi regime then interfered by closing down one of these mosques for quartering such groups. Abu Hareth whose brother is a member of these groups says "My oldest brother is member of these groups, and he was discharged from the army for his affiliation to these people and he became unemployed, and he started to spend most of his time in the mosque. The Ba'athists were closely following him, and whenever they could they would arrest some of the members of this group. This happened many times in the city of Fallujah and the city of Abu Gharib, my oldest brother was never imprisoned because my youngest brother was a member of the Ba'ath party, and he always protected him." [Ibid]

That passage describes the Saddam regime that we have been presented with by the American media—Secular Ba'athists in hot pursuit of Islamic extremists in Iraq. But it is not the entire story:

> It seems to very clear the level of tyranny the city of Fallujah witnessed from the groups and the regime itself. The rise of such groups can be attributed to lack of authority of the regime. The regime is derives in essence its power and legitimacy mainly from these areas, and according it is very difficult to exercise total control over these areas, and a compromise was always reached. [Ibid]

A compromise was always reached. Saddam needed the support of the men directly involved in the oil smuggling. The greatest threat to the Saddam regime was insurrection. To forestall it he had to keep the support of the Anbar province. Ba'athists got to pocket oil-smuggling money; Islamic extremists got funding to replace lost Saudi sponsorship and were allowed to spread their ideology under controlled conditions as long as it did not threaten but in fact enhanced Saddam's grasp on the power. Hazem tells us further:

> Among the citizens of this city who were well know and their reputation far exceeded the city and even the county [sic] are Dr. Ahmad Al Kabissi and Sheik Abdulaziz Al Samarrai. (Ibid)

So it seems clear that Dr. Ahmad Kabissi listed in the Saddam memo is a real person. He was involved with Islamic extremists in Fallujah. It is a nice bit of validation for the Lebanese article that some of its claims are validated by the Saddam regime documentation. Other documentation provides evidence to support the article's claim that the Saddam regime found common ground with the Islamic extremists when it was beneficial. Because the article seems to have gotten it quite right with other facts we have found in the documentation it provides the basis of this book's working theory of the nature of the Saddam regime in regards to Islamic extremists.

Some corroboration of this hypothetical motivation can be found in a Fox News article, Possible Saddam-Al Qaeda Link Seen in U.N. Oil-for-Food Program by Claudia Rosett and George Russell. (In the interest of full disclosure, George Russell has edited the work of a co-author of this book, Ray Robison, for Fox News but is in no way affiliated with this work.) The article discusses a company favored by the Saddam regime for trading, MIGA, or the *Malaysian Swiss Gulf and African Chamber.*

Shortly after the September 11, 2001, attacks on the United States, both MIGA and its chief founder and longtime president, Ahmed Idris Nasreddin, landed on the U.N. watchlist of entities and individuals belonging to, or affiliated with, al-Qaeda. Nasreddin is a member of the terror-linked Muslim Brotherhood.

Nasreddin's longtime business partner, Egyptian-born Youssef Nada, also of the Muslim Brotherhood, likewise appears on the U.N.'s al-Qaeda watchlist, as do a slew of both Nasreddin's and Nada's enterprises. Former Treasury Secretary Paul O'Neill described Nada and Nasreddin in August 2002 as "supporters of terrorism" involved in "an extensive financial network providing support to al-Qaeda and other terrorist-related organizations."

Far less attention has been paid to the small, select band of MIGA's other charter members. But one of them, Iraqi-born Ahmed Totonji, set up shop years ago just outside Washington, D.C., and is now among those named by U.S. federal authorities in an investigation into a cluster of companies and Islamic non-profits based in Herndon, Virginia, which are suspected of having funneled money to terrorist groups.

MIGA had other founders as well. One of them, who does not appear on the U.N. terror list, is an Arab businessman now in his early 60s named Abdul Rahman Hayel Saeed.

Described by an acquaintance as urbane, polite and fluent in English, Hayel Saeed was born into one of Yemen's most prominent business clans, the owners of a family-held global conglomerate based in the Yemeni capital of Taiz and named for its founding patriarch—the Hayel Saeed Anam Group of Companies, or HSA.

So a founder of MIGA owns a conglomerate called HSA, Rosett and Russell tell us:

HSA is unquestionably a company involved in legitimate business. But given the involvement of Abdul Rahman Hayel Saeed, it is striking that between 1996 and 2003, while the United Nations ran its Oil-for-Food relief program in Iraq, the HSA Group — via U.N.-approved Oil-for-Food contracts — sold at least $400 million worth of goods to Saddam. [Ibid]

And to understand why this is significant, you have to understand the corruption of the oil-for-food program:

Saddam's standard scam was to underprice oil sales and overpay for relief supplies, thus generating fat profits for his business partners. Many of those contractors would kick back part of the take to Saddam's regime — or divert it to whatever uses Saddam might fancy. By various accounts, those uses ranged from building palaces to buying arms to supplying Saddam's sadistic son Uday with equipment for torturing Iraqi athletes.

One of the big questions is whether any of the money skimmed from Oil-for-Food also slopped into terrorist-financing ventures such as MIGA. [Ibid]

A major beneficiary of Saddam's contracts, Saeed was also a founder of another company that has significant ties to Islamic terrorism. While it may not be possible to prove that Saddam's funds found their way straight into Islamic terrorism it does help to illuminate that web of interdependency and mutual interest between Islamic terrorists who needed funding and the Saddam regime which had the oil that it undersold for kickbacks with both sides sharing in the illicit, undeclared profits.

Thus, the reasons why Saddam worked with Islamic extremists can include:

- The Saddam regime was not a strictly secular regime.
- The regime used Islamic terrorists to influence and attack enemies.
- Saddam was forced into accepting Islamic extremists in the Anbar province because they were connected to and needed by his military and political support base at the command level of his regime.
- They Islamic extremists provided revenue generation in the smuggling of oil.
- Saddam placated them to keep them from attacking his regime.
- Because of the strategic location of Afghanistan in relation to Iran it would have been essential that he have influence over the Islamic extremists in Afghanistan lest they fall under Iranian control.
- They provided Saddam potential access to the good graces of Pakistan, a nuclear state, which would have been a powerful ally.
- They provided a connection to his Sunni power base and were a tool to use directly against Shi'ite and Kurdish antagonists in Iraq.
- Some of Saddam's key leaders genuinely embraced Sunni fundamentalism.
- Saddam supported Egyptian and Saudi Arabian opposition groups because of the mutual objective of driving the United States from the Middle East to end its support of those governments and then deposing those governments.

- Even though Islamic extremism is anathema to the west, it is not for many of the governments with which the Saddam regime wanted to form alliances. Therefore, political influence in other Arab and South Asian governments was enhanced by the regime's relations with leaders of the *global Islamic jihad movement.*

These reasons are far more compelling than the simple claim of a secular/Islamic divide.

CHAPTER 4:
THE IIS AGENT'S NOTEBOOK
PART ONE

Background

IN OCTOBER OF 1999, the Pakistani military began a *coup d'état* to replace Prime Minster Nawaz Sharif with General Pervez Musharraf. Musharraf retains power in Pakistan as of this writing. The timing is important to note because it relates directly to why Maulana Fazlur Rahman was in Baghdad a month later negotiating between the Taliban, his own sizable Islamic jihad-centric political parties, and the Saddam regime.

The Taliban in Afghanistan had enjoyed support and legitimacy from Pakistan prior to this coup. The Taliban was largely of Pakistani origin. Many of its leaders had ethnic ties to Pakistan and had lived and trained there. The Pakistani government considered the Taliban the surest route to stabilizing its western border and securing trade routes across Afghanistan. For many reasons, including Islamic identity, Pakistan provided essential support to the Taliban via their intelligence services and military. In fact, before the Taliban moved into more progressive regions of Afghanistan in 1997 and highlighted the brutality of their brand of Sunni Islamic extremism, many foreign governments considered them a potentially unifying factor that might stop the internal warring. As it happens, this view was mistaken as the Taliban subsequently brutally suppressed even non-aggressive elements of Afghan society and began to focus its Islamic extremism outwards via international Islamic terrorists groups such as al Qaeda.

The support of Pakistan had eroded by October of 1999 because of the Taliban's nurturing of international Islamic extremism in Afghanistan. Even though a Pakistani-Islamist shadow government still provided support to the Taliban overt political support was waning under pressure from the United States which was a significant benefactor to Pakistan. When the Pakistani military staged a coup and supplanted a more Islamist Prime Minister with a more secular military dictatorship the Taliban had to see it as a threat.

Maulana Fazlur Rahman had enjoyed influence with the Islamist Pakistani governments beforehand. He was now on the outs along with the Taliban, the group he helped to create. His political faction would become known as 'the opposition' of the Pakistani government. He had here-to-for held positions of power that supported his globe-trotting Islamic militant life style. But now he was relegated to relying on the influence of his Pakistani political base and whatever international support he could bring to the table. In this case, as evidenced by this document and others what he brought was Saddam Hussein.

IRAQI INTELLIGENCE DOCUMENTS

Highlights

This document, evidently captured shortly after the start of the Iraq war (March 2003), is a handwritten notebook kept by an Iraqi intelligence agent describing meetings with Islamic terrorists in 1999.

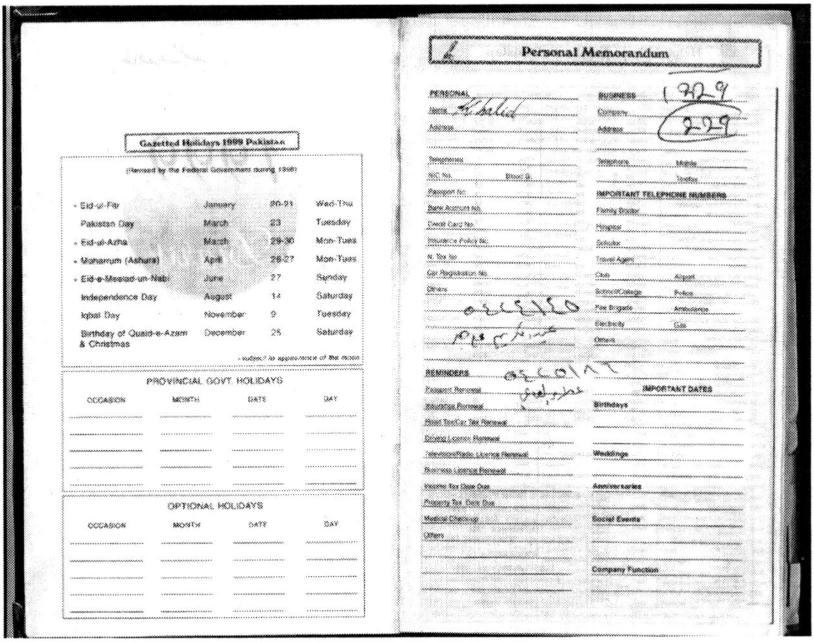

Figure 1. IIS notebook (Page 1)

The most revealing portions include meetings between Ba'athist government and intelligence officials with terror leaders including the Taliban, al Qaeda, and their Pakistani supporters.

Narrative

The document is a notebook kept by an Iraqi intelligence agent. He used it to keep track of his meetings and instructions. Sometimes, fortunately for history, he transcribed meetings with terrorist leaders.

This portion deals extensively with meetings between Maulana Fazlur Rahman who supported al-Qaeda and the Taliban as an unofficial ambassador, and Taha Yassin Ramadan, a former vice president of Iraq. Ramadan was called Saddam Hussein's chief enforcer because he tortured and murdered Iraqi officials who failed Saddam. In 2002 and at his hanging in 2007, the BBC covered him:

> "Washington showed considerable interest in him well before the Iraq war this spring, after opposition forces claimed he hosted Usama bin Laden's deputy, Ayman al-Zawahiri, in Baghdad in 1998." —
> (http://news.bbc.co.uk/2/low/middle_east/2333287.stm)

It is a claim that might have been easy to dismiss coming from opposition forces, but now appears to be quite possible considering the meeting this notebook attributes to Taha Yassin Ramadan.

Maulana Fazlur Rahman is a Pakistani cleric described in a November 6th, 2002 article from the BBC entitled Profile: Maulana Fazlur Rahman by Haroon Rashid as "A pro-Taliban cleric in Pakistan ... one of the two main contenders for the post of the country's prime minister." The BBC also said that "Maulana Fazlur Rahman ... is known for his close ties to Afghanistan's ousted Taliban regime."

Maulana Fazlur Rahman is mentioned by name in this meeting transcript. Another man present in the meeting is Abdul Razaq (alternate spelling Razzak) called the Defense Minister of the Taliban in this notebook. Most western media reports peg him as the Interior Minister of the Taliban. But there are several Southwest Asia media references that claim he was the Taliban Defense Minister. Whatever the case the IIS agent called him the Defense Minister of the Taliban on page sixty-nine of this notebook.

This portion of the notebook provides evidence that in 1999 the Taliban welcomed "Islamic relations with Iraq" to mediate between the Taliban, Hekmatyar and Russia. It provides evidence that the Taliban invited Iraqi officials to Kandahar, Afghanistan also known as the base of operations for al-Qaeda before the U.S. invasion of Afghanistan.

As noted previously there is a corroborating document that mentions the relationship between Maulana Fazlur Rahman and Saddam. It was captured in Afghanistan and used by the U.S. Army in a report about al Qaeda. The document is posted under the identifying administrative number AFGP-2002-601693 at the West Point Combating Terrorism Center website. The government-provided translation used here describes the document as a July 26, 2002, four-page, typed letter from Abu Mus'ab to Abu Mohammed (apparently al-Qaeda operatives) in reply to his inquiry about the status of jihad in Afghanistan.

The letter does not clarify who Abu Mus'ab is but he seems to be high ranking as he has conversations with other high ranking al-Qaeda leaders. Also of note is that the al Qaeda letter makes another revelation where it reads "Aymen went to Iraq." This statement is in the context of a clear conversation about Dr. Ayman al Zawahiri, co-leader of al-Qaeda. The letter was written before the start of Operation Iraqi Freedom. Therefore, it provides evidence that another al-Qaeda leader was in Iraq. It is not stated that he was in Iraq as a guest of the Saddam regime and he could have been there against Saddam's wishes. In another passage the author says about other mujahideen "Some of them went to Saddam". This is an explicitly indication that these al Qaeda men were in Iraq as guests of Saddam. As such it increases the likelihood that Ayman al Zawahiri was a guest of Saddam and provides further indication that the Saddam regime was linked to al-Qaeda.

Here is the passage from the al-Qaeda letter connecting Maulana Fazlur Rahman to Saddam. The authors add bold for ease of reference.

Notes about the passage:

Fadhlu Rahman is an alternate spelling for Fazlur Rahman.

Banazeer is a reference to Benazir Bhutto, a former Pakistani Prime Minister.

Qaddafi is the ruler of Libya.

Sheikh Mohammed 'Omar is Mulla Omar the leader of the Taliban.

Hikmatyar is an alternate spelling for Gulbuddin Hekmatyar. The reference means that the Pakistani government supported the Taliban over Hekmatyar, to replace or substitute Hekmatyar as the central power of Afghanistan. He had previously been the Afghanistan Prime Minister on two occasions.

> After my release I found that people came from the Sudan and everywhere, and began fighting alongside the Taliban movement, which for Pakistan was a substitute for Hikmatyar. Everyone, even children in the streets knew that they were created and controlled by Pakistan. **Their leader Fadhlu Rahman is a friend of Banazeer, Saddam and Qaddafi.** They comprise of the veteran sheikhs (religious scholars) from the schools of Mujaddidi and Mohammed Nabi such as Sheikh Mohammed 'Omar the movement leader.

This second source describes both Fazlur Rahman and Mullah Omar as leaders of the Taliban. The simple fact of the matter is that both men held sway over the Taliban, Mulla Omar in Afghanistan and Fazlur Rahman in Pakistan. Thus, this al Qaeda leader makes the claim that a man he considers the leader of the Taliban is a personal friend of Saddam Hussein.

So what is the relationship between Maulana Fazlur Rahman, the Taliban, and al-Qaeda? Rahman is often described in news articles as the father or godfather of the Taliban. It seems clear that Rahman was close to al Qaeda through his friend Mullah Omar who sheltered Usama bin Laden prior to the allied invasion of Afghanistan in response to 9/11.

Rediff.com, a leading news website in India, ran an article on July 23rd, 2003, entitled <u>Beware the Maulana</u>. It gives an extensive history of Rahman and explains how he helped to organize the men who would later become the Taliban under his friend Mullah Omar. It also describes links to al Qaeda. Most of the details in this article are supported by other reporting. Previously we mentioned that the Maulana was a hard-line fundamentalist with one exception:

> Rahman is a fundamentalist with a difference, known for his proximity to Benazir Bhutto and her Pakistan People's Party. Despite his fundamentalist orientation, he supported her right to become prime minister and opposed the Jamaat-e-Islami campaign in the 1990s against a woman heading the government of an Islamic country.

So Maulana Fazlur Rahman appears to be able to put his Islamic fundamentalism aside when it keeps him in power. One should know that ideology is secondary to benefit for the Islamic jihadists. Islamic extremism is merely a means to an end.

> Benazir rewarded him by making him Chairman of the Parliamentary Foreign Affairs Committee and allegedly asked the Inter-Services Intelligence to place a large amount from its secret fund at his disposal during his travels abroad. (Ibid)

His proximity to Prime Minister Benazir Bhutto is what ultimately led him to create the Taliban:

> In 1993-1994, Pakistan's cotton crop was practically destroyed by
> insects for two years in succession and many textile mills were threat-
> ened with closure. Asif Zardari, Benazir's husband, through a business
> crony in Hong Kong, entered into a contract with Turkmenistan for
> emergency supplies of cotton. The responsibility for transporting
> them to Pakistan by road via Afghanistan was given to the Hong Kong-
> based Pakistani businessman.
>
> His cotton convoys were attacked and the cotton looted by armed
> followers of Gulbuddin Hekmatyar of the Hizb-e-Islami and Ismail Khan,
> the pro-Teheran warlord of Herat.
>
> Zardari then asked retired Major General Naseerullah Babbar, Bena-
> zir's interior minister, to organize a special force to escort the cotton
> convoys through Afghanistan. Naseerullah, with Pervez Musharraf's
> help, organized the Taliban by rallying round many of the dregs of the
> Afghan war of the 1980s against the Soviet troops under Mullah Mo-
> hammad Omar's leadership.
>
> They were helped in this by Fazlur Rahman and his protégé, Mufi
> Shamzai of the Binori madrasa of Karachi. Thus, the Taliban came into
> existence in 1994. (Ibid)

Maulana Fazlur Rahman organized one of the most ruthless regimes in modern history for the purpose of protecting Pakistani
trade routes. Ironically, Benazir Bhutto was not supportive of the
creation of an Islamic state in Afghanistan. She was, rather, led
to do so by her military advisors who saw them as a useful tool for
stabilization. As this Afghani protective force coalesced behind
an Islamic ideology derived from Deobandi and ultimately Saudi

Islamic teachings and began to use its muscle to take control of Afghanistan, the Pakistani intelligence services began to see it as a movement that could be used to secure Afghanistan under Pakistani influence. They then applied pressure to the Prime Minister to fund and control the Taliban. Fazlur Rahman became even more powerful because of his influence over the Taliban.

The *Rediff* article also explains how Maulana Fazlur Rahman is connected to al-Qaeda. But first, the reader must understand the hierarchy and structure of Pakistan's Islamic jihad centric political parties of which the Maulana is a major leader.

One of the most powerful political parties in Pakistan today is the Muttahida Majlis-e-Amal (MMA), or the United Action Front. It is considered the opposition to the current Pakistan government. The Maulana is the Secretary General of the MMA. *Global Security.org* states that the MMA is an alliance composed of 4 powerful religious parties: Jamaat Islami (JI), Jamiat Ulema-e-Islam (F), Jamiat Ulema-e-Islam (S), and Jamiat Ulema-e-Pakistan (N). Other resources give the same or similar description of the MMA.— (http://www.globalsecurity.org/military/world/pakistan/mma.htm)

Maulana Fazlur Rahman is the head of Jamiat Ulema-e-Islam (F), or JUI (F). According to the Federation of American Scientists (*FAS.og*), the JUI (F) in turn has its own subgroups, including the HUM (Harakat ul-Mujahidin) or Movement of Holy Warriors. The *Federation of American Scientists* website describes the HUM. Similar descriptions are found in other references:

The HUM is an Islamic militant group based in Pakistan that operates primarily in Kashmir. It is politically aligned with the radical political party. Jamiat Ulema-i-Islam Fazlur Rehman faction (JUI-F). Longtime leader of the group. Fazlur Rehman Khalil, in mid-February 2000 stepped down as HUM emir, turning the reins over to the popular Kashmiri commander and his second in command, Farooq Kashmiri. Khalil, who has been linked to Usama Bin Ladin and signed his fatwa in February 1998 calling for attacks on U.S. and Western interests, assumed the position of HUM Secretary General. HUM operated terrorist training camps in eastern Afghanistan until Coalition airstrikes destroyed them during fall 2001.—

[http://www.fas.org/irp/world/para/hum.htm]

[FAS references listed as:

• Explaining the Kashmir Insurgency: Political Mobilization and Institutional Decay, Sumit Ganguly, International Security, Vol. 21, no. 2, (Fall 1996)

• Patterns of Global Terrorism 2003 Report)

To summarize, Maulana Fazlur Rahman is the leader of JUI (F) which incorporates the HUM. Fazlur Rahman Khalil was the leader of the HUM. Fazlur Rahman Khalil signed Usama bin Laden's 1998 *fatwa* in the name of the HUM. The HUM was in fact a founding organization of the alliance of Islamic jihad-centric political parties that comprised the World Islamic Front. Although the 1998 *fatwa* is typically called Usama bin Laden's by convention a technical examination shows that the *fatwa* was actually a declaration of war against the U.S. made by several jihadist organizations. The HUM, a subgroup of the JUI (F), was one of them. Shaykh Mir Hamzah, secretary of the Jamiat-ul-Ulema-e-Pakistan, also signed the *fatwa*. His party is also a member of the MMA and the World Islamic Front. The fact of the matter is that the 1998 *fatwa* was a declaration of war against the United States by al-Qaeda and these Islamic jihad-centric political parties led by the Maulana. The Maulana's religious position provided the 'religious authority' needed by Usama bin Laden to attack the U.S. on 9/11.

So when Maulana Fazlur Rahman was meeting with the Iraqi VP in Baghdad he did so as the *father of the Taliban* and as a leader of the World Islamic Front which declared war on the U.S. the year before. The *Rediff* article also defines the relationship of Maulana Fazlur Rahman to the HUM:

> In October 1997, the U.S. State Department designated the Harkat a foreign terrorist organization under the Anti-Terrorism and Effective Death Penalty Act of 1996. Consequently, it is a crime for anyone in the U.S. to be associated with it and foreigners associated with it are not entitled to U.S. visas. Fazlur Rahman, as a suspected supporter if not the Harkat's mentor, is covered by this ban. After the ban, the Harkat-ul-Ansar ostensibly split into two organizations, the Harkat-ul-Mujahideen and the Harkat-ul-Jihad-al-Islami. The Maulana is viewed by many in Pakistan and the U.S. as the patron of both.

According to *Rediff* and other sources, Maulana Fazlur Rahman is the mentor and patron of the HUM (Khalil's group) which is an Islamic jihad organization that was designated a foreign terrorist organization by Madeline Albright, former Secretary of State during the Clinton administration. Rahman is a politico-terrorist which is not an uncommon condition when you view other terrorist leaders such as Yassir Arafat. The *FAS* article about the HUM also mentions that Ahmed Omar Sheik, was convicted of the abduction/murder in January-February 2002 of U.S. journalist Daniel Pearl. Khalid Sheik Mohammed, the mastermind behind 9/11 and the 1993 WTC attack has admitted to beheading Denial

Pearl by his own hand. Thus, it becomes clear that the Maulana is another portal for Saddam's entry into the *global Islamic jihad movement* and a link for Saddam's involvement with the groups that have spawned the most heinous attacks on America.

The *Rediff* article also mentions that the Maulana is a mentor to the Harkat-ul-Jihad-al-Islami, (HUJI) the Islamic jihad organization that was implicated in a recent large-scale plot in Britain to blow up airliners over the U.S..

In his book *Taliban: Militant Islam, Oil and Fundamentalism in Central Asia,* Ahmed Rashid mentions Fazlur Rahman (Rehman):

> However the Taliban's closest links were with Pakistan where many of them had grown up and studied in madrassas run by the mercurial Maulana Fazlur Rehman and his Jamiat-e-Ulema Islam (JUI), a fundamentalist party which had considerable support amongst the Pashtuns in Baluchistan and the North West Frontier Province (NWFP). More significantly Maulana Rehman was now a political ally of Prime Minister Benazir Bhutto and he had access to the government, the army and the ISI to whom he described this newly emerging force.

The Maulana, as leader of the JUI (F), is heavily involved in supporting the madrassas and terrorist camps that churn out Taliban and al-Qaeda fighters. The ideology that spurns these men is called Deobandi. Deobandi traces its lineage to wealthy Saudis who spread their Islamic sectarian theocracy, called Wahhabi by some, to Pakistan. *Global Security.org* has an entry on *Deobandi Islam:*

> Although the majority of the Islamic population (Sunni) in Afghanistan and Pakistan, belong to the Hanafi sect, the theologians who have pushed Pakistan towards Islamic Radicalism for decades, as well as

the ones who were the founders of the Taliban, espoused Wahabi rhet-
oric and ideals. This sect took its inspiration from Saudi Hanbali theo-
logians who immigrated there in the 18th century, to help their Indian
Muslim brothers with Hanbali theological inspiration against the British
colonialists. Propelled by oil-generated wealth, the Wahhabi worldview
increasingly co-opted the Deobandi movement in South Asia. –

[http://www.globalsecurity.org/military/intro/islam-deobandi.htm)

(Global Security references listed as:

Deobandi Islam: The Religion of the Taliban, U. S. Navy Chaplain
Corps, 15 October 2001)

It should be noted again that the Wahhabi or Salafi sect co-exists
with the Sufi/Sunni sect within these terror groups, they are not
identical, but are similar. The same article from *Global Security.org*
mentions the Maulana:

The fundamentalist Deoband Dar-ul-Uloom brand of Islam inspired
the Taliban movement and had widespread appeal for Muslim fundamentalists. Most of the Taliban leadership attended Deobandi-influ-
enced seminaries in Pakistan. The Taliban was propped up initially by
the civil government of Benazir Bhutto, then in coalition with the Deobandi Jama'at-ulema Islam (JUI) led by Maulana Fazlur Rehman [who by
2003 was the elected opposition leader at the Center in Islamabad and
whose protégé is now the chief Minister in the NWFP]. (Ibid)

The Maulana is a major figure of a religious sect, Deobandi
which shares its ideology with the Wahhabis. Usama bin Laden, a
leader of the *global Islamic jihad movement* is the undeclared leader
of the Wahhabi sect in the form of al Qaeda.

It is here that we understand the prominence of the Maulana. He is a leader of the Deobandi much like Usama bin Laden's role as leader of the Wahhabis. The Deobandi, Wahhabi and Sufi Sunni sects came together in 1998 to declare war on the United States. A year later the Saddam regime was having meetings with them at the highest levels.

While the Taliban and al-Qaeda are two distinct organizations, they share an ideology, a common mission, some of the same leaders, and culpability for 9/11. The fact that the Saddam regime was negotiating mutual support with them flies in the face of the supposed secular/Islamist divide in Baghdad.

To further illustrate the point, a report from the Institute for Afghan Studies concerns a Deobandi conference held in April of 2001 in Pakistan which was organized by Maulana Fazlur Rahman:

> The highlight of the three-day conference near Peshawar from April 8 to April 11 was the prominence given to the messages of Qadhafi (BIOT note: the Libyan leader), the Taleban leader Mullah Omar and the international terrorist, Usama bin Laden." The report indicates the conference "concluded after adopting resolutions challenging the hegemony of the U.S. and its allies in world; demanding an end to U.N. sanctions against Afghanistan, Iraq and Libya, and early withdrawal of U.S.-led Western troops from Arab lands."—
> [http://www.institute-for-afghan-studies.org/ AFGHAN%20CONFLICT/TALIBAN/deobandi_conf_2001.htm]

The Deobandi conference report provides evidence of a *quid pro quo* agreement between the Saddam regime and the *global Islamic jihad movement* centered around Pakistan's Islamic jihad-centric political parties. Here the jihadists are demanding an end to UN sanctions on Iraq—the ultimate goal of Saddam Hussein—after meeting with officials from Saddam's regime in Baghdad. Now consider that this demand concerning Iraq was also made in the World Islamic Front's 1998 *fatwa*. Is it not reason to suspect that the Iraq justifications included in the 1998 *fatwa* was also a result of a previous *quid pro quo*?

If there is evidence that the Deobandi were meeting with the Saddam regime and responded to Saddam's requests for help in removing UN sanctions after 1999 does that suggest that the motivation was the same for the 1998 *fatwa*? The same people with the same arguments were supporting Saddam at different times. Doesn't it make sense that since this support for Iraqis existed before, in the 1998 *fatwa*, then the *global Islamic jihad movement* was benefiting from Saddam before? If the religious authorization that was obtained by al-Qaeda from the Paki clerics under the Maulana for the war against America incorporated the desires of Saddam Hussein then that is a massive indicator that the Saddam regime was central to the *Global War on Terror*. There is significant evidence that this is exactly the case.

It appears quite likely that Saddam co-opted the al-Qaeda cause via the Pakistani end of the World Islamic Front. Al Qaeda needed the Pakistani clerics to authorize the *fatwa*. The Pakistanis were cooperating with Saddam. Therefore, they incorporated Saddam's needs into the 1998 *fatwa* and Usama bin Laden allowed it as long as the public emphasis was on Iraq and not Saddam Hussein. To be sure, this in no way limits the mutual support between these two elements to these terms alone. The evidence presented here shows a much more interdependent relationship between the World Islamic Front and the Saddam regime.

The Deobandi conference also demonstrated that another state sponsor of terrorism, Muammar al Qaddafi is given a prominent voice among the jihadists. Some terrorism experts have argued publicly that the *global Islamic jihadist movement* has moved beyond and is indeed distrustful of state sponsors. While it is likely true they are distrustful, these relationships are not built on trust. They are built on common need, needs that put them "both in one trench." Here the jihadists are providing Qaddafi a platform. In the previously referenced al Qaeda letter the writer says Qaddafi had built them a hospital. This is yet another example of an existing quid pro quo arrangement between a supposedly secular Arab government and Islamic terrorists. Libya provided military support for Islamic militants in return for their support to Libya.

Just as the Ba'athists and Saddam ruled in Iraq, Libya is governed by an Arab secular-socialist revolutionary regime under Qaddafi that suppressed internal Islamic radicalism. Both of these leaders should be precluded from involvement with the *global Islamic jihad movement* if they were true to their ideology and western preconceptions. Yet we find again that the secular vs. Islamic fundamentalist rift can be overcome when both sides have the need.

Findings

This document provides significant evidence that Maulana Fazlur Rahman and the Defense Minister of the Taliban were in Baghdad in 1999 to negotiate for support with the Saddam regime.

- This document provides significant evidence that the Saddam regime was not ideologically opposed to the Taliban or to al-Qaeda.
- This document provides significant evidence that the Saddam regime understood the importance of an alliance with Afghanistan.
- This document provides significant evidence that the Sad-

dam regime was negotiating with the Pakistani political parties for continued support. We can conclude that to secure this support the Saddam regime must have offered something though we cannot determine what precisely in return to the Pakistani political parties.

- This document and the al-Qaeda letter substantiate a secret relationship between the Saddam regime and Maulana Fazlur Raman which ties the regime to a major Deobandi leader and 'religious authority' for the World Islamic Front's 1998 *fatwa*.

Translations

The following is a translation by our translator-colleague, who goes by the *nom de guerre* of "Sammi." It is the first part of three that will come from a notebook kept by an Iraqi intelligence agent. This document was previously reported by Fox News Channel and the Fox News website as part of the *Saddam Dossier* series authored by co-writers Sammi and Ray Robison of this book.

Because of the administrative number—called a Harmony number for the database these documents were stored in—this document appears to have been captured in Iraq in 2003. Sammi adds notes for clarity in parenthesis with 'TC' for 'translator comment'. The authors add informational notes, which are indicated by 'BIOT'. The bold typeface is our addition, and it indicates emphasis or reference material.

Translation for ISGP-2003-0001412 Part One follows:

Meeting of Mr. Vice-President with the Pakistani Fazlur Rahman

Location: Office of Mr. Vice-President in al Zaqqura

Date: Sunday 10:30 AM

Present: Mr. Vice-President, Maulana Fazlur Rahman, Taher

Krichi (TC: family name not very clear), Jamal Abdul Razzak

Meeting session

Words of welcoming.

Questions about the situation in Pakistan

Fazlur Rahman: The situation is good and the Pakistani people have agreed to fight against America.

Unknown: The new humanitarian method of human rights of the American people in the United Nations... (TC: Fragmented notation)

Fazlur Rahman: What is happening in Afghanistan is a violation of the human rights of this country, where Usama bin Laden is one person and the fate of millions cannot be tied to him. (TC: the U.S. is forcing sanctions or pressures on Afghanistan because it is providing sanctuary to bin Laden)

Vice-President: The American method is clear. First I discover many times some Islamic organizations which are not themselves and Islam is innocent from them (BIOT: probably means Islamic organizations that he believes do not behave like Islamic organizations). Those could be a cover for the American deviation like Kosovo. Muslims are known where they are and America is one of the fiercest enemies of Islam. Muslims in Palestine are slaughtered and they support the Jews, but they were provided this cover. America wants to control the world through human rights (TC: following word unclear, possibly democracy) and multiple parties so it can form collaborating parties and create unrest.

Unrest serves America's purpose. The Security Council (BIOT: United Nations) is a tool in the hand of America. Can you blockade a country (BIOT: Afghanistan) because of the presence of one man (BIOT: Usama bin Laden)? This time she (America) got the resolution from the Security Council and it is number 77 (TC:

or 771; BIOT: probably UNSCR 771 in 1992 concerning Bosnia) relative to Iraq (BIOT: probably is making a comparison between 771 and a new resolution on Iraq most likely UNSCR 1284 passed Dec 1999 about WMD and humanitarian efforts). And it is the first time that the parliament of a country (TC: U.S. Congress) speaks after a resolution (TC: unclear) and comes out through the Security Council.

It is ignorant to send memos and complain to the Security Council because it is a tool in the hands of America the master of oppression and if we do that it does not mean that we are boycotting the diplomatic process. Also the monetary fund (TC: probably the International Monetary Fund) is in the hand of America and she helps according to her interests. My personal stand is with his (BIOT: probably UBL) call to fight America.

(Probably) Rahman: I support him body and soul and if it is true (TC: probably referring to the UBL call to "fight America") then it is the right thing to do. I personally do not know him and never met him (BIOT: probably UBL) and he is not the issue. There is the port of Gwadar (in Baluchistan area) under construction in Pakistan, and Europe and America wants to use it instead of (TC: unclear possibly Bankham) to trade with Asia. After the fall of the Soviet Union they wish to expand trade to Central Asia through Afghanistan and Afghanistan is against their wishes (BIOT: opposed to the U.S.) and they want to bring the Taliban government down. (BIOT: Rahman is saying that the Americans are using bin Laden as an excuse to attack Afghanistan so they can control a port).

Vice-President: They (BIOT: Americans) are controlling Turkey.

Fazlur Rahman: Gwadar is the shortest road for them and we spoke with the Afghani government. **I met Mullah Omar the**

leader of Afghanistan (BIOT: leader of the Taliban) **and he welcomed the establishment of Islamic relations with Iraq and we foresee to tell them about our needs and they would like to have contacts with Russia** but they feel that the Russians (unclear) with Afghanistan, they go to America (BIOT: probably means that the Russians side with the U.S. against the Taliban). And they (BIOT: probably the Taliban) say that now we do not feel that Russia is our enemy and we do not know why they support the Northern Alliance (BIOT: non-Pashtun Afghani militant groups seeking to topple the Taliban). **They (BIOT: probably the Taliban) want Iraq to intervene with Russia.**

And Russia thinks that the Taliban are supporting the Chechens through providing them 5 million dollars in weapons so the question is from where do they have all this money and weapons and they want Iraq to know their problems and needs.

Concerning Hekmatyar (BIOT: this is Gulbuddin Hekmatyar, leader of the Islamic Party, a faction that vied for control of Afghanistan before the Taliban victory and who has since pledged his allegiance to Usama bin Laden) I delivered him your letter and his reply was positive for **"they are our brothers"** (BIOT: Fazlur Rahman apparently delivered a note from the VP of Iraq to Hekmatyar—an Islamic terrorist—in response to which he called the Ba'athist regime "our brothers"). But in this case the news from Hekmatyar is that he still has contacts against us (BIOT: referring to the Taliban as "us") so how can we have trust between each other (BIOT: Hekmatyar's party and the Taliban were also in conflict). We wish to see Afghanistan as an independent country. We (BIOT: the Taliban) will basically agree with them (BIOT: Hekmatyar's party) and later the details will come after Afghanistan is under our (BIOT: Taliban) control. His (BIOT:

Hekmatyar's) answer was positive and he thanks Iraq for its role in this matter (BIOT: for helping as intermediary between Hekmatyar and the Taliban).

Vice-President: Afghanistan has a domestic issue but now we have some insight about it and we feel pain for what is happening. Iraq is the first country which objected to Russia's entering Afghanistan with a "liberating" message, and is this the way you (BIOT: as if addressing a rhetorical question to the former leaders of the U.S.S.R.) are going to deal with the countries you have a friendship agreement with? The Russians were not happy about the message we sent them. Most important is that the situation settles in Afghanistan and that the bleeding between brothers stops. It is better that Afghanistan solves his own problems and not depend on foreign countries.

(Probably) Rahman: I support that Afghanistan and the Taliban, from a religious stand point, do not hand over bin Laden (BIOT: to the U.S.).

(Probably) the VP: The agreement between Afghani parties should not be delayed because the U.S. policy is to keep the world in trouble.

(At the end of page 21, right side)

Fazlur Rahman: **One more time concerning Afghanistan I have a suggestion that a delegation should visit Kandahar and a schedule should be set concerning this issue.**

Vice-President: We will study this in the future.

(Page 21 left side, top.)

Vice-President: Last time you saw Mullah Omar?

Fazlur Rahman: **Last July and I proposed to him the subject that I was assigned to and I wanted to meet Mr. President (Saddam Hussein).**

Vice-President: I gave Mr. President an overview about Afghanistan and its issues.

End Translation

The following is the U.S. government provided translation of the al-Qaeda letter regarding the status of jihad that was captured in Afghanistan. Comments in parentheses start with *TC* for the government translator's comments. It is not clear what *EC* stands for, but it appears to be from a government analyst. The letter is written shortly after U.S. forces and the Northern Alliance toppled the Taliban. Al-Qaeda and Taliban forces were on the run. This appears to be a status letter of those who were left.

It is important to note that the letter was included in a West Point, United States Military Academy study of al Qaeda and that it shows that even within al Qaeda there are deep theocratic divisions. The letter indicates that the writer had the highest contacts within al Qaeda.

Bold is added for emphasis and reference. The authors of this book add comments that are not part of the original translation that are annotated with 'BIOT'.

Begin Translation for the first two pages of AFGP-2002-601693

Date: July, 26 2002

All praise is to Allah and blessing and peace is upon his messenger, family, companions and all who follow them.

Beloved brother Abu Mohammed (EC: Could be Abu Mohammed Al-Meqdese who is jailed in Jordan). (BIOT: The authors disagree with the guess that this is Meqdese because he is talked about by the letter writer—referred to by his alias al Barqawi—in a way that doesn't make sense for him to have been the recipient of the letter).

(TC: The writer is pleased and expresses his joy and thanks

God for Abu Mohammad's release from prison, especially after his second release. This letter is a reply to Abu Mohammad's letter which he had sent previously, in which he questioned what is going on now).

I met Abu Musab Al-Zarqawi (BIOT: al-Qaeda leader killed by U.S. forces in Iraq) and we sat together at his request, and he said to me: Abu Muhammad talked to me a lot, but he did not show up. I am suffering more than anyone else accused of Takfeer (EC: A faith sect accuses believers with infidelity) because I don't believe in fighting under the banners of the party or Bosnia or Tajikistan or Chechnya and or Kashmir. I say that all of these banners represent polytheism and call for democracy under secular rule. The Tajik cause ended after they kicked Ibn Al-Khattab out from north Afghanistan because he wanted to fight. They came to an agreement with the government and were given two ministries. I also spoke about the Bosnia secular rule and their killing of Anwar. I was surprised of what Anwar Sha'aban (I think you know him well) (BIOT: Anwar Sha'aban was an al-Qaeda operative responsible for providing safe houses in Europe and was part of the jihad in Bosnia in the mid to late 90's) and the Egyptian Islamic Jama'ah (group) (BIOT: A group closely related to the Egyptian Islamic Jihad or EIJ) have done in Bosnia while and receiving orders directly from Saudi Arabia.

As usual, I have my archives; I collect and distribute information proving that they do not want Islam. This is clearly a banner of infidelity. It happened that they issued a Fatwa (ruling) permitting the killing of some brothers. Fighting broke out while we were living in Babey (Afghani village) and they supported the Pakistani army. They were three thousand and the brothers were seven (three Arabs and four Tajik). I was detained and handed over to the Pakistani government who was nobler than them. By God they did not raise their voices with one word to and I stayed with them for 15 months before releasing me and Brother Abu Zaid.

After my release I found that people came from the Sudan and everywhere, and began fighting along side the Taliban movement, which for Pakistan was a substitute for Hikmatyar. Everyone, even children in the streets knew that they were created and controlled by Pakistan. **Their leader Fadhlurahman is a friend of Banazeer, Saddam and Qaddafi.** They comprise of the veteran sheikhs (religious scholars) from the schools of Mujaddidi and Mohammed Nabi such as Sheikh Mohammed 'Omar the movement leader, and Gilani and Peer barah (TC: I was informed that Gilani is a relative of the former king of Afghanistan Thaher Shah. The other name "Peerbarah" is unknown)—(BIOT: the authors can not confirm it but the translator seems to be referring to Pir Sayed Ahmed Gilani who received payments from Saddam according to another captured document. He was a former Mujahideen commander though he is not an Islamic terrorist and in fact cooperates freely with the U.S. government. He is related to the former Afghan King. He initially supported the Taliban until its' true extremist nature became obvious. "Peerbarah" is probably a misidentification for Pir—a religious title- Barah who is probably Sheikh Ahmed Abu al-Baraa, a former—now dead—leader of an Algerian terrorist group strongly affiliated with Al Qaeda and Ayman al Zawahiri.)

They are extremists of the Sufi sect and straying from the right path. (BIOT: the letter writer appears to be a Salafi or Wahhabi—probably a Saudi or Egyptian—who is criticizing Sufi Islamists whom he calls extremist. He probably means not religious enough. He is essentially criticizing the Taliban for not adhering to Wahhabi tenants. It should be noted that the Sufi in Afghanistan are generally moderate, like Pir Gilani but a Sufi terrorist by definition would be an extremist unlike a Wahhabist who is widely expected to go to jihad). The governor of Jalalabad is one of them whom your friend Al-Zarqawi accuses of infidelity. Unfortunately, his love of leadership and the organization kept him from coming to me although I met before. Once he said to me "I do not envision fighting", but another time he said "I do envision fighting. In a (200) page research by Abu Mus'ab Al-Souri; he said that it is permissible to fight under the banner of infidelity supporting his opinion with quotes from here and there (BIOT: the writings of al Souri—alternate spelling al Suri—can be found in the West Point study referred to previously.— (http://iis-db.stanford.edu/ pubs/21057/Harmony_and_Disharmony-CTC.pdf).

It was my turn and brother Abdul Hameed Shareef to speak. Abu Mujahid (he remained unchanged after I discussed the tombs infidelity with him) was sitting with us. I said each one should present his physical proof keeping in mind that the claim of a general banner would not be sufficient. Their reply was: what are you saying? I said that it is a banner of infidelity, and infidelity exists in requesting to join the United Nations. They do not see our leaders as infidels but they see them as Moslems and make alliances and agreements with them. They went to Qaddafi and he built a hospital for them in Kandahar. As for the Cross (TC: Probably he is referring to the Christians), they said it happened and there is no prohibition about it especially a brother by the name of Abu Hammam, who memorizes the Koran. They asked us to present a study supported with proof. I and brother 'Abd Al-Hameed prepared the study titled (Exposing the fighters' suspicions under the banner of those who violated the essence of the religion) and gathered all the proof we have. We distributed it to the officials and sent a copy to Abu Qutada, who promised to respond. He responded by saying that the writer of the study is a member of the "Khawarej" (TC: Khawarej are an extremist group of the Shiite) then he wrote "Ju'nat Al-Muttayebeen" (liars). He accused us that we consider the Taliban, Hamas, Al-Tali'ah and others of being infidels although our study was not about believing and infidelity but a response to those who permit fighting under any banner even if an infidel one. In addition, it was an exoneration of the scholars including Ibn Taymiyyah. (BIOT: It appears that the letter writer was at an Al Qaeda council meeting held to determine who they can work with and what justifications they can use for jihad. The letter writer appears to consider the Taliban and its supporters and pretty much anyone who works with someone other than a Wahhabist to have strayed from the path. He appears to be arguing against al Souri in the council meeting. However, this does not mean they were enemies, there was and is constant theocratic discord within Al Qaeda.)

God willing, we will publish the third edition to clarify the suspicion that Imam Ahmad and 'Abdullah bin al-Mubarak fought with the "Juhmiyah" (TC: Moslem sect changed the Koran verses contents to suit their needs); and also the suspicion of those who hide behind "Hilf al-Fadoul" (TC: A council which was formed by Prophet Mohammad prior to the spread of Islam. This council was composed of tribal elites in the Arab Peninsula to deal with issues of their people. The Saudi scholars referred to this council to justification the Saudi government's request for U.S. assistance in the Gulf War).

Everything was supported with proof from the Koran and the Sunna. Besides, we only wrote the name "Abdullah Al-Muwahhid" on the study, and wrote another one titled "Revising the methodologies from the innovations of the Khawarej" and also the one titled "Faradhiyat al Kufr bi Al-Taghoot" (TC: The duty/theory of disbelieving in Satan). We replied to Abu Qutada (BIOT: A UK Times article entitled *Al-Qaeda cleric exposed as an MI5 double agent* from March 25th, 2004 reveals that a man named Abu Qutada was an al-Qaeda leader in Britain who the MI5 used as an inside source to Islamic extremism among Britain's youth, though the authors can not be certain it is the same man) in a letter titled "Proof and Clarification and Refuting the Fabrications of the Writer of Ju'nat Al-Muttayebeen". You will see the lies and fabrications against us and others. Hamad Bin Ateeq was accused of being an extremist. Some of them even prohibited coffee drinking. All of this because we issued a Fatwa concerned with ruling the country.

Would someone who accused an infidel of infidelity become an outsider even if disagrees with him on the ruling?

I know this man (TC: Referring to Abu Qutada) well and want to expose him to everybody. At the time when everyone was fighting, he was an advisor to the devil. He came to Peshawar after everything was over, and started to make fatwas in return for few dollars from the Saudi Islamic Relief Center, stating that the Sudan government is an Islamic government. He later on with others went to Europe and achieved Bush's wishes and what the Americans had planned for (BIOT: this may be a reference to Qutada acting as an MI5 source in Britain). And now, they want to bring the people to exile, especially the Jordanian youth to clear the arena for the Jews and apostate governments.

I read your criticism of the doctor (BIOT: This is almost surely Dr. Ayman al Zawahiri, al Qaeda co-leader). My opinion is that you rushed in replying, and it would have been better if you read the entire book. (BIOT: Zawahiri writes on Islamic theology)

Then I read a letter for Abu Al-Buraa' titled "The Oneness of the Almighty, the Praiseworthy" (TC: He is referring to God). I do not know him and my advice to you is leave him alone and do not answer him back. His understanding is limited (as Egyptians say), (TC: He used a known phrase among Egyptians to describe someone of his limited knowledge in a derogatory manner), because he considered you and the doctor of the "Murji'ah group" (TC: A division of the Shiite), and he became as low as your friend Al-Barqawi (BIOT: A reference to Zarqawi's mentor, Isam Mohammad Taher al-Barqawi a.k.a Sheik Abu-Mohammed al-Maqdisi—http://www.windsofchange.net/archives/007175.php) and accused everyone who holds a passport of being an infidel, and of course it is hard to believe but that's what he along with Abu Hammam and others have done. **Some of them went to Saddam**; others went to Iran and so on. (BIOT: The letter writer is clearly talking about Barqawi's followers, chiefly Zarqawi who did in fact go to Iraq prior to the Iraq war. The matter of whether Zarqawi was in Iraq at the approval of Saddam or despite Saddam is a controversial one. Clearly, this al Qaeda leader believes Zarqawi and his men are there to support Saddam, which the letter writer criticizes them for doing.)

May Allah make us steadfast to his religion and I praise him for making me say everything had happen. When Ibn Baz and Ibn Othaymeen (TC: Two famous dead Saudi scholars) sent a missionary to learn the reason behind accusing them of infidelity; I was the only one present. He asked about you and Ahmed. I told him that you did not object to them being called infidels, and that they are being accused because of their alliance with the government (TC: Saudi government) and not for any other reason. I told him that I considered them infidels too. Afterwards, Ayedh

Al-Qarni came and the incident at Dar Al-Ansar took place. I held a private meeting with him in the presence of Abu Shaheed Al-Yemeni (from the Moslem Brotherhood) and Abu Al-Faraj Al-Yemeni Al-Misri. The discussion was about the Saudi government. He said that he is not a scholar and we should judge to scholars, he took with him the book titled "Al-Kawashif Al-Jaliyah" and the Saudi law encyclopedia, and I have not heard from him.

Best regards to all believers, and do not forget us in your prayers. Peace and blessings of Allah be upon you.

As for your criticism of the doctor for being too hasty regarding Jihad activities; he speaks of experience about both the Islamic and Jihad groups. Al-Jamaatul Islamiyah (TC: Islamic group) did not seeking a fighting Jihad in the Shari'ah, (TC: Islamic law) sense, rather they just wanted to pressure the government to allow them to call people to Allah. As you see, they got entangled without any military preparedness. They only wanted a revolution similar to that of Khomeini. As for the Jihad group, the doctor left them in 1995 and they did not announce it. (TC: Sentence structure in what follows indicates that the writer is not Arab or he is using a dialect in his writings for that the wording is grammatically wrong). When the rest knew that Aymen is the leader, and at the same time he and the others knew of all the people that had been arrested during the past seven months and the government did not announce that until it gathered them and named the organization "Talae' Al-Fath". To increase the division, the government incorporated more than 95 groups and only one Jihad group under this name. Thus, the government achieved its goal of solving the conflict over the name, and deeply infiltrated the ranks of the Jihad group in Peshawar. It also succeeded in infiltrating the Jordanians, 'Azzam Abu 'Adel's family, Abu Al-Harith, the office of services and Abu Zubaydah. (TC: two words are illegible) (BIOT: Abu Zubaydah is a well known al Qaeda leader held in U.S. custody. Zubaydah is not Jordanian but strongly connected to Jordanian Islamic jihad. He was captured in Pakistan a few months before this letter was written.) They were friends of an Egyptian intelligence officer named Hilmi who lived in Peshawar for the past 19 years and owns a gold and currency exchange shop. They were selling gold to him and exchanging money because he was paying much more than the market. So he succeeded in recruiting their children with the exception of a few of all nationalities, especially Abdul Salaam's children who was working at the Office of Services. When I realized this, I cautioned everybody from him and the campaign against me increased and accused me of infidelity because of their involvement with this man.

The Jihad group is in prison; the people inside want a political party and so does the Islamic Jama'ah; and the people on the outside are careless for decisions taken inside the prison while the government is involved through the lawyers. The people in prison are divided now; those who accepted the government initiative are awarded with visitation rights, and the unlucky ones are tortured daily. (BIOT: The two previous paragraphs seem to discuss Egyptian intelligence activities against the mujahideen and how many of them are now in prison.)

This is what happened on the outside of unbelievable events. **Aymen went to Iraq and Iran,** (BIOT: The letter writer reveals that al Qaeda leader Ayman al Zawahiri was visiting Iraq) and now he told Abu Mujahid Al-Filistini (BIOT: This may be Abu Qatada al-Filistini, a Jordanian and an adherent to the teaching of al Barqawi, al Zarqawi's mentor. He led al Qaeda in Britain, but not confirmed.) that he regretted writing "Al Hasad Al Mur" (Bitter Envy) and thinks that he rushed in writing it. They also did a lot to the doctor other than the matter of the book. They took his personal money and accused him of infidelity among other things. He prayed that God will punish them. He was treated unjustly, and so were I and many others. For example, they killed 'Abd Al-'Aleem while torturing him; another was beaten, imprisoned, the escaped and surrendered to the Egyptian embassy, and many others as well. What took place require volumes to write it, but that is enough for now. (TC: The contents of the last paragraph are just reminders and advice to be patient and not to care about what others say. He is also referring to a verse of the Koran to carry on with calling and guiding the people to the path of God by explaining the oneness of Allah).

Abu Musab

End Translation

CHAPTER 5:
THE IIS AGENT'S NOTEBOOK
PART TWO

Background

ON THE SAME day (November 28th, 1999) that Maulana Fazlur Rahman met with Vice President Ramadan in Baghdad he had an evening meeting another regime official. Although the second meeting was with a person of lesser rank than a Vice President it is perhaps more telling that this second meeting took place. The evening meeting was with Tahir Jalil Habbush al Tikriti, the Director of the Iraqi Intelligence Service. The collaboration in Baghdad between the Saddam regime and a leader of the *global Islamic jihad movement* left the political stage and entered the realm of security and secrets.

The translation of part one from this notebook indicated that the Taliban was seeking Iraq's support in mediating with Russia and Hekmatyar in Afghanistan. This translation reveals that the Saddam regime had expectations of assistance from the Taliban, and that the two agreed to a secret intelligence relationship. The Iraqi official tells the Maulana that they want the Taliban to support Iraq against U.S. actions. It must be emphasized that this is not a meeting between diplomats, trade ministers, or national leaders. It is a meeting between a leader of Islamic jihad (whose terror groups had just the year before declared war on the United States) and Saddam's intelligence director. There is one ultimate reason for meeting with an intelligence director—to secure intelligence and military cooperation. Although Abdul Razaq, the Taliban Defense Minister, is not listed in this meeting it is more than likely that he is there as a part of the Afghani delegation.

According to the notebook, Maulana Fazlur Rahman approached Taliban leader Mulla Omar with the idea of seeking support from Iraq. Omar sent Rahman and his defense minister to Iraq for this task. As previously mentioned, Pakistani support to the Taliban was fading in 1999. This couldn't have come at a worse time for the Taliban. As stated in the transcript, they faced the wrath of the Russians who believed that the Taliban was supporting the Chechnyan jihadists. The United States was probing and preparing to attack in covert operations to hunt Usama bin Laden in Afghanistan. The United Nations had taken steps to oppose the Taliban and even Arab leagues or coalitions of Arab governments were sending signals of opposition. Pakistan had been the Taliban's only succor and with the recent coup that no longer seemed secure.

Narrative

The Taliban was seeking to "establish relations with Iraq and Libya." Fazlur Rahman as a leader of the Pakistani "Association of Islamic Scholars," according to Tahir Jalil Habbush al Tikriti, told the IIS Director "our association has taken this responsibility upon her." The usage of the term "Association of Islamic Scholars" can also be translated as "Organization of Islamic Clerics" or JUI, the Maulana's Pakistani political party. Therefore, the Maulana is telling the IIS director that the Taliban needs support and his Pakistani associates in the JUI (and other associated Pakistani

Islamic jihad-centric political parties) are taking it upon themselves to find the Taliban new backing. He states explicitly that he wants Iraq to intervene with Russia and mediate with Afghani opposition.

It is interesting to note that although there is considerable discussion of the United States as an enemy, no explicit statement is recorded in regards to doing something about it. Such commiseration inevitably involves discussion of what should be done. This hole in the conversation indicates that such talk was not recorded. The Maulana does mention, "They are ready for this matter and they prefer that the relation between Iraq and Taliban be an independent relation from Hekmatyar's relation with the Taliban." Thus we learn that although the explicit purpose of the meeting is about negotiating with Afghani opposition and Russia the Maulana has made a subtle statement that the Taliban wants a relationship with Iraq beyond the mediation. In other words 'let's work together.'

Tahir Jalil Habbush al Tikriti, the Director of the IIS makes some very interesting points. He states "We already believe that there are no points of disagreement between us and the Taliban because we are both in one trench facing the world's oppression." The context is critical here. Usama bin Laden, under the protection of the Taliban and in conjunction with the Islamic jihad-centric political parties of Pakistan had just previously declared war on the United States. Although the Taliban continues to claim ignorance it is no secret that Mulla Omar is harboring and facilitating Usama bin Laden. Yet the IIS director says the Saddam regime has "no points of disagreement between us and the Taliban". Saddam's later claims to have been averse to working with Usama bin Laden are proven wrong.

Al Tikriti makes three points:

- Iraq wants a relationship with the Taliban that is independent (or rather more than) the issue of mediation.
- Iraq wants the Taliban to control Afghanistan.
- Iraq wants the Pakistani Islamic jihad centric political parties to support opposition to the Dutch-British UN draft resolution that sought to reinstate the inspection process in Iraq.

Al Tikriti states: "But the details of the relation and its management are linked to the facts of the international situation." In other words, our relationship has to be a secret as evidenced by this statement: "For the future we think that we will arrange relations between us, as an intelligence service, and them in a secret way to establish the strong base of this relation." The Director of the IIS explicitly stated that Iraq wanted a secret intelligence service based relationship with the Taliban. That means Saddam agreed to support the Taliban prior to 9/11.

Then he states: "We look forward to security and stability in Afghanistan, the control of the Taliban and the construction of a political system according to the political and ideological choices of the Taliban." The supposedly secular Ba'athist regime specifically endorsed the ideology of possibly the most strictly fundamentalist regime ever in the Islamic world. Why would the Ba'athists do such a thing if the secular/Islamic divide was so absolute that it prevented Saddam from working with Islamic terrorists?

By this time—late 1999—the Taliban had already secured most of Afghanistan. It was clear the Taliban had the covert support of powerful political figures and organizations in Pakistan, but was losing official support. A quick look at a map shows that Afghanistan is essentially on the opposite flank of Iran in relation to Iraq. Because Iran was still Saddam Hussein's arch nemesis (the U.S. was secondary because Saddam never really believed the U.S. would remove him whereas the Iranians unquestionably would) it is a simple matter to see the strategic significance of Afghanistan's location. If Saddam successfully wooed the Taliban and their important supporters in Pakistan he could use them to provide significant pressure on Iran as military allies. Imagine if the Taliban and a nuclear-armed Pakistan were backing him. Iran would be extremely exposed should it ever attack Iraq again as it would have been essentially surrounded. Thus the Saddam regime hoped the Taliban "will win and control" Afghanistan because he needed their support.

This once again demonstrates that the concept of a Ba'athist regime incapable of dealing with Islamic extremists is flawed. The Saddam regime was coveting the cooperation of Islamic extremists in Afghanistan in order to protect his own interests, a recurring them of these documents.

Further, the IIS director tells them: "The third point which is important for us is outside Afghanistan. It is the spiritual relation which ties us with the Association of Islamic Scholars and we know your role in supporting the Iraqi cause and the effect you have on the Pakistani street." The Maulana did in fact lobby for the removal of UN sanctions on the Saddam regime as had Usama bin Laden and the World Islamic Front in the 1998 *fatwa*. Furthermore, the Maulana's support continued right up to the start of the Iraq War according to press accounts. A BBC article Anger and Dismay in South Asia quoted the Maulana:

"Saddam Hussein is a hero of Muslims," a protester cried at a rally in the northwestern city of Peshawar. AFP reports. "We want the government to give us permission to go to Iraq to fight against the U.S. forces," another protester told hundreds of supporters. Supporters of the Islamic Jamaat-i-Islami party assembled in the eastern city of Lahore, chanting "Bush is a dog," and "Save Iraqi children," AFP reports. "America has signed its own death warrant," Islamist leader Maulana Fazlur Rehman said.

Because the Iraqi official in this meeting is referred to by codename, we have to deduce that it is Tahir Jalil Habbush al Tikriti. There are several strong clues. It is clear Rahman has high level access and would most likely be meeting with a senior member of the government, such as a department head. This official talks about an intelligence-based relationship which indicates that this is the chief of the IIS, the former Iraq Intelligence Service. The Maulana says, "I already met with Mr. the Vice President and the previous head of the directorate, may God rest his soul." This seems to indicate he is speaking to the current head of the directorate.

Another excerpt from the notebook provides further evidence. It states:

> the mentioned person arrived to the country on 11/27/1999 and he was hosted in Al Rachid Hotel suite number 526. He will leave on 12/1/1999.

That entry encompasses the date of the transcripted meeting presented here. The notebook also tells us:

> He visited Iraq on the beginning of April 1999 and the ex-director of the intelligence, may God rest his soul, instructed him to mediate between the Taliban and the leader of the Afghani Islamic party, Hek-

matyar following the request for mediation done by Hekmatyar to the leadership of Iraq during a visit when they met us on 3/19/1999.

The notebook shows that a previous meeting in April of 1999 occurred between a person who was later in Iraq on November 28th, 1999 (the date of the meeting translated here) and the previous IIS director in which they discussed the Taliban and Hekmatyar. There is every reason to conclude that this person was Fazlur Rahman and that this transcript is of a follow-up meeting with the new director. Therefore 'M.O.M' as listed in the following translation is the codename for the IIS Director.

The previous IIS director, Rafa Daham Mujawwal Al-Tikriti died a few weeks prior to this meeting. He died within days of being fired in what was likely a Saddam directed political assassination. The new IIS chief was Tahir Jalil Habbush al Tikriti who as of this writing is still at large. In July 2006, the Iraqi government placed him on a list of the forty-one most wanted in Iraq for insurgent activities.

The new director Tahir Jalil Habbush al Tikriti came to public attention in December of 2003 when the *Telegraph UK* reported Terrorist Behind September 11th Strike was Trained by Saddam by Con Coughlin:

> Details of Atta's visit to the Iraqi capital in the summer of 2001, just weeks before he launched the most devastating terrorist attack in U.S. history, are contained in a top secret memo written to Saddam Hussein, the then Iraqi president, by Tahir Jalil Habbush al-Tikriti, the former head of the Iraqi Intelligence Service.
>
> The handwritten memo, a copy of which has been obtained exclusively by the Telegraph, is dated July 1, 2001 and provides a short resume of a three-day "work programme" Atta had undertaken at Abu

Nidal's base in Baghdad.

In the memo, Habbush reports that Atta "displayed extraordinary effort" and demonstrated his ability to lead the team that would be "responsible for attacking the targets that we have agreed to destroy".

Atta, of course, led the execution phase of the 9/11 attacks. Let's be clear here. The *Telegraph* reported that the Director of the IIS was training Atta. The contents of this memorandum may have sounded outlandish at the time of the report. Now, this IIS agent's notebook tells us that Tahir Jalil Habbush al Tikriti was also entering into secret operations with the Taliban and the Maulana Fazlur Rahman, a man we can now identify as essential to supporting the World Islamic Front's jihad, a group that included al Qaeda. Thus, there are two documents that show an operational connection between the Saddam regime and the groups that attacked the U.S. on 9/11 in the time frame of the planning for 9/11. The Atta memo does not sound quite so farfetched in the context of a second source to the operational relationship.

Subsequent to the *Telegraph* article, *Newsweek* ran an article with several experts who claimed the document was a fraud. The authors of this book contacted the *Telegraph* author who wrote the article and he states that the document was from a trusted source who had given him valuable intelligence before. The authors of this book take no position about the validity of this report, but we note that none of the experts who decried this document had seen it. Their argument was based on four points:

- The FBI has investigated and has a detailed timeline of Atta's movement before the attack.
- There are other items in the document that pertain to the acquisition of uranium. Since Ambassador Wilson said

the Niger intelligence (yellowcake) was flawed, it cannot be true.

- A document expert who stated that Iraq was never so explicit in its documentation.
- It can't be true because Saddam wouldn't work with Islamic terrorists so it is a fake.—(http://www.msnbc.msn.com/id/3741646)

However, the *Newsweek* article said that the FBI was unable to account for Atta's whereabouts for days at a time during the summer of 2001. The Wilson argument was completely discredited by a Senate Intelligence Committee report that stated the acquisition of yellowcake was still an open question and Ambassador Wilson had in fact validated the CIA's concerns about the matter—according to the CIA. The document expert never saw the document, which begs the question why the report even used him as a source unless the intent was to mislead. This work provides overwhelming evidence that the secular/Islamic divide is a fiction so that theory does not discredit the document. The bottom line is that the authors have no evidence to prove that the document was authentic or not, but to dismiss it reflexively is not good investigation.

Findings

This document provides evidence that the IIS entered into covert security and intelligence agreements with the Taliban.

- This document provides significant evidence that the IIS wanted a relationship to the Taliban that was more than negotiating with Afghan and Russian opposition.
- The document provides significant evidence to counter the theory that the Saddam regime would not work with Islamic extremists.
- This document provides significant evidence that the Sad-

dam regime understood the importance of an alliance with Afghanistan.

- This document provides significant evidence that the Saddam regime was negotiating with the Pakistani political parties for continued support. We can conclude that to secure this support, the Saddam regime must have offered something to the Pakistani political parties, though we cannot determine what precisely, it probably involved money.

- This document and the al-Qaeda document substantiate a secret relationship between the Saddam regime and Maulana Fazlur Raman and thus it links the regime to the World Islamic Front and al Qaeda.

- This document provides evidence that the Saddam regime dealt with Islamic extremists to garner political support. If it desired political support from Islamic extremists known to be deeply involved with international Islamic terrorism there is reason to conclude that the support would encompass other activities such as terrorist activities. For if Saddam was only seeking political support there were other places to find it than in terrorist enclaves.

- This document provides significant evidence to explain why the Taliban sought the support of the Saddam regime. It needed support to maintain stability and security in Afghanistan. It was inundated with powerful enemies at the time. Chief among them was the United States.

Translation

The following is a translation by our translator-colleague, who goes by the *nom de guerre* of "Sammi." It is the second part of three from a notebook kept by an Iraqi intelligence agent. This document was previously reported by Fox News Channel and the Fox News website as part of the *Saddam Dossier* series authored by co-writers Sammi and Ray Robison of this book.

The administrative number, called a Harmony number for the database these documents were stored in, shows this document appears was captured in Iraq in 2003. Sammi adds notes for clarity in parentheses with 'TC'. The authors also add informational notes with 'BOIT'. The bold font is our addition, and indicates emphasis or reference material.

Translation for ISGP-2003-0001412 Part Two follows:

Meeting of Mr. M.O.M. with Sheikh Maulana Fazlur Rahman on Sunday, 11/28, 7:45 PM

Words of welcoming.

M.O.M.: We are aiming to arrange a meeting between you and Mr. President Leader (TC: this is how Iraqi officials refer to Saddam). But in the beginning we were instructed that Mr. Vice-President will meet you. I personally met Hekmatyar and he asked us to intervene to bring closer relations with the Taliban. And he sent us emissaries concerning this issue.

Fazlur Rahman: **I am the one who started with this issue, the relation between Taliban and Iraq, and it is our idea. The brothers in Afghanistan are facing the pressure of America, and are struggling against America and aim to have some connections between Afghanistan and Iraq, and it is a good start to establish relations with Iraq and Libya and our association has taken this responsibility upon her.** I already met with the Vice-President and the previous head of the directorate, may God rest his soul (TC: apparently the head of the directorate passed away) and both proposed that Hekmatyar and the Taliban should get to an agreement. I spoke with the Taliban about this issue and they started meeting with delegations from the Islamic Party (BIOT: this is the name of Hekmatyar's party), and I met Mullah Omar and his reply was positive.

As a party, our stand is that there should be an agreement between the Taliban and the rest of the opposition, Shah Ahmad Massoud and Rabbani (BIOT: Afghani opposition to the Taliban). And Mullah Omar said that we are looking towards this and that (not clear) and (not clear) and Ahmad Al Kilani and Jalal Al Din Hakkani do not oppose us. Therefore, Hekmatyar is favorable to a settlement but we are still fighting and we require a lot of trust, and there are hurdles to this because he fought us and killed us and he has problems with the opposition in the North and with us. After repeated contacts we will reach an agreement, but in the form of steps.

Concerning the relations with Iraq, he (BIOT: Mulla Omar) said that they are our brothers and Muslims and are facing pressures from America, like us and like Sudan and Libya. **And he (Mullah Omar) desires to get closer relations with Iraq and that Iraq may help us in reducing our problems. Now we are facing America and Russia. He requested the possibility of Iraq intervening to build a friendship with Russia since Russia is no more the number one enemy. And we request Iraq's help from a brotherly point of view. They are ready for this matter and they prefer that the relation between Iraq and Taliban be an independent relation from Hekmatyar's relation with the Taliban. We want practical steps concerning this issue and especially the relationship with the Taliban and (translator's note: not clear, but could be Iraq).**

M.O.M.: I want to discuss three points.

The first is the relation with Taliban. **It should be understood** that this issue is completely independent from the mediation requested by Hekmatyar to get to an agreement with the Taliban. Developing the relation with Taliban is essential and this development requires meetings to create a common ground of understanding. We already believe that there are no points of disagreement between us and the Taliban because we are both in one trench facing the world's oppression. But the details of the relation and its management are linked to the facts of the international situation.

I find that by simply meeting with you (BIOT: Fazlur Rahman) is a step forward in the relation with Taliban because we know well how much they trust you and what you represent for them. And when you relay our point of view for them they will understand it.

For the future we think that we will arrange relations between us, as an intelligence service, and them in a secret way to establish the strong base of this relation. In the meeting (TC: future meeting) and after reviewing the Taliban's point of view, we would discuss the possibility of us making an effort to stabilize the situation between Taliban and Russia. We could discuss the subject through the intelligence channel. We look forward to security and stability in Afghanistan, the control of the Taliban and the construction of a political system according to the political and ideological choices of the Taliban. We look forward to assure the Russians that Afghanistan does not constitute a threat to Russia. Afghanistan is a country that wants to live in independence and by dialogue it is possible to reach common grounds to finally get to the result hoped for.

The second point is the subject of the agreement between Hekmatyar and the Taliban.

We proposed it for a single reason related to our psychological stand concerning Taliban. **We hope that they will win and control.** We felt that Hekmatyar hopes that Taliban will control the situation and his intentions are true. Because when he sees the different political and military parties in Afghanistan he knows that the best choice is Taliban.

(TC: the Iraqi continues to expand his view on how all parties should come together through trust and negotiations.)

The third point which is important for us is outside Afghanistan. It is the spiritual relation which ties us with the Association of Islamic Scholars and we know your role in supporting the Iraqi cause and the effect you have on the Pakistani street. In the coming two weeks we are going to a confrontation with America because the U.S. has put all its weight in the Security Council to publish the Dutch-British resolution. We refuse this resolution and view it as a life-long embargo. We look to our Muslim brothers in particular to support us and especially our brothers in the Association of Islamic Scholars to organize protests in Pakistan against the resolution when it is made official. We ask our Muslim brothers in Pakistan to do this effort. We are trying and we have contacts with Muslims all over Asia and especially in Pakistan, Indonesia, Malaysia, Bangladesh and India. We hope that during the two coming weeks you will ask our friends in those associations to demonstrate.

Fazlur Rahman: **Concerning the relations between the Taliban and Iraq I was informed that they are going to start those relations in a secret manner and they are waiting for the answer and I will inform them that you will answer them through the embassy** (TC: could be through the Iraqi embassy of Kabul, if they had one, or Islamabad in Pakistan). Concerning the agreement with Hekmatyar, we are going to proceed with this issue. **Concerning the third point, the Association of Islamic Scholars has a popular voice in Pakistan and we will always side with Iraq and we hope that the new government will have a positive stand with Iraq.** (BIOT: These meetings occur a few weeks after the Pakistani military coup of 1999.)

Last July we received information that America wants to attack Afghanistan because of Usama bin Laden so we did a (not clear) and agreed to contact the Taliban to be sure and they said it was true. We received information about CIA and U.S. commandos reaching the Pakistan-Afghanistan border and they started dropping bombs on Afghanistan and they used the Pakistani airfields to bomb important positions in Kandahar. We as a Muslim people do not accept the American presence on our soil. A representative from the U.S. embassy came and told me, "You said that America was your enemy, how can you say that we are your enemy and the enemy of Islam?" So I told them that you took Russia's role in bombing Afghanistan and you are bombing Muslims. Then they said that they wanted Usama so I told them that Usama is in Sudan and that he was in Afghanistan during the rule of Rabbani and I added that they do not have a treaty to hand over criminals, as they pretend, with Afghanistan.

End Translation

CHAPTER 6:
THE IIS AGENT'S NOTEBOOK
PART THREE

THE FIRST TWO parts of the IIS agent's notebook revealed that Maulana Fazlur Rahman and the Taliban Defense Minister met with the Saddam regime in November of 1999 in Baghdad. The third part of this notebook is a collection of separate entries, not presented as a transcript of one specific meeting like the first two segments.

A notebook entry records a meeting with Gulbuddin Hekmatyar, an Afghani Islamic jihadist and leader of the Islamic Party in Afghanistan. In this translation Hekmatyar makes specific requests for a "center" in Baghdad and/or Tajikistan.

Another entry involves an Islamist representative of Bangladesh that we identified as Fazlur Rahman Khalil, an al-Qaeda and Taliban operative who signed the 1998 *fatwa*. The notebook indicates Khalil was scheduled for a meeting and he was considered very important.

"Sammi" puts translation clarifications in parenthesis with 'TC'. Informational notes are added with 'BIOT'. Bold type is added for ease of reference and for emphasis. It is important to remember that Arabic is written right to left and so the page numbers in the notebook are in reverse chronological order.

Translation begins for part three of ISGP-2003-0001412:

Left Side of Page 70:

Saturday March 20th [1999] at 11:45.

Met with him Mr. MS4 [TC: MS4 is the code name for the high rank-ing IIS official].

1. Intelligence and security cooperation.

2. Mr. MS4 informed him that the Iraqi president and Iraqi leader-ship are interested in him.

3. "We are ready to help you in any country and against your en-emies". [TC: most probably this is MS4]

4. Fadlul Haq—The governor of Peshawar that was assassinated.

[TC: points 5 and 6 are direct quotes from the Afghani]

5. "We are facing a vicious international plot against the Islamic Party and cannot find any country to help us at the time being".

6. "Iran helped us at the beginning and we brought 2,000 fighters but things changed at the time being. Also the Russians called to help but we do not trust them. Moscow and Iran want the war to drag on." [BIOT: this is probably the Taliban vs. Islamic Party conflict]. This is why he is coming to Baghdad for help. **Asked Baghdad to help open a center in Tajikistan or in Baghdad and they will bring them** [TC: not clear what them refers to] **in through Iran or Northern Iraq.**

He asked for help in printing Afghani money in Baghdad or help in printing it in Moscow.

Page 69, Right Side:

Stinger missiles have a range of 5 kilometers. [TC: there is only this one sentence on this page]

Page 27, Left side:

[TC: contains notes with information on prior meetings recorded in the notebook.]

The mentioned person arrived to the country on 11/27/1999 and he was hosted in Al Rachid Hotel suite number 526. He will leave on 12/1/1999.

[TC: note No. 1 in a list of notes.]

He visited Iraq on the beginning of April of 1999 and the ex-director of the intelligence. may God rest his soul. instructed him to mediate between the Taliban and the leader of the Afghani Islamic party. Hekmatyar following the request for mediation done by Hekmatyar to the leadership of Iraq during a visit when they met us on 3/19/1999.

End Translation

On page twenty-seven of the notebook we learn that Hekmatyar had a meeting in Baghdad on the 19th of March [1999] with regime officials. Again, the pages are in reverse chronological order so page twenty-seven seems to be a reminder that the notebook's author has written to keep the previous meetings straight. The meeting excerpt on page seventy is dated March 20th, which fits the time frame that Hekmatyar was in Baghdad according to page twenty-seven. In the meeting on page seventy, the man states: "We are facing a vicious international plot against the Islamic Party". Hekmatyar is the leader of the Islamic Party in Afghanistan. The evidence is strong to conclude this meeting on page seventy is with Hekmatyar.

How do we know that 'MS4' from the Hekmatyar meeting on page seventy is the former Director of the IIS? Because of this entry on page sixty-nine, left side:

Meeting of MS4 with 6951 on 4/10 at 8 p.m. in room 710.

The entry (which the authors will examine in further detail

later) goes on to describe the meeting and the context makes it clear this early April meeting is with Maulana Fazlur Rahman. On page twenty-seven it states that the Maulana met with the former IIS Director in early April. It is strong evidence that 'MS4' is the former Director of the IIS, Rafa Daham Mujawwal Al-Tikriti. The authors believe the excerpt from page sixty-nine is a continuation of the Hekmatyar meeting since no new header is provided.

The IIS director tells the Afghani warlord, Hekmatyar, that Saddam Hussein is interested in him. Hekmatyar is a power-hungry Islamic extremist who has shown a propensity to gravitate toward whatever option will bring him control of Afghanistan. He was part of the mujahideen resistance against the Soviets only to later side with a former communist to fight against the mujahideen after they took power. He eventually accepted the position of Prime Minister of Afghanistan from 1993-1994 only to split away to fight for full control of the Afghan government. In 1996 he was again given the Prime Minster position only to be toppled by the Taliban. Most likely, he was a major benefactor of CIA support in order to oust the Soviets in the 80s, but Hekmatyar seems to be willing to work with anyone to get what he wants. And now we have a record of him in Iraq trying to get what he wanted from Saddam in 1999 after he had become tied to al Qaeda.

Although atrocity has been a part of daily life in Afghanistan for decades Hekmatyar seems to have been one of the worst warlords. He indiscriminately shelled cities killing thousands. He was identified as a major terrorist trainer in the 1996 edition of the Department of State report Patterns of Global Terrorism:

Plagued by the absence of a cohesive central government and ongoing fighting among rival factions, Afghanistan remained a training ground for Islamic militants and terrorists in 1996. Ahmed Shah Masood, Gulbuddin Hekmatyar, and Abdul Rasul Sayyaf all maintained training and indoctrination facilities in Afghanistan, mainly for non-Afghans. They continue to provide logistic support and training facilities to Islamic extremists despite military losses in the past year. Individuals who trained in these camps were involved in insurgencies in Bosnia and Herzegovina, Chechnya, Tajikistan, Kashmir, the Philippines, and the Middle East in 1996.

[http://www.fas.org/irp/threat/terror_96/asia.html]

The IIS Director began the conversation with the Islamic terrorist trainer by discussing intelligence and security cooperation. Specific terms are not recorded, but the fact that this meeting occurred once again provides evidence that the Saddam regime was not averse to working with Islamic terrorists. One of the meeting participants (Sammi believes it is the IIS director due to the flow of the conversation) says that "we are ready to help you in any country and against your enemies." Coming from either of the parties, it is a powerful statement.

The subject of someone named Fazle Haq came up in the meeting. In an article entitled Osama and his Shi'ite nemesis that appeared in the *Asian Times*, writer B. Rahman, a widely regarded terrorism journalist in Pakistan reported that Lieutenant-General Fazle Haq, a retired Pakistani army officer close to Zia, the former Pakistani military ruler was killed by Shia fighters partially in response to Usama bin Laden's fighters slaughter of Shi'ites at the request of Zia. We do not know why they talk about this assassination (if that is the correct Fazle Haq). But the murder of Fazle Haq was a stab at General Zia-ul-Haq the Pakistani leader who strongly supported the Mujahideen in Afghanistan against the

Soviets. He died in 1988 in a mysterious plane crash. The authors of this work believe that this entry in the notebook concerned a conversation about the threat to the Sunni Islamists posed by the Shi'ites; that it was a commiseration.

The conversation then turned to specifics: "Iran helped us at the beginning and we brought 2,000 fighters but things changed at the time being. Also the Russians called to help but we do not trust them. Moscow and Iran want the war to drag on." It is not clear if these are Iranian army or Islamic fighters. It would seem, however, that the Iranians provided recruits to Hekmatyar's terror training camps. The most reasonable guess is that they are Hezb'allah fighters based in Lebanon and sponsored by Iran. The Russian's appear to have wanted to use Hekmatyar to fight the Taliban—which they suspected of supporting Chechnyan mujahideen. Probably rightly so since al Qaeda principle Ayman al Zawahiri was arrested in Russia for doing just that although they failed to identify him.

At this point our record of this meeting turns from transcription of a conversation back into notation or narrative form. The IIS agent writes: "This is why he is coming to Baghdad for help. Asked Baghdad to help open a center in Tajikistan or in Baghdad and they will bring them in through Iran or Northern Iraq." While 'them' is not specifically stated, it seems obvious. Hekmatyar is known for his terror training camps. He is talking about receiving 2,000 Islamic fighters from Iran. Then the note says this is why he came to Iraq. He wants Saddam to open a center in Tajikistan or Baghdad and they will smuggle them in through northern Iraq. The meaning is clear; Hekmatyar is asking for a terror-training center in Baghdad and says the fighters can be smuggled in.

This makes sense. It is no secret that Saddam sheltered terrorists in Baghdad. For Hekmatyar, Baghdad would provide a relatively secure location for the training where the Taliban couldn't get to his men. He is asking Saddam to help train international terrorists since that is what Hekmatyar does. It is worth noting that in the fight between Hekmatyar and the Taliban there were no good guys; these were bad men fighting each other for control. Both sides were central to the *global Islamic jihad movement.* Hekmatyar then asks Saddam to print counterfeit Afghani money to support his terror training.

The idea that a request for a "center" in Tajikistan is really a request for a terror camp can be supported. There are many references in the media to Taliban and al-Qaeda associated terror-training camps located in Tajikistan. In a January 12th, 2005 article entitled International Terrorist Reveals All, *The Moscow News* interviews Shukhrat Masirokhunov, a former chief of the IMU (an Islamic terrorist group) counterintelligence service. When asked where the training camps are based, Shukhrat replies:

> Where they have always been based — in Afghanistan and Pakistan. Those that I know of are located on the border between these two countries — in the Khanta Thal gorge and near the village of Wana. Each has about 100 men — from Central Asia and Russia, and there are also Arabs. There are camps in Tajikistan and there are plans to set them up in Kyrgyzstan.
> [http://www.mosnews.com/interview/2005/12/01/terroristreveals. shtml]

The *Washington Post* wrote about these camps in an article entitled Borderless Network of Terror in September of 2001.

Although the Bush administration has identified the IMU as part of bin Laden's network, its links to al Qaeda are fuzzy. It enjoys a haven in Taliban-controlled Afghanistan, and is said to receive funding from bin Laden. With camps in Tajikistan and an ability to launch raids into Kyrgyzstan and Uzbekistan, U.S. analysts worry that one day it could strike near the oil fields of the nearby Caspian region.

(http://www.washingtonpost.com/ac2/wp-dyn?pagename=article& node=&contentId=A10543-2001Sep22)

So why would Saddam be entertaining requests from Hekmatyar? The most generous answer would be to buy influence in Afghanistan. Afghanistan's location would make it a key ally. The converse is also true. As an ally of Iran it could pose a huge threat. As Hekmatyar had already been the Prime Minister of Afghanistan twice there is no reason to believe he could not rule again if he defeated the Taliban. And as the Iranians were already supporting him in his quest to become the ruler of Afghanistan (by sending him fighters to train thus financial support as well) he would have been in Iran's pocket. It cannot be emphasized enough that this would be a huge misfortune for Saddam. He had to maintain a supportive relationship with Hekmatyar. To do so, he would have used the influence of his treasury, military and intelligence assets, and his Sunni ties.

In effect, although it is Hekmatyar who is coming hat-in-hand to Baghdad it is Hekmatyar that had the stronger hand. Hekmatyar had indeed lived in Iran prior to this meeting and would have been considered a major risk to Saddam if he took control of Afghanistan unless he was allied with Saddam. Saddam would have had to appease him in case he did take over Afghanistan, or he had to make the choice to kill him and risk the wrath of his supporters. Hekmatyar was a major force of Afghanistan; Saddam would not have taken him lightly.

Another entry is made about stinger missiles. This is most likely a request for military hardware which makes sense in a conversation about terror training camps and funding. Stinger missiles were part of the U.S. covert aid to mujahideen leaders like Hekmatyar during the Soviet jihad so he may have been talking about his own supply.

There is little media or government reporting to substantiate the relationship between the Saddam regime and Hekmatyar. The only news article the authors found that provided further evidence of this relationship was reported in October of 2004. CNSNews.com (*Cyber News Service*) ran an article in which it claimed that an official with the Iraq Survey Group provided them with documents collected in Iraq. Many commentators immediately disregarded them because there was no way to validate the documents. They had apparently been handed over to CNS in an unauthorized fashion. No government statement on the documents has been released. The authors of this book have had a Freedom of Information Act request with the Defense Intelligence Agency for information concerning these documents since the fall of 2005.

The article entitled Exclusive: Saddam Possessed WMD, Had Extensive Terror Ties by Scott Wheeler contains purported Saddam regime documents that detail its' relationships to terrorist groups. One of those documents was described as a memo from the Iraqi Intelligence Service to Saddam (via his secretary) on Jan. 25, 1993. The document is basically a list of terror groups that the IIS can work with to "hunt the Americans" in Somalia. Under the section detailing relations with Asian groups it lists Hekmatyar's group the Afghanistan Islamist Party:

The Afghani Islamist party:

1. Established in 1974, the leader fled Afghanistan to Pakistan.

2. Considered amongst the fundamental religious/political movements against the West and amongst the strongest seven "Sunni" parties politically & from military point of view.

3. They are against the current president of Afghanistan. The party has influence on "Pashto" clans that consists of about 70% of the population.

4. Financially: the party relies on its supporters and through helps from Iraq & Libya.

5. Our system has relationship with the party since 1989, the relationship was improved & become directly between the leader "Hekmatyar" and Iraq, or through his representative Dr. Gherat Baheer" whose also his cousin and his son in law at the same time.

This document matches what we have seen from the IIS agent's notebook. Hekmatyar worked with the Iraqi Intelligence Service. The implications are staggering. Either forger of the CNS documents got very lucky or this CNS document is authentic. It is far more probable that it is an authentic document. Which increases the likelihood that all the CNS documents are authentic. The document from 1993 shows that terror trainer Hekmatyar was supported by Saddam. The memo says the IIS began working with him in 1989 which is when the Soviet Army withdrew from Afghanistan leaving a power vacuum. Because of the importance of the location of Afghanistan to the security of Iraq it makes complete sense that Saddam tried to fill the power vacuum with Iraqi money and influence. Other documents provide further evidence of this strategy.

Furthermore, the CNS documents reveal that the relationship with the Maulana Fazlur Rahman is nothing new either:

The (J.U.I)/or the Islam Clerks [sic] (BIOT: Clerks) Society:

1. Established in 1948, it's considered as a political party that has an influence in Pakistan, especially in northern parts of Pakistan, Blojestan & the Punjab. The leader is "Mawlana Fadhel Al-Rahman". [TC: alternate spelling for Maulana Fazlur Rahman]

2. Financially: it depends on its organizations inside Pakistan plus the foreign helps from Libya & Iraq.

3. The secretary general of the party "Mawlana Jaweed Ahmed Ne'amatee" has good relationship with our system since 1981 and he is ready for any mission.

According to the document released by CNS the Saddam regime had a relationship with the Maulana and his organization for decades. The IIS was funding the JUI and the Maulana and thus the JUI was "ready for any mission." Such a revelation is powerful considering the supporting role played by members of the Maulana's groups to al Qaeda.

The next excerpt from the IIS notebook is from an April 10th, 1999 meeting between the former IIS Director, codenamed MS4 and Maulana Fazlur Rahman codenamed 6951.

Translation begins for part three of ISGP-2003-0001412:

Page 69, Left Side:

Meeting of MS4 with 6951 on 4/10 at 8 p.m. in room 710.

He (6951) inquired about our relation with Usama (bin Laden). (TC: The Maulana asks the question, the Iraqi answer is not recorded.)

He (6951) proposed to the Taliban to form a front with Iraq, Libya and Sudan.

He met some of them in Hajj (TC: Pilgrimage to Mecca in Saudi Arabia, it is one of the five pillars of Islam) and he came to the conclusion that they do not know anything about Foreign

Relations. (BIOT: Unsure who says this but in our studies, the authors have come to realize that the Hajj pilgrimage is used as cover for a lot of jihad activities—and state spying—to move men and equipment and conduct high level meetings.)

The Taliban defense minister is Abdul Razzak (unclear) Association of Muslim Clerics.

They openly claim that they are against America.

He said that he was ready to build relations between the Taliban and Iraq.

(TC: The meeting continues on both sides of page 68/76, with questions about Pakistani politics and the other Islamic parties.)

The Iraqi official says, "I suggest that the parties come closer together because that means power to Islam against the American and Zionist policies".

End Translation

Because of the note on page twenty-seven, it is apparent that 6951 is the codename for the Maulana. From this passage we learn that the Maulana believes the IIS has some type of relationship with Usama bin Laden. We also learn that Abdul Razzak (alternate spelling Razzaq or Razaq) is noted as the Defense Minister of the Taliban making it likely that he was present at this meeting and was introduced. The entry also tells us that the Taliban sought the support of Libya.

Translation begins for part three of ISGP-2003-0001412:

Page 73, Left Side: a list of Islamic clerics coming to Iraq:

With him in the delegation:

1- Munir al Kilani / member of the presidency and former secretary / Democratic Islamic Front

They came on Tuesday:

2- Saber Hussein Shah / Jaafari / Sajed Tatawi

3- Raja Basset association of the Iraqi-Pakistani Friendship

4- Fadel Al Hussein / Union of Islamic Parties

5- Sardar

The parties which took a good stand and participated in the demonstrations with him

- Popular Pakistani Party

Page 72/76R *(continuation of page 73)*

Al Rabita party and mostly all parties participated in the demonstrations.

The Muslim Brotherhood is weak unlike the previous years.

He made clear that the political situation is unstable and yesterday there were large demonstrations in Islamabad numbering 50 or 60 thousands led by Benazir Bhutto and deputy Zawa (unclear) but America wants Nawaz Sharif to stay in power for the time being..

Union of opposition / Hamed Nasser Jatta / president of the opposition party of Islamic Party.

Very important.

Fadlur Rahman Khalil leader of the Ansar Movement. He does not have a position inside Pakistan, he has positions inside Afghanistan and Kashmir.

He does not have a position on Iraq he does not have a direct relation with him.

End Translation

Included in a list of men coming to or having already met with the regime is Fazlur Rahman Khalil. The IIS agent records that Khalil is ambivalent about the Iraqis. Nothing can be said about the meeting, if it actually took place since there is no guarantee he actually showed up. But it is yet one more example of the Saddam regime networking with Islamic terrorist leaders.

CHAPTER 7:
PAYMENTS TO AFGHAN MUJAHIDEEN

Background

IN 1988, THE former Soviet Union began a military withdrawal from Afghanistan. The mujahideen dealt the Soviet Army a critical blow that ultimately contributed to the downfall of the U.S.S.R. The mujahideen consisted of a collection of native Afghani anticommunists and nationalists or royalists, Afghani tribal fighters under varying degrees of Islamic influence, and foreign Islamic extremists.

Among the mujahideen commanders was an Afghani named Pir Sayed Ahmad Gailani (alternate spellings Kilani or Gilani; Saed; Ahmed), leader of the National Islamic Front of Afghanistan (Mahaz-e Melli-ye Islami-ye Afghanistan). During the Afghan insurgency against the communist government backed by the Soviets, Gailani was a supporter of deposed former king Mohammad Zahir Shah. By most accounts although he was a devout Muslim involved in fighting he is not an extremist and is considered by some to live a secular life style. His daughter is actively involved in the issues of women's rights in Afghanistan. Although a mujahideen commander, he was not a particularly active or aggressive fighter against the Soviets. There are no indications that he is a supporter of the *global Islamic jihad movement* and is self-admittedly a supporter of U.S. action in Afghanistan.

Several of the documents released through the now defunct Department of Defense Iraqi document archive mention his relationship to the Iraqi Intelligence Service. According to the documents he had a relationship with the IIS beginning in 1980. The IIS also states that his family is Iraqi.

The historical context of these documents is complex. To summarize, the former U.S.S.R. invaded Afghanistan in late 1979 to secure its southern border by supporting the Afghani communist government. Despite the superior technology the U.S.S.R. lost tens of thousand of soldiers in a nine year wasted effort to secure Afghanistan for the communists. The Soviet army was mostly gone from Afghanistan by 1989, but the communist Afghani government managed to stay in power for some time afterwards while fighting the mujahideen. It is during this time that we see the payments going to Gailani. Most likely Saddam believed the communist Afghan government would quickly fall as most observers did at the time, and he wanted an alliance with the likely new Afghan government even possibly the return of the King. But that is speculation.

Iraq was also engaged in a near decade long war that was just ending. The Iraq-Iran War ended in mid 1988. It was a very costly war for Iraq which was a factor in Iraq's invasion of Kuwait to expand Saddam's oil holdings. Documents show Saddam paid at least eleven million dollars. That was a significant investment at the time for one person which would seem to indicate Gailani's importance to Saddam. While there is no way to know exactly what this money was for there is a most likely explanation.

The Saddam regime realized that the withdrawal of Soviet forces would create a power vacuum in Afghanistan. Hussein sought a position of influence. Afghanistan is located on the east side of Iran with Iraq on the west. For Saddam, it would be a great strategic move to secure cooperation with Afghanistan. A coalition between the two governments would put Iran in a geopolitical vice.

Narrative

Of particular interest in the records is the eleven million dollars Saddam paid Gailani during the redeployment of Soviet forces from Afghanistan. Iraq was a client state of the Soviets. The Soviets continued to support the communist Afghan government with covert funding and military aid even after the army retreated. Therefore, it is a most unlikely scenario that Saddam would be paying eleven million dollars to a relatively insignificant mujahideen commander. The plausible explanations run from a "humanitarian contribution" to buying influence should Gailani become the next Afghani leader (being more politically than militarily significant) to paying Gailani for information. But speculation is fruitless as the documents give no obvious purpose for the payments.

But it does however once again demonstrate that Saddam was actively involved with expanding his sphere of influence in Afghanistan. Understanding the importance of Afghanistan to Saddam is important to understanding his support of the *global Islamic jihad movement.*

These records provide strong evidence that Saddam Hussein was actively engaged in buying influence with Afghani mujahideen commanders which demonstrates the strategic importance of Afghanistan to Iraq.

Gailani would have been a weak ally for Saddam. But considering that the documents show Saddam was courting the Taliban and Hekmatyar as well it is clear Saddam was covering all bets in Afghanistan. Gailani does not appear to be connected in any way to terrorism, and by all accounts he was and is relative moderate, especially for a mujahideen commander. He was very much opposed to the Taliban and even appreciative of the U.S. efforts to remove them. His relevance to Afghani issues is evidenced by other documents. He is mentioned on page twenty of the IIS agent's notebook. Maulana Fazlur Rahman states "...Ahmad Al-Kilani [alternate spelling for Gailani] and Jalal Al-Din Haqqani do not oppose us [the Taliban]." There is also a reference to him in the al-Qaeda letter.

> "They comprise of the veteran sheikhs (religious scholars) from the schools of Mujaddidi and Mohammed Nabi such as Sheikh Mohammed 'Omar the movement leader, and Gilani and Peerbarah (TC: I was informed that Gilani is a relative of the former king of Afghanistan Thaher Shah)."

The government translator comments that the man named *Gilani* in the al-Qaeda document is a relative of the former Afghan King, which is supported by other references that also make the same claim about Sayed Ahmad Gailani. Gailani initially supported the Taliban (as many others did) before they demonstrated their true brutality against moderate Afghans. At the time that Saddam was paying Gailani the Taliban did not exist as such.

It is interesting to note that in a second document the IIS claims Hamed Gailani, Sayed's son, was cooperating with the IIS as late as March of 2002 effectively naming him as a spy for Saddam. That fact reveals a great irony because during the January of 2006 State of the Union Speech Hamed Gailani sat with the First

Lady as her guest. At the time he was the First Deputy Speaker of the Afghan parliament's upper house. In the *realpolitik* of Afghanistan and Iraq Saddam's spies sit with First Ladies.

It is quite likely that vetting was conducted before the State of the Union speech. Vetting seems to have failed to detect his past involvement with the IIS. Or there may have been such a limited involvement that it was considered insignificant. In the tumultuous world of Afghan politics, it is not unheard of for a person to take a payoff and then not perform a single service or even have the intent to act. In other words, the Gailani's could have been ripping Saddam off for all we know. Or it could even be that they were taking money for 'humanitarian aid' and not realizing it was coming from the IIS. In the Middle East and Southwest Asia alliances shift like the sand they are built upon.

The Harmony number for the first document begins with IISP, a strong indication it was recovered from an Iraqi Intelligence Service facility. The following translations are the original work of Sammi.

Translator's notes:

- Document IISP-2003-00040598 contains 64 pages regarding memos and transfers of money to the Afghani opposition in 1988-89-90.

- All transfer documents are in English, $500,000.00 per month.

Begin translation for IISP-2003-00040598; Translation of page 13/64:

Council of Revolutionary Command

Intelligence Directorate

Top secret and private

To: Respected director

Subject: The Afghani Ahmad Hassan Al Gailani

Sir,

The President Leader (May God protect him) had previously ordered us, through the Secretary's memo number 560/K on 2-2-1990 to provide a monthly amount of half a million dollars from the account of the Presidency to be transferred to the account of Mr. Ahmad Al Gailani in a Swiss bank, starting from 1-1-1989 and until the opposition controls the government in Afghanistan. Since 1-1-1989 we have been continuously paying half a million dollars monthly.

Please review, with respects

11th March 1990

Translator's Gist (summary):

On page 61 a top secret and private memo (dated 2nd of November 1988) says that the half a million dollars transfers started in October 1988.

On page 29 an intelligence memo (dated 5th of January 1991) mentions that the last half a million dollar payment took place on the 9th of August 1990 (BIOT: 7 days after he invaded Kuwait).

End translation

Other documents illuminate the relationship a bit more.

Translator's notes:

- This record was a collection of 59 pages and contains dozens of documents.

- Page 7 of 59 is a congratulation letter sent from Sayed Ahmad Gailani to Saddam Hussein on the Eid Al Adha, a religious holiday.

- Page 6 of 59 is an official memo sent from the press secretary, Ali Abdallah Salman to Saddam's secretary regarding the Gailani letter.

Begin Translation for ISGP-2003-00014647

Page 6

Republic of Iraq

Office of the Presidency

Press Secretary

March 6, 2002

Respected Mr. Secretary

Subject: Message

Enclosed a message of congratulations for Eid Al Adha to Mr. the President Leader, May God protect him, from Mr. Sayed Ahmad Al Gailani the leader of the National Islamic Front of Afghanistan.

We asked the Intelligence Service about Mr. Gailani and his National Islamic Front and we got the following:

Mr. Gailani was born in 1928, has a Saudi passport, leader of the National Islamic Front and one of the leaders of the jihadist parties, from the Iraqi Gailani family, he immigrated with his father in the forties, has a religious and spiritual influence in many Afghani tribes, is a moderate politician, has contacts with Jordan, Saudi Arabia, Britain and America, he is loyal to the King (TC: Afghan king). He has a relation of cooperation with the Service (TC: Iraqi Intelligence Service) since 1980 and he used to receive help from the Service at the rate of half a million dollar monthly-which stopped with the beginning of the Mother of All Battles (TC: Desert Storm). His son Hamed is cooperating with the Service and occupies the position of vice-President of the Islamic Front.

Opinion:

We do not approve the publication of the letter at the time being

Please review...the decision is yours...

Respects

End Translation

CHAPTER 8:
HAMAS IN IRAQ

Background

A MONG SADDAM'S WELL-DOCUMENTED terrorism activities is his support to Palestinian terrorists. Most observers agree that Saddam assisted Palestinian terrorists but he is most associated with leftists like Yassir Arafat of the Palestinian Liberation Organization considered to be politically oriented instead of Islamic jihad oriented. For this reason some experts do not consider his support to Palestinian terror groups to be congruent with support for Islamic terrorism. However, with the increasing influence of Islamic jihad propaganda of the Muslim Brotherhood, al-Qaeda, and the Wahhabists, many Palestinian militants have become indistinguishable from Islamic jihadists since at least the early 90's. Perhaps the most notorious of these Islamic terror groups is Hamas which was kind enough to dispel notions of secularism by naming their group the Islamic Resistance Movement thereby disentrancing any such "secular terrorist" arguments about this terror group. Hamas was declared a foreign terrorist organization by former Secretary of State Madeline Albright under the Clinton Administration. The term 'Hamas' is actually an acronym and as such should be written as 'HAMAS' but the convention is distracting in text and this work will use 'Hamas'.

Narrative

Two documents captured in Iraq demonstrate that the Saddam regime was strongly connected to Hamas. Both were written by Saddam's spying apparatus the Iraqi Intelligence Service (IIS). According to one memorandum which was written during the opening days of Operation Iraqi Freedom (OIF) the leaders of Hamas requested permission to send fighters to Iraq to conduct suicide bombings against American soldiers. The Iraqis replied to the request by urging Hamas not to send fighters to Iraq but instead to launch a "campaign aimed at the American and Zionist interests inside and outside of the occupied territories." The statement does not rise to the level of directing Hamas to act but reads more along the lines of 'if you are going to do something it would be better to attack the Americans outside of Iraq'.

This document is further evidence to support the hypothesis that the Saddam regime did not want Islamic radicals operating freely inside Iraq, but had no compunction with them operating in Iraq's interest outside of Iraq by attacking their common enemy—the United States. The Saddam regime coordinated with Hamas via a liaison living in Baghdad with his family. To put it another way, an Islamic terrorist group had an ambassador to the Saddam regime in Baghdad. The memo shows Hamas had students living and studying in Iraq. In other words, Islamic radicals of a known Islamic terror group were training in Baghdad with the approval of the Saddam regime. This revelation alone flies in the face of the secular/Islamic divide theory.

A second document from March of 2001 recommended a "media campaign" to "strike the presence and interests of America" under the guise of the "Palestinian cause." This plan was in retaliation for what the IIS perceived as a political attack on the regime by the newly elected President George W. Bush. The IIS believed that President Bush had a plan to ease the import restrictions on humanitarian goods to Iraq "to make the leadership in Iraq responsible for the starvation of the Iraqi people and not the responsibility of the United Nations."

Broader Context

Just days before the start of OIF and the writing of the Hamas memorandum, the BBC reported in a March 13th, 2003 article entitled Palestinians get Saddam funds that Iraqi agents were paying $25,000 dollars to the families of Hamas members. They appear to have offered to fight for Saddam in return. This is independent confirmation from a second source that Saddam was supporting Hamas.

The first IIS memo describes a Hamas leader in Damascus who is almost certainly Khalid Mashal. Mashal recently resurfaced as the suspected mastermind behind the kidnapping of an Israeli soldier. This attack by Hamas sparked the latest round of Middle East fighting in the summer of 2006.

Khalid Mashal is discussed at the website *Global Security.org*:

Khaled Mashal, a physics teacher, who directs Hamas's political bureau from Damascus, will be what he called the group's "first head," its world leader. After the killing of Abdel Aziz Rantisi in 2004, he is considered to be the highest-ranking member of Hamas.

In October 1997 men carrying forged Canadian passports and believed to be agents of Mossad, the Israeli secret service, tried and failed to poison Khaled Mashal in Amman, Jordan. Two of the agents were chased and captured, while the HAMAS official was taken to a hospital and, although seriously ill, recovered. The event caused an uproar in Israel, the Middle East generally, and beyond. Canada recalled its ambassador from Israel over the used of forged Canadian passports. Jordan's government demanded the antidote for the poison used in the assassination attempt, and Jordan's King Hussein then brokered a deal that saw the ailing Muslim religious leader who founded HAMAS, Sheik Ahmed Yassin, released from an Israeli prison and eventually returned to Gaza. Several other HAMAS activists were also released from Israeli jails, presumably in return for the two Israeli agents being held in Jordanian police custody. Israeli Prime Minister Benjamin Netanyahu was reported to have personally ordered the assassination effort.

After the killing of al-Rantisi in April 2004, Israel's minister for parliamentary relations, Gideon Ezra, also warned that Khaled Mashal will meet a fate identical to that of al-Rantisi.

Following the election victory of Hamas, in the January 2006 Palestinian parliamentary elections, Mashal has declared that Hamas will not disarm. Many Western countries have asked Hamas to disarm and have threatened to cut off aid to Palestine if they do not lay down their weapons. Mashal has even suggested that Hamas could create a Palestinian army to defend Palestine against aggression. But he also announced that Hamas will be working with Fatah to form a partnership in order to govern the Palestinians.

(http://www.globalsecurity.org/military/world/para/hamas-leaders.htm)

President Bush cut off funding for the Palestinians after they elected the political wing of Hamas to leadership in the occupied territories. This evidence demonstrates that Hamas was trying to kill American soldiers. Clearly, President Bush made the right call in denying Hamas support.

It is interesting to note that Mashal lived in Kuwait at the time of the Iraqi invasion in 1990. He was a Palestinian student studying in Kuwait with thousands of others. The Palestinian students were so subversive to the Kuwaiti government and complicit to the Iraqi invasion that the Kuwait government kicked hundreds of thousands of Palestinians out after liberation from Iraq. The transgression was so egregious that years later the Palestinians would apologize to the Kuwaitis for supporting Saddam Hussein in Kuwait. (http://news.bbc.co.uk/2/hi/middle_east/4089961.stm)

It was at this time, while the Iraqis held Kuwait, that Mashal left Kuwait to later co-found Hamas. It is shear speculation but not without precedent that Mashal began a relationship with the IIS while in Kuwait and thus the IIS gave him the backing to form Hamas. In other words, the Iraqi Intelligence Service which was already neck deep in other Palestinian terror groups may have created Hamas. This document is not direct evidence of such a relationship but it certainly provides a reason to investigate the theory now that we know Mashal did have a relationship with the IIS, that Hamas members were being trained in Baghdad and Hamas fighters or their families were being paid by Saddam.

In fact, many terrorist leaders would spring forth from Saddam-occupied Kuwait. Many of those were of Palestinian heritage. Some of those would go on to become the backbone of al Qaeda. Often, this expulsion is mischaracterized as flight from the Iraqi invasion. The fact is that these terror leaders supported Saddam's invasion while living in Kuwait. The phenomenon is detailed in a study reported on by the Middle East Media Research Institute (MEMRI) entitled Special Dispatch Series—No. 848 in January of 2005:

Al-Zarqawi's Organization: Made Up of Extremist Palestinian Sheikhs Who Emigrated from Kuwait to Jordan

The inquiry noted that following Iraq's invasion of Kuwait and the 1991 Gulf War, 250,000 Palestinians emigrated from Kuwait to Jordan.

This phenomenon was called "those who returned from Kuwait." The inquiry stated: "According to calculations by Jordanian experts and researchers, some 160,000 of these displaced persons came only to Al-Zarqaa. The experts noticed a connection between their return and the flourishing of the Salafi **Jihad** trend in Jordan, particularly in Al-Zarqaa."

According to the inquiry, the phenomenon of "the returnees from Kuwait" was perceived by many in Jordan as "a turning point in social change." The Jordan Center for Research at the University of Jordan conducted a survey on the matter and found that beginning in 1993, "the youth [in Jordan] became more conservative than the youth of preceding generations, and a large percentage of them supported polygamy and gave priority to educating boys rather than educating girls."

Among the returnees from Kuwait were "a number of people belonging to the **Jihad** stream, and at their head Sheikh Abu Muhammad Al-Maqdisi, [whose real name is] Issam Muhammad Taher Al-Burqawi. [He is] a Palestinian who lived in Kuwait, who later became the spiritual teacher of this stream in Jordan, and in 1989 became Abu Mus'ab Al-Zarqawi's teacher.

"[Al-Maqdisi] went from Kuwait to Afghanistan with the Palestinian sheikh Omar Mahmoud Abu Omar, known by the nickname Abu Qatadah. When Al-Maqdisi returned to Kuwait and then to Jordan, Abu Qatadah found refuge in London. [But] these two figures became the main source of authority of the Salafi **Jihad** ideology in Jordan...

"Also among the returnees from Kuwait was Abu Anas Al-Shami, the jurisprudence authority of Al-Zarqawi's organization, who was killed several months ago in Baghdad, as well as Abu Qutaybah, senior military official in the Al-Qa'ida organization. Also Ghazi Al-Tawba, a prominent leader in Al-Zarqawi's organization, lived in Kuwait.

"These and others, with Abu Mus'ab [Al-Zarqawi] at their head, constituted the nucleus of the Salafi **Jihad** movement. They met in the mid-1990s at one of the mosques in the Ma'ssoum neighborhood in the city of Al-Zarqaa."

It seems an odd convergence that the *"jihad* stream" from Kuwait supported the supposedly secular Ba'athists over the Islamic (though moderate) Kuwaiti government. But Saddam's support to the Palestinian cause in the occupied territories surely gained him favor with the Palestinians in Kuwait; Palestinians who were becoming Islamic radicals under the influence of the Muslim Brotherhood based in Egypt. Therefore, the support of the Palestinian jihad was another portal of influence for Saddam into the *global Islamic jihad movement.*

Some of these Palestinian terrorists who were booted out of Kuwait are named in the captured al Qaeda letter. Al-Burqawi, Zarqawi's mentor was named in the al Qaeda letter in reference to a group of men who "went to Saddam". That reference was to Zarqawi's group (sometimes called *al Tawhid*) going to Iraq prior to OIF in 2002. Zarqawi's men were in northern Iraq attacking Saddam's Kurdish enemies in the north as opposed to attacking Saddam. Many of these men had collaborated with the Iraqis in Kuwait and were sympathetic to Saddam because of his support to the Palestinians.

The article also tells us:

> The **Jihad** fighters "related that Abu Mus'ab [Al-Zarqawi] used the experience of the [Iraqi] Ba'th[ists] in his war on the Americans and Iraqis, including regarding the security issue. [A man named] Ahmad clarified that this was particularly true regarding the city of Al-Fallujah,

which contained hundreds of former Iraqi military intelligence officers with great experience in the security sphere. (Ibid)

So dozens of IIS officers joined with Zarqawi. Why? Remember the insurgency plan that directed the IIS to join with those returning from abroad?

But after the regime was toppled and Zarqawi went on a rampage killing thousands of Muslims, things changed.

Burqawi had sent Zarqawi to Iraq to support Saddam. Zarqawi and Burqawi were already affiliated with al Qaeda as evidenced by the al Qaeda Millennium plot and their participation. Zarqawi joined with IIS officers in Iraq.

But as the insurgency developed Zarqawi began to slaughter Muslims so terribly that even his mentor Burqawi tried to rein him in. This enraged Zarqawi's followers who then distanced themselves from Burqawi.

> The inquiry showed the Al-Zarqaa **Jihad** fighters' attitude towards the dispute between Abu Muhammad Al-Maqdisi and Al-Zarqawi in the matter of the path of Al-Zarqawi's **Jihad** in Iraq. Recently, he published an article in which "he expressed his reservations regarding the behavior of his disciple Abu Mus'ab Al-Zarqawi in Iraq.
>
> "This enraged the young **Jihad** fighters, who see Abu Mus'ab [Al-Zarqawi] as 'divine grace, and it is heresy for anyone to think he made a mistake, even regarding his teacher and guide Abu Muhammad Al-Maqdisi.'" (Ibid)

It was probably at this time, late 2004, that Zarqawi swore his oath to al Qaeda. Zarqawi distanced himself from the Palestinian-Jordanian jihad stream—which was one part of al Qaeda—and aligned himself more directly with the Zawahiri/Bin Laden branch. Why? Because he still needed external support to recruit and send jihadist fighters to Iraq.

Also at this time, it was clear that the Ba'athist party was not coming back even to his holdouts. IIS agents who had been assigned to work with them under Saddam then defected to the Zarqawi group.

> Dozens of them took an oath of allegiance to Abu Mus'ab [Al-Zarqawi], and renounced the previous secular regime..." (Ibid)

This all provides interesting context to reexamine the case of Ramzi Yousef who led the 1993 WTC bombing and his uncle Khalid Sheik Mohammed, mastermind of the 1993 WTC attack and 9/11; both of whom supposedly lived in Kuwait prior to the Iraqi invasion according to Kuwaiti documents. Dr. Laurie Mylroie, an expert on the Saddam regime has postulated the theory that Yousef and possibly KSM are actually Iraqi agents with cover stories (legends) planted in Kuwait during the occupation. Although the theory does indeed sound like something out of a spy novel, the evidence disclosed here and supported by independent reporting lends credence to her hypothesis. With all the terror leaders emanating from Saddam-occupied Kuwait and all the portals of entry between the IIS and the *global Islamic jihad movement*, specifically the "returnees from Kuwait" it is beyond absurd to consider them happenstance. They are outward signs of hidden directed effort. When combined with the direct evidence provided by this work the erroneous secular/Islamic divide theory is swept away. Thus, there is no reason not to reconsider the depth and nature of this collaboration.

Yousef entered the U.S. on a forged Iraqi passport. It is worth noting that both of these men (Yousef and KSM) were also of Baloch lineage emanating from the Baluchistan region of Pakistan—which is generally sympathetic to al-Qaeda and the Taliban—and is a support base for the Islamic jihad-centric political parties of Pakistan, the Maulana's base. We know that the Maulana's followers gave al Qaeda safe passage and hid them in Pakistan as well as the religious edict to carry out the war on the U.S. We know that a member of the Maulana's group was with KSM when he murdered Daniel Pearl.

Another Hamas leader mentioned in the document was Dr. Aziz al Rantisi, the Hamas leader in Gaza before he was killed by an Israeli air-strike in April of 2004. He has a listing at the website of *MIPT: Terrorism Knowledge Base*, a well regarded research tool for tracking terrorism:

'Abd al-Aziz Rantisi was born in 1947 in Yabna and grew up in the Khan Yunis refugee camp. He was educated as a medical doctor (pediatrician) at Alexandria University (1972. 1974-1976) where he first came into contact with the Muslim Brotherhood. He helped establish the Islamic Center in Gaza in 1973 and joined the Muslim Brotherhood in 1976. He worked at Khan Yunis hospital as head of pediatrics but was dismissed by Israel in 1983 and was imprisoned multiple times. He led Hamas after April 1989 but was deported by Israel to Marj al-Zuhur in Lebanon in 1992. In Lebanon, he served as the spokesperson for the deportees. On his return, he was rearrested by Israel in December 1993 and held until April 1997. He was then held by the Palestinian Authority in detention for 21 months until February 2000. He was arrested again in July 2000 after calling the Palestinian participation in the Camp David talks an act of treason. He was released in December 2000 but has been rearrested multiple times since 2000. He currently operates out of the Shaykh Radwan area of Gaza City where he served as the Gaza spokesman for Hamas. Following the killing of Sheikh Ahmed Yassin, Hamas' founder, Rantisi was elected as the group's leader. Rantisi was killed by an Israeli missile strike on April 17, 2004.

[http://www.tkb.org/KeyLeader.jsp?memID=63]

His death provoked international outrage against both Israel and the United States even though the United States denied involvement. President Bush was roundly criticized. Considering that we now know Rantisi was personally trying to orchestrate homicide bombings by Hamas terrorists against American soldiers it seems that those who criticized the president and Israel for the attack were in error. The killing of Rantisi was a justified defensive act against an Islamic terrorist group.

Rantisi was a prime example of the Islamic radicalization of the Palestinian cause which occurred largely due to Egyptian influence. Dr. Rantisi was trained in Egyptian medical schools under the influence of the Muslim Brotherhood. The Muslim Brotherhood has successfully infiltrated Egyptian professional colleges. These schools turn out Islamic radicals like Rantisi as a matter of course. The co-leader of al-Qaeda, Dr. Ayman al Zawahiri is a similar example of a Muslim professional radicalized by the Muslim Brotherhood (which he later rebelled against for being too weak) at an Egyptian medical school. He is also a portal between Saddam and the *global Islamic jihad movement* based upon the mutual opposition to the Egyptian government and support for the Palestinian cause.

For its part, the IIS recommended that Hamas attack U.S. interests inside and *outside* of the occupied territories. The document is undated, but it is grouped together with a document from late March of 2003 and the content matches the time frame. It is unlikely that a week into the war, the Iraqi government would consider a few hundred fighters worth the effort of coordinating command and control on the battlefield. But that doesn't mean the Saddam regime didn't want their help. They just suggested attacks on Americans outside of Iraq.

It is worth noting that the Senate Intelligence Committee on Pre-war Iraqi Intelligence stated in its report:

> The CIA was also reasonable in judging that Iraq appeared to have been reaching out to more effective terrorist groups, such as Hizballah and Hamas, and might have intended to employ such surrogates in the event of war.

So it would appear that the CIA nailed it. This really begs the question: Why are some former CIA officials currently proclaiming that Saddam Hussein would not work with Islamic terrorists like al-Qaeda because of the secular nature of the Saddam regime? Especially considering that the CIA itself determined that he would do so before the war and the Senate Intelligence Committee validated the finding during an investigation of the prewar intelligence.

The 2001 IIS memorandum shows that the IIS believed the easing of humanitarian goods restrictions was a threat to the regime. It appears they cared little about how the easing of these restrictions would benefit their own people. They seem to have preferred to have the political argument against the U.N. than actual assistance to the Iraqi people. It is a telling comment on the brutality of the Saddam regime. It also demonstrates that the Saddam regime considered the Palestinian conflict with Israel a *Causa belli* for terrorists to attack American interests.

This document confirms that the mere election of President Bush as U.S. president was enough for the Saddam regime to encourage attacks against the United States prior to 9/11. It has been noted in many references—including a U.S. government study entitled *Iraqi Perspectives Project*—that Saddam Hussein considered Iraq in a state of war with the United States from the time of the first Gulf War. He had good reason considering that the United States bombed Iraq nearly continuously from the mid-90's on because he engaged U.S. military aircraft with air defense forces and attempted an assassination of George Bush senior among other things. Considering that the CIA concluded Saddam would call upon Islamic terrorists during a time of war, and considering that Saddam viewed Iraq as being at war with the U.S. since the Gulf War, it is not too much of an extrapolation to determine that Saddam would have used Islamic terrorists at any time since the Gulf War.

The originals copies of the following documents are in Arabic. Sammi, our translator provides an original translation work below.

Begin Translation for Page 22 of IISP-2003-00026588

Respected Director of the Intelligence Service

Subject: Hamas Movement

We would like to inform you about the following:

The Hamas representative in Baghdad called us and informed us about the following:

The leadership of the Movement in Damascus called him (BIOT: the Hamas representative in Baghdad) several times since the beginning of the brutal American aggression on Iraq and he renewed their agreement with us including all the capabilities of the *Movement* (BIOT: Hamas is an acronym for the Islamic Resistance *Movement*) and that the leadership of the Movement saluted the Jihad resistance stand of our heroic people in all its social classes, and our courageous confrontation of the enemy attack while showing courage, patience and absolute faith.

Dr. Abdel Aziz Al Rantisi (member of the Movement political bureau) contacted him from Gaza and he sent his and the Palestinian people's regards to the leadership and people of Iraq and they acclaimed their heroic stand against the American barbaric attack. They also renewed the stand of the Palestinian people inside the occupied territories with Iraq in body and mind. Rantisi confirmed that he wanted open Arab borders (BIOT: most likely Iraq's border with Syria) so volunteers can participate with the Iraqi people in his (BIOT: Saddam Hussein's) honorable war against the infidel forces and they will conduct demonstrations and suicide operations in support of the honorable stand of Iraq.

The representative informed us about the departure of his family and he is standing by for our instructions to execute what is wanted from him and his followers of the Movement who are studying in the country.

We assured him of our gratitude for their offer and that it is in keeping with principles of the Movement, its work and the sincerity of its intentions. But we will be happier if we heard about any campaign aimed at the American and Zionist interests inside and outside of the occupied territories.

Please review, with regards.

End Translation

The next document provides validation that the concept of using Palestinian terrorists to attack American interests was nothing new to the Saddam regime. As early as March of 2001, the IIS was encouraging Saddam Hussein to do so. This document was initially discovered, translated, and disclosed among the Iraqi documents by the website *Free Republic*. Citizen translators and analysts of the *Free Republic* performed an invaluable service by translating and researching the Iraqi documents from the U.S. government's repository. The following is an original translation by Sammi. Bold is added for reference.

Begin Translation for CMPC-2003-006758

In the name of Allah the Merciful

Presidency of the Republic

Intelligence Service

To: Respected Assistant director of Operations

Subject: The new American policy towards Iraq

Enclosed is the letter of M10 and attached is the note of the Assistant Director of the Service on 24/3/2001 that your Excellency and both directors of M4 and M10 read from the letter of M10 and which includes:

1- The available signs confirm America's intentions, under the son of Bush's Presidency, to damage the political leadership of the nation to include what they calls smart sanctions, which are:

   A) To allow the flow of humanitarian products to Iraq without prior approval which will make the Iraqi leadership responsible for the starvation of the Iraqi people instead of the United Nations.

   B) Bring back the inspectors.

   C) Unify international opinion regarding the special procedures intended to contain Iraq.

   D) A travel embargo on Iraqi officials and freezing of their private accounts.

2- M10 proposed the following to counter the above:

   A) Prepare a media campaign to plead Iraq's case; **use**

the Palestinian cause and call for strikes against the American presence and interests.

B) Work on joining with some countries, like France, China, Russia and Japan in economic treaties which would cause the smart sanctions to have a negative influence on the interests of those countries.

C) Reinforce our embassies with new and expert staff which would target new opportunities in our international relations.

D) Prepare a list of the state officials including those of the Service (TC: IIS) who have foreign bank accounts under their name, so protective measures can be taken to protect those accounts from any hostile action.

E) Make sure that the money of Iraq is kept in Iraq.

F) Inform the President about the above issue.

Please review and we suggest that you get the opinions of M4, M5 and M40 concerning what was mentioned above....With respects.

Signed

28/3/2001

End Translation

CHAPTER 9:
THE INSURGENCY PLAN

Background

AS PREVIOUSLY MENTIONED, a plan has been found among the Saddam documents to instruct the Iraqi Intelligence Service on what to do should the regime fall to the coalition. The eleven directives mirror what really happened in Iraq.

One directive tells Ba'athist officials to burn all records, especially those of the IIS. The Saddam regime managed to burn a significant portion of its records at the beginning of Operation Iraqi Freedom. A statement by David Kay on the *Interim Progress Report on The Activities of the Iraq Survey Group (ISG)* before House and Senate committees given October 2, 2003 mentions the destruction of records:

> In addition to the discovery of extensive concealment efforts, we have been faced with a systematic sanitization of documentary and computer evidence in a wide range of offices, laboratories, and companies suspected of WMD work. The pattern of these efforts to erase evidence—hard drives destroyed, specific files burned, equipment cleaned of all traces of use—are ones of deliberate, rather than random, acts. For example,

- On 10 July 2003 an ISG team exploited the Revolutionary Command Council (RCC) Headquarters in Baghdad. The basement of the main building contained an archive of documents situated on well-organized rows of metal shelving. The basement suffered no fire damage despite the total destruction of the upper floors from coalition air strikes. Upon arrival the exploitation team encountered small piles of ash where individual documents or binders of documents were intentionally destroyed. Computer hard drives had been deliberately destroyed. Computers would have had financial value to a random looter; their destruction, rather than removal for resale or reuse, indicates a targeted effort to prevent Coalition forces from gaining access to their contents.

- All IIS laboratories visited by IIS exploitation teams have been clearly sanitized, including removal of much equipment, shredding and burning of documents, and even the removal of nameplates from office doors.

- Although much of the deliberate destruction and sanitization of documents and records probably occurred during the height of OIF combat operations, indications of significant continuing destruction efforts have been found after the end of major combat operations, including entry in May 2003 of the locked gated vaults of the Ba'ath party intelligence building in Baghdad and highly selective destruction of computer hard drives and data storage equipment along with the burning of a small number of specific binders that appear to have contained financial and intelligence records, and in July 2003 a site exploitation team at the Abu Gharib Prison found one pile of the smoldering ashes from documents that was still warm to the touch.

(http://www.fas.org/irp/cia/product/dkay100203.html)

The sabotage of Iraqi utilities, another directive in the memo, by the insurgency was and is still well marked by reporting and continues to be an insurgent tactic years after the overthrow of the Saddam regime.

Directives five, six and seven are perhaps the most controversial:

- Recruit reliable sources and direct them to the mosques.
- Join with the Islamic Hawza `Alemiya in Najaf. [Translator's comment: The Hawza is an Islamic religious teaching institution.]
- Associate with the national and Islamic groups and parties.

Even in post-Saddam Iraq, certain American intelligence officials believe that the ideology of the Ba'athists prevented them from working with Islamic extremists. In February of 2005, the Iraqi government became so convinced that former Ba'athist leaders were working with al-Qaeda and other foreign and domestic Islamic terrorists that they issued a most-wanted list including references to a collaborative relationship.

From that most-wanted list comes a bit of validation for the insurgency plan document:

Shaykh Mahmud Al-Hasani al-Sharqi—Shaykh Mahmud Al-Hasani al-Sharqi is a former Shia clerical **student at the An-Najaf Hawza.** He is responsible for attacks on coalition forces and undermining the reconstruction of Iraq. In October 03, he organized the ambush in Karbala that resulted in the death of two Iraqi policeman and four coalition soldiers. Hassani is also implicated in the rr Feb 2004 attack on Spanish forces and Iraqi Police in Diwaniyah. He is believed to be hiding in the Karbala/Najaf areas and may be disguising himself by dressing as a woman. The Multi National Force in Iraq is offering a reward of $50,000 for information leading to the capture of Shaykh Mahmud Al-Hasani al-Sharqi.

(http://www.arcent.army.mil/media_releases/2005/february/feb11_01.asp)

This statement describes the insurgent as a student of the An-Najaf Hawza. The IIS insurgency plan directed coordination with the Hawza in Najaf. This is independent evidence that a portion of the IIS directed insurgency emanated from the Hawza. But since the Hawza is a Shi'ite institution, it would be nearly inconceivable to find collaboration with Saddam.

Narrative

The Hawza in Najaf is a centuries old Shi'a religious institute that is the heart of the city. As the center of Shi'a theology, although finding competition for eminence from a center in Qum, Iran the Hawza was particularly unfriendly to the Sunni-backed Saddam regime. The murders of several Shi'a leaders of the Hawza have been laid at the feet of Saddam and the Ba'athists. So for the Saddam regime, sending IIS officers to the Hawza is indeed a peculiar move. Why would they? The easiest answer can be found in directive eleven, which reads "assassinate the clergy in the mosques."

The covert assassination of clergy might be viewed as an attack by rival religious sects and would sow the seeds of sectarian violence which is the main destabilizing factor in Iraq at the time of this writing. But directive six doesn't say, "join the Hawza and assassinate its clerics." It says "Join with the Islamic Hawza `Alemiya in Najaf." The tenor of this directive sounds collaborative, not threatening.

So the question becomes did the Saddam regime have a plan to work with a religious leader from the Hawza to lead the insurgency? Perhaps we should also ask if there is a religious leader affiliated with the Hawza who leads a portion of the insurgency.

The questions lead to a bit of theorizing. Given that the Saddam regime was making an insurgency plan against the occupation forces and that the majority of Iraqis are Shi'ite, would it not be likely that the Ba'athists knew they needed to turn Shi'ites against coalition forces? It was a given that the Sunni's would fight the American forces but not the Shi'ites. The Saddam regime existed under the constant threat of a Shi'a uprising, and it knew that the Shi'ites would help the coalition forces thus giving the Ba'athists no chance of regaining power.

So how could the Saddam regime incite Shi'ites to fight the Americans? It seems an impossible task. Yet there was and is a 'Shi'ite branch' of the insurgency that has been laid at the feet of Iran and one cleric in Iraq. However, it should be noted that other prominent clerics came back to Iraq from Iran after the war started and they counseled cooperation not conflict.

When the regime was planning the insurgency it needed to find a Shi'a cleric to fight the occupation forces; one with the power and legitimacy of the Hawza to back him. This could potentially shift the balance of power to the insurgency and drive out the coalition forces, a definitive starting point for the Ba'athists to retake power.

But why would a Shi'a cleric fight forces that were obviously benefiting his religious sect in Iraq? How could the Ba'athists entice a Shi'a cleric to support the insurgency? Wouldn't it take a particularly brutal Shi'a cleric to lead Shi'ites against the coalition and inevitably, the fellow Shiites who would cooperate with the coalition? So the key to detecting evidence of this hypothetical musing based on the directive would be to find a Shi'a cleric who fights coalition forces, fights Shi'ites who cooperate with the coalition forces, is particularly brutal and power hungry, and is associated with the Hawza. And there is a Shi'a cleric who fits that description named Muqtada al Sadr.

Almost all observers indicate that Muqtada al Sadr is using the insurgency to attain personal power. His methods are brutal and his Mahdi army has been compared to the Taliban. He has waged war on coalition forces and on his own fellow Shi'ites. He is considered to be personally responsible for the assassination of senior clerics who stand in his way.

In spite of the fact that virtually all of his senior clerics in the decidedly hierarchically structured Hawza urged him to work with the coalition Muqtada fought coalition forces. These actions have led him into a condition of war against the Hawza of which he was affiliated with before the war. In our theoretical musings al Sadr perfectly fulfills the requirements for a Shi'a cleric who would be an insurgent ally of the Ba'athists, except in one aspect—he hated Saddam Hussein.

So why would Muqtada al Sadr agree to accept the IIS into his Mahdi army to fight an insurgency for the Ba'athists? To many observers, this undoubtedly flies in the face of his history with Saddam.

Muqtada al Sadr's father, Ayatollah Muhammad Sadiq al-Sadr was assassinated by what is generally accepted to be Saddam's orders in 1999. His father-in-law, Muhammad Baqir al-Sadr was an even more heralded Shi'a cleric who Saddam executed in 1980. Muqtada's family is steeped in historical leadership of the Hawza and the Shi'ites. Muqtada wears the black turban, which indicates lineage to the prophet Mohammed. He has every reason to detest the Saddam regime.

Still, al Sadr may be exactly what the Ba'athists needed if they had any hope of defeating American forces. But then how would it help Muqtada to fight an insurgency and how can a man whose father was killed by the regime possibly think of working with that regime?

He was probably given an ultimatum from the Saddam regime—fight for us, or be killed like so many others in your family (including two older brothers). It is likely he wasn't the only Shi'a cleric to whom the regime made "an offer you can't refuse." This type of manipulation was an every day occurrence under the Saddam regime. Pitting the regime's enemies against each other, the Shi'ites versus the Americans in this case, was a central tenant of the Saddam regime's retention of power. It would have been the first thing they thought to do in planning an insurgency.

If Muqtada al Sadr took the only option that would have left his head on his shoulders and agreed to accept the IIS into his Mahdi army to fight the insurgency along side his own followers what would be the benefit other than keeping his head? The regime would most likely have guaranteed its support in placing him at the head of the Hawza if it returned to power. The IIS agents that integrated into the Mahdi army to fight the coalition would also have killed other Hawza clerics putting Sadr in a position to gain control of the Hawza. In this way the assassination of other clerics would not be traceable to known elements within his Mahdi army as the acts would have been committed by covert agents, probably unknown in even their own communities as former members of the secret Saddam security apparatus.

As the leader of the Hawza in Najaf a Shi'a cleric holds much power. But the older, established clerics of the Hawza already had this theocratic power. So it would serve them nothing to work with the Ba'athists. It would make a lot more sense for the Ba'athists to illicit cooperation from a brash, younger cleric with historical backing for a claim to the leadership of the Hawza, but who was many years behind the senior clerics who already held the authority. In effect, the Ba'athists were the only hope Sadr had for immediate ascension to the leadership of the Hawza and Iraqi Shi'ites.

This would save Sadr decades of study and toil to attain a position of leadership that would not be guaranteed to him even if he took the traditional route of ascension through the hierarchy. A position he undoubtedly feels is his by divine right of ascension from lineage to the prophet Mohammed. But in addition to this potential outcome Muqtada al Sadr would probably see this as a path to direct control of Iraq using his theocratic authority over his Mahdi army and his integrated Saddam regime assets. He may have envisioned taking direct control over Iraq's majority Shi'a population in a double-cross of the Ba'athists once the Americans had been driven out. This scenario would put Sadr in direct control of the nation and he would get to betray the Ba'athists to boot.

To investigate this theory, we have to validate certain elements of it with what is known about the situation in Iraq. The Middle East Forum website has an article written by Nimrod Raphaeli called Understanding Muqtada al-Sadr in the Fall of 2004 edition of the *Middle East Quarterly*. The article discusses the situation with Sadr in great detail and includes this interesting passage:

> The Hawza was not blind to the threat posed by the Jaysh al-Mahdi. In a July 26, 2003 declaration to the "honorable sons of Najaf," the Hawza condemned the Jaysh al-Mahdi, declaring:
>
> This army is composed of suspicious elements, [including] individuals from the extinct regime and its security officers and members of the [Baath] party who have wrapped their heads with white and black rags to mislead people into believing that they are men of religion when in truth they are only devils... We do not need your army, which you have slanderously and falsely called the Mahdi army ... The Imam [al-Mahdi] is in no need of any army made up of thieves, robbers, and

perverts under the leadership of a one-eyed charlatan.

[http://www.meforum.org/article/655]

Jaysh al Mahdi is the Muqtada al Sadr army. According to an official statement of the Hawza, former regime security officers, or IIS agents, infiltrated the Mahdi army. This provides evidence to support our theory that the IIS coordinated with Muqtada al Sadr to send IIS agents to the Hawza. Surely al Sadr knew this if others did and he allowed them into his army.

The article also supports many of the elements of our theory. The information validates that this possible Ba'athist collaborator joined the insurgency against the objections of the Shi'a clerics and targeted them, as well as the coalition forces:

> When U.S. forces rolled through Iraq in March and April 2003, most Shi'ites greeted them as liberators. But, the demise of Saddam Hussein's regime in Iraq unleashed an array of forces that had been dormant or suppressed for more than three decades. From almost total political marginalization, the Iraqi Shi'ites found themselves at the center of political power. While some political parties such as Da'wa and the Supreme Council for Islamic Revolution in Iraq participated in the U.S.-sponsored political process, it was not long before U.S. forces became aware of a new force among the Shi'ites.
>
> Muqtada al-Sadr, a young cleric from a prominent family, almost immediately launched a fierce campaign of resistance, first against competing clerics and then against the coalition forces. [Ibid]

The article also discusses Sadr's potential for power within the Hawza:

> Muqtada may not have inherited his father's religious legitimacy,

but the large number of Shi'ites who follow him do so not because of his status as a marja' or religious authority, but because for them, he is the symbol and the personification of Sadr's legitimacy. Shi'ite Islam is hierarchical. At the top of the Shi'ite pyramid is the marja'. The marja' is usually a senior cleric, such as an ayatollah who, after years of study, may issue fatwas (religious edicts) on a wide range of political, social, and legal matters to which his followers adhere. The seat of the marja' is referred to as marja'iya. Unlike the Catholic church, where the pope is the undisputed leader, Shi'ite individually choose a living marja' to emulate so that any time, there might be a handful of prominent ayatollahs or grand ayatollahs who fit the bill. Since Muqtada has not reached the rank of Ayatollah, let alone Grand Ayatollah, he cannot be a marja', but this has not hurt his ability to mobilize the young and disaffected. A personality cult has developed with Muqtada pictures adorning shops, stores, mosques, and public buses. (Ibid)

We see that Muqtada al Sadr had little chance to gain Hawza leadership in the short term unless some external force emplaced him as the leader. He had the lineage and some popular support, but he did not have the legitimacy of theocratic sanction. How many other historical examples are there of those on the cusp of power who side with an enemy to usurp the hierarchy?

Power-hungry Sadr needed a religious *coup d'état*. That was his only chance to immediate power. To rise to power, he needed to eliminate all of the leading Shi'a clerics and drive out the coalition forces, which is exactly what the Ba'athists needed as well:

Muqtada's rise to prominence came shortly after U.S. forces marched through the country. On April 3, 2003, as U.S., British, and Polish forces pushed through southern Iraq on the path to Baghdad, Hojjat ul-Islam Abdul Majid al-Khoei returned to Iraq. Less than two weeks later, he was dead, hacked to death with two of his supporters in the mosque of Imam 'Ali, perhaps the holiest shrine in Shi'ite Islam.[9]

The death of the 40-year-old Khoei reverberated around the world for he was the son of Grand Ayatollah Abulqasim Musawi al-Khoei, the Iranian-born architect of a prominent school of thought in the principles of jurisprudence and Islamic law. Abulqasim Musawi al-Khoei had also been the teacher of Grand Ayatollah 'Ali al-Sistani, perhaps the most prominent living Shi'ite religious scholar today. Abdul Majid was prominent in his own right, however. Following the failed Shi'ite rebellion against Saddam in 1991 and the subsequent liquidation of many clerics, Abdul-Majid al-Khoei fled to London to head the Al-Khoei Foundation, a charitable organization active not only in southern Iraq but also across Africa and Asia. Many Shi'ite and Iraq watchers considered Khoei both a religious moderate and a rising young star. Following Khoei's assassination, supporters of Muqtada demonstrated outside the home of Grand Ayatollah 'Ali al-Sistani, the most senior ayatollah in the Hawza, calling on him to go back to Iran. The siege ended only after Sistani called in 1,500 tribesmen from surrounding areas to disperse the crowd.

Khoei's assassination removed from the Iraqi political and religious scene one of Muqtada al-Sadr's chief competitors. Hawza officials put together the details of Khoei's murder and named Muqtada al-Sadr's supporters as responsible.

...Shortly afterward, another prominent Shi'ite figure was assassinated, again apparently at the hands of Muqtada al-Sadr's followers. Assailants murdered Hayder ar-Rifa'i, the klaydar (keeper of the key) of the tomb of Imam 'Ali. (Ibid)

So the Mahdi army began a systematic campaign to "assassinate the clergy in the mosques," just as the insurgency plan from the Ba'athists directs. And the article speaks directly to his brutality:

> The two murders mark the beginning of the abuses by Muqtada. But there were others as well, many of which created friction between Muqtada's followers and ordinary residents of Najaf and elsewhere. For example, there were arbitrary arrests and sentencing by unofficial Shar'ia courts he established; forced veiling of women; acts of violence against liquor stores and merchants, many of whom were either killed or received public lashings; closure of cinemas; and confiscation of money and property under the guise of religion. His excesses have led people in Karbala to declare Muqtada's people "worse than Saddam." (Ibid)

This definitely fits the profile of a brutal thug who would sell out his own people to gain power much like Saddam Hussein the very man who killed his father. In fact, it might be said that Saddam met his match in Muqtada al Sadr. The article illuminates the reasons why a Shi'a cleric would overthrow his religious hierarchy:

> The conflict between Muqtada and the Hawza, particularly its most senior leader Grand Ayatollah 'Ali al-Sistani, is more political than theological. The 31-year-old Muqtada lacks the intellect, scholarship, maturity, experience, and balance to challenge Sistani on issues of Islamic jurisprudence. It would be the equivalent of a college freshman challenging a tenured professor. However, Muqtada does enjoy some advantages. His name is magic, particularly among the young and downtrodden. While Muqtada hails from Iraq, Sistani is Iranian born and hence lacks the young cleric's purity in the nationalist context. The willingness of Muqtada to use violence to achieve his goals also is significant.(Ibid)

It should also be pointed out that reporting on Muqtada al Sadr has indicated that he makes a logical distinction between "Saddamists," or those who are loyal to Saddam directly and Ba'athists or those who were part of the party but not particularly loyal to Saddam. In fact, this distinction turned up in a few different media reports of interviews with other Iraqis. Considering that Saddam was undoubtedly target number one of the coalition forces Sadr may have considered it likely he would be quickly captured or killed and may not have considered Saddam as a factor in his decision to work with the IIS.

While this theory is controversial and is far from proven the authors wish to provide this evidence for further investigation. If more inquiries turn up significant evidence that those IIS agents who were directed to join with the Hawza were also told to join with Muqtada al Sadr it may be the key to de-legitimizing one of the most stubborn elements of the insurgency. Proof that Sadr was working with the Ba'athists might go a long way toward reducing his prestige and quelling at least one aspect of the insurgency. It is interesting to note that following the hanging of Saddam Hussein, Sadr left Iraq and has since told his followers to lay down their arms—for now.

Broader Context

The most wanted list produced by the Iraqi government in 2005 also includes an IIS agent believed to be working directly with Islamic terrorists:

Ahmad Hasan Kaka al-'Ubaydi—Ahmad Hasan Kaka al-'Ubaydi is a former Iraqi Intelligence Service officer, and is now believed associated with Ansar Al Islam affiliate. He is believed to be a leader of an insurgent and criminal network that is conducting attacks against coalition forces, the Interim Iraqi Government, Iraqi National Guard, the

Iraqi Police and the Iraqi people. The Multi National Force in Iraq is also offering a reward of $200,000 for information leading to his capture.

Ansar al Islam received Abu Mus'ab al Zarqawi and his fighters in Northern Iraq. Previously, the evidence showed that Zarqawi's group was under the influence of al Barqawi a man who was among the Palestinians kicked out of Kuwait for supporting Saddam during the occupation. Zarqawi's group included others who had supported Saddam in Kuwait. The evidence also includes an al Qaeda letter in which the writer is speaking about Barqawi and his Jordanian group (Zarqawi's group) and he states they "went to Saddam".

We then postulated that many of these terror groups and leaders were in a position to be influenced if not directly controlled by the IIS relating to the invasion of Kuwait. In the most-wanted list, the Iraqi government claimed in 2005 that an IIS officer was fighting for Ansar al Islami.

Put together, this provides evidence that the insurgency plan directed the pre-war coordination between the IIS and what would become al Qaeda in Iraq. It also appears that the coordination was based upon a pre-existing relationship between the IIS and al Qaeda elements. It may even be that the collaboration with the IIS was not directed by Usama bin Laden. It is conceivable Zarqawi acted on his own authority (and Barqawi's and maybe even Zawahiri's as a Saddam collaborator) in the name of al Qaeda and Usama later acquiesced once the deal was done.

It is a contentious issue as to whether or not Ansar al Islam was working for or against the Saddam regime. Because Ansar al Islam attacked Kurdish separatists (opposed to Saddam), some see that as evidence they cooperated with the Saddam regime. At the start of Operation Iraqi Freedom (OIF) some journalists in the Kurdish region reported witnessing Saddam regime military vehicles supplying military hardware to Ansar al Islam. The issue is well explained by Jonathan Schanzer, a Soref Fellow at the Washington Institute for Near East Policy. His article entitled Ansar al-Islam: Back in Iraq which can be found at the website Middle East Forum under the publication *Middle East Quarterly,* lays out the controversy as of winter 2004:

Months before the Iraq war of 2003, The New Yorker, Christian Science Monitor, and The New York Times published reports about Ansar al-Islam ("Partisans of Islam"), a brutal band of al-Qa'ida guerrillas based in a Kurdish area of northern Iraq near the Iranian border. U.S. officials pointed to Ansar al-Islam as the "missing link" between al-Qa'ida and Saddam Hussein. When Secretary of State Colin Powell made the U.S. case for war against Saddam at the United Nations on February 5, 2003, he cited Ansar al-Islam as a key reason for invasion. Powell drew links among the group, al-Qa'ida, and Saddam, citing Central Intelligence Agency (CIA) documents declassified upon the request of the White House.

As war approached, however, the Bush administration said less about Ansar al-Islam and al-Qa'ida. Rather, the administration focused on Saddam's attempts to develop weapons of mass destruction. After the war, it became a matter of common wisdom that Saddam had no links to al-Qa'ida. Carl Levin, chairman of the Senate Armed Services Committee, said that the case linking Saddam to al-Qa'ida was never "bullet-proof." Former vice president Al Gore denied that such ties existed at all.

But since the defeat and dispersal of Saddam's regime, U.S. officials have begun to talk of Ansar al-Islam once more. In July 2003, U.S. joint chiefs of staff chairman General Richard Myers stated "that group is still active in Iraq." A week later, Myers revealed that some cadres from the group had been captured and were being interrogated. The U.S. top administrator in Iraq, Paul Bremer III, reiterated Myers's message in August, saying that there were "quite a number of these Ansar al-Islam professional killers on the loose in the country," that they were staging attacks against U.S. servicemen, and that U.S. forces were trying to track them down.

[http://www.meforum.org/article/579]

This document adds to the evidence that during the pre-invasion planning the Saddam regime considered Islamic extremists to be an ally which does make it more likely that Zarqawi was in Iraq at Saddam's acquiescence.

The BBC reported in a July 24th, 2002 article entitled 'Al-Qaeda' influence grows in Iraq that the Kurds had captured an Iraqi intelligence officer who claimed Saddam was working with Ansar al Islam:

One of those leaders [of Ansar al Islam] is Abu Wa'il, a former Iraqi army officer.

Shadowy connections

A captured Iraqi intelligence officer of 20 years' standing, Abu Iman al-Baghdadi, who is held by the PUK, said Abu Wa'il is actively manipulating the Ansar on behalf of Iraqi intelligence.

"I was captured by the Kurds after Iraqi intelligence sent me to check what was happening with Abu Wa'il, following rumours that he'd been captured and handed over the CIA," al-Baghdadi said.

He added that Baghdad smuggles arms to the Ansar through the Kurdish area, and is using the group to make problems for the PUK, one of the opposition factions ranged against Saddam Hussein.

"The Ansar's basic allegiance is to al-Qaeda, but some of them were trained in Iraq and went Afghanistan," he said, interviewed in a Kurdish prison.

"When the Americans attacked, they [al-Qaeda] came here through Iran. Iraq is supporting them and using them to carry out attacks."

[http://news.bbc.co.uk/1/hi/world/middle_east/2149499.stm]

The claims of opposition groups should always be viewed with a good measure of skepticism. But this evidence points to collaboration between the Saddam regime and the *global Islamic jihad movement* that allowed al-Qaeda affiliated fighters to infiltrate into northern Iraq for training and staging for the insurgency as part of the *Insurgency Plan*. As this portion of Iraq was "not under his control," Saddam could maintain deniability. But the term "not under his control" is a bit misleading as Saddam could and did carry out covert operations according to media reports and other captured documents.

Perhaps the definitive work on the subject of Saddam and terrorists in Iraq comes from Stephen Hayes in his writing for the *Weekly Standard*. His January 16th, 2006 article entitled Saddam's Terror Training Camps claims voluminous evidence exists that the Saddam regime was collaborating with Islamic terrorists inside Iraq:

THE FORMER IRAQI REGIME OF Saddam Hussein trained thousands of radical Islamic terrorists from the region at camps in Iraq over the four years immediately preceding the U.S. invasion, according to documents and photographs recovered by the U.S. military in postwar Iraq. The existence and character of these documents has been confirmed to THE WEEKLY STANDARD by eleven U.S. government officials.

The secret training took place primarily at three camps—in Samarra,

Ramadi, and Salman Pak—and was directed by elite Iraqi military units. Interviews by U.S. government interrogators with Iraqi regime officials and military leaders corroborate the documentary evidence. Many of the fighters were drawn from terrorist groups in northern Africa with close ties to al Qaeda, chief among them Algeria's GSPC and the Sudanese Islamic Army. Some 2,000 terrorists were trained at these Iraqi camps each year from 1999 to 2002, putting the total number at or above 8,000. Intelligence officials believe that some of these terrorists returned to Iraq and are responsible for attacks against Americans and Iraqis. According to three officials with knowledge of the intelligence on Iraqi training camps, White House and National Security Council officials were briefed on these findings in May 2005; senior Defense Department officials subsequently received the same briefing.

The photographs and documents on Iraqi training camps come from a collection of some 2 million "exploitable items" captured in postwar Iraq and Afghanistan. They include handwritten notes, typed documents, audiotapes, videotapes, compact discs, floppy discs, and computer hard drives. Taken together, this collection could give U.S. intelligence officials and policymakers an inside look at the activities of the former Iraqi regime in the months and years before the Iraq war.

The discovery of the information on jihadist training camps in Iraq would seem to have two major consequences: It exposes the flawed assumptions of the experts and U.S. intelligence officials who told us for years that a secularist like Saddam Hussein would never work with Islamic radicals, any more than such jihadists would work with an infidel like the Iraqi dictator. It also reminds us that valuable information remains buried in the mountain of documents recovered in Afghanistan and Iraq over the past four years.

[http://www.weeklystandard.com/Content/Public/Articles/000/000/006/550kmbzd.asp]

The Insurgency Plan document, part of what Hayes refers to in his article as the "mountain of documents" indeed provides strong evidence that the Saddam regime was planning an Islamic jihad based insurgency to drive out American forces. We find evidence that the directives match with what actually happened in post-Saddam Iraq.

To put it simply the Saddam insurgency plan wasn't relying on the kindness of strangers.

The following translation is provided by the U.S. government. The Harmony number indicates that it was captured in Iraq in 2003.

Translation begins for CMPC-2003-016373

In the Name of God, most Merciful, most Compassionate

Republic of Iraq

Presidential Office

Iraqi Intelligence Service

Top Secret

Number: 549

Date: 23 January 2003

To / All National Offices [directorates] listed below

Reference / Emergency Plan

- Security [Service]

- [Military] Intelligence

- Intelligence [Service]

In reference to our secret letter, numbered 3870, dated 19 January 2003, please do what is necessary if, God forbid, the Iraqi Command falls to the Coalition Forces—the Americans, British and Zionists. To all the associates in your offices, and specifically the departments mentioned above, proceed in accordance with the following instructions:

1. Demolish and burn all offices in the country, especially [those] associated with ours and other departments.
2. Change your residence from time to time.
3. Sabotage electrical power stations.
4. Sabotage water stations.
5. Recruit reliable sources and direct them to the mosques.
6. Join with the Islamic Hawza `Alemiya in Najaf. [Translator's comment: The Hawza is an Islamic religious teaching institution.]
7. Associate with the national and Islamic groups and parties.
8. Cease all internal and external communications.
9. Purchase stolen weapons from the public.
10. Develop relationships with those returning from abroad.
11. Assassinate the clergy in the mosques. [Translator's comment: Clergy here includes both Imams and orators (guest speakers).]

A copy to the [Illegible signature]
Baghdad Intelligence Directorate

Comrade
Ninawa Intelligence Directorate

General Intelligence Director
Al Basra Intelligence Directorate

23 January 2003
End translation.

CHAPTER 10:
HOW TO REMAIN INCOGNITO IN AFGHANISTAN

Background

THE WEALTH OF documentation provided in this book shows the Saddam regime was working deals with Islamic terrorist groups so it should not come as a surprise to find evidence that the Iraqi military was conducting covert operations in Afghanistan. A document captured in Iraq provides a clear indication of an Arab military presence in Afghanistan although it does not specifically state it was the Iraqi military.

The circumstances of how this document came to be released by the Defense Department are clear to someone with knowledge of the document exploitation process conducted by ISG. The first thing that can be determined by the Harmony number, '2RAD-2004-600760-ELC' is that the document was processed into the U.S. database 2004. The ELC designation means the document was an electronic document removed from a computer or computer media such as a thumb drive or CD.

When computer media was processed at the combined media processing center for the ISG, it was assigned a Harmony number. That Harmony number applied to the physical media item itself, not files contained on the media. It could be thought of as a parent number. As documents were discovered and identified by media processes on that piece of media the documents with intelligence value were assigned a secondary Harmony number. Often these numbers were designated by the '2RAD' number found at the beginning of this Harmony number.

Thus the authors are able to deduce with much confidence that this is an electronic copy of an electronic document removed from computer media that was captured in Iraq. How that document came to be in Iraq is another matter. It is possible the document could have been brought from Afghanistan on a computer or computer media device.

Narrative

The document is an informal letter of instruction or training manual. It is clearly not a formal military publication. It looks very much like an instruction letter written at an operational level for a small team on a specific mission—a team with computer resources.

The training manual warns about the danger of "information leaks," and it instructs Arab operatives residing in or on their way to Afghanistan to dress like Afghan tribesmen, to avoid being followed ("Routine is the enemy of security"), to always be armed, and "to behave as if enemies would strike at any moment."

The manual also cautions the Arabs soldiers who hold military ID's to "beware of rapid and spontaneous friendships with Afghans who speak Arabic," and "always make sure about the identity of your neighbors and classify them as regular people, opponents or allies."

This seven-page document contains instructions for a group of Arab men, military ID holders, and their families joining other military men already in Afghanistan who are hosting volunteers. These facilities appear to be safe houses or training facilities. Afghanistan was full of Arabs since the time of the Soviet invasion, so it is unusual that Arabs would be so concerned about their identities.

As a general rule the Arab mujahideen were proud to announce their national identity, but not these men. Their nation of origin was a secret not even revealed in the document. However, it makes sense that a document about concealing their nationality would not state their nationality.

The argument that this document provides compelling evidence that Iraqi forces were conducting covert training operations in Afghanistan to train Islamic terrorists is supported by:

- The covert nature of the instructions.
- The fact that they are Arabs.
- The fact that these are military men working for an intelligence service.
- The fact that they are hosting volunteers in safe houses in Afghanistan.
- The fact that there is other documentary evidence that links the Iraqi Intelligence Service to Hekmatyar, notorious for training camps in Afghanistan.
- The fact that Iraq was one of only two Arab state supporters of terror.

Broader Context

The instruction letter indicates that the secret mission was located in Kandahar, Afghanistan. Kandahar is notable as the base of Usama bin Laden's operations and site of a major terror training facility. The Saddam regime had expertise in chemical weapons production. Reports indicate that training camps in Afghanistan included training and experimentation with chemical weapons. Al-Qaeda has repeated expressed its desire for WMD.

Al-Qaeda had the desire for WMD and associated training. Iraqi intelligence had the know-how for WMD (the IIS was the proponent of WMD activity in Iraq even though such activity was carried out by the Iraqi military) and the capabilities to train. Both had motive to attack the U.S. with WMD. According to an al-Qaeda detainee description, both were involved in a plot to use WMD on a U.S. embassy. According to government documents, the detainee was an Iraqi working with the IIS and al Qaeda in a chemical weapons plot in Pakistan. (U.S. claims Iraqi detainee plotted embassy attacks, Associated Press, 3/30/2005 - http://www.usatoday.com/news/world/2005-03-30-iraqi-pakistan_x.htm)

This document is an indicator that Iraq was running a covert training mission in Afghanistan. It is quite possible that this training could have been the source of al-Qaeda's WMD capabilities discovered in its abandoned terror training camps.

And Maulana Fazlur Rahman invited the IIS to Kandahar according to the IIS notebook.

The following is an original translation by Sammi. He adds notes, and bold type is added for emphasis.

Begin Translation of 2RAD-2004-600760-ELC

In the Name of God the Merciful

Personnel Security:

Respected brother,

Know that one of the main causes of information leaks is from personnel who talk. This is why we try to cooperate with you so that neither you nor one of your brothers becomes the cause of a catastrophe that might hit one of the brothers or all of them.

Please follow these instructions:

1- Know as much as you need. (TC: don't ask too many questions)

2- Don't talk too much; it is said that "silence is wisdom."

3- It is recommended that all personnel wear Afghan clothing so they do not stand out from other people. (BIOT: An Arab mujahideen would typically dress as an Arab, not an Afghani, since they considered themselves superior to the backwards natives. This is a strong indication this is not a letter for jihadists.)

4- All the brothers should go to the market by themselves, alone.

5- It is not advised to move alone at night. (At night, walk the streets on foot)

6- As much as possible **do not disclose your identity as an Arab.**

7- Avoid excitement whether by glorifying or bashing.

8- Avoid being observed (TC: being followed and observed) and always notice who is walking behind you or following you from a distance; review the observation manual (BIOT: Apparently they have a counterintelligence manual, another indicator it is a professional military organization and not mujahideen.)

9- All brothers should be always armed even if with a small knife in their pockets.

10- Check your pockets and never leave important papers in them when moving around.

11- Always be careful in personal relations with Afghans or Pakistanis.

12- Avoid giving any information about the locations of your brothers.

13- It is forbidden to discuss work issues with the women.

14- It is forbidden to take children to parks and offices.

15- It is forbidden to talk about your work or the nature of your mission with anybody who is not related to it.

16- Beware of habit in your daily routine because the rule says, "Routine is the enemy of security."

17- If you are moving and have a large amount of money, beware of showing it in the market so you do not attract robbers.

18- Always beware when you are talking about the work because somebody not related to your work, the women or the children, might hear you.

19- Beware of rapid and spontaneous friendships with Afghans who speak Arabic.

20- In public places beware of talking about work issues because some Afghans know Arabic but you cannot notice this.

21- Always be forgiving when you are buying from, selling to or dealing with Afghans and avoid trouble.

22- Children are not allowed to go out by themselves whether to buy stuff or play.

23- Always make sure about the identity of your neighbors and classify them as regular people, opponents or allies.

Security of compounds:

The security of the house or the living quarters is one of the most important aspects of security because the house contains the personnel, the equipment and the important documents. Make sure the house is secure and that these measures seriously. There are important precautions, to the security of the house, that have to be taken before renting but it is not practical to list them here.

(TC: several instructions for securing the houses are listed, including location, neighborhood, weapons inside, rules for children, night-time policy, and patrolling the surroundings)

Security of the hosting places:

A hosting place is the place where most infiltration takes place. What we mean by hosting place is a public place where people, who most of the time are not related to the work, are received. But in case we are receiving special guests or others, it is not considered a hosting place but it is affiliated to the security of the special offices. (TC: there are 23 instructions for the security of the hosting places; here are 10)

At the hosting place a room for the security unit is necessary for observation:

1. The hosting place should be away from the living space of the brothers and their meeting areas.

2. Brothers should not go often to the hosting place except for a purpose.

3. It is forbidden to practice any private or secret matter in the hosting place.

4. The hosting place where our brothers are grouped, like Kandahar

a. Anybody who enters it should be known

b. Nobody lives in it unless a known party recommends him

c. Persons living in the hosting place should be organized and authorized by the brother in charge of the hosting place. It should be known where the brother is going and when he is coming back.

5. Brothers living in Kandahar and who repetitively visit the hosting place should abide by the Holy Hadith (a sacred text of Islam), "The virtue of one's Islam is to leave what does not belong to him," and not to start a relation with the brothers living in the hosting place.

6. The brother in charge of the hosting place should assign a private place for each brother living in the hosting place and not leave the decision to the visitor.

7. There should be a schedule for night guard in the hosting place.

8. The communication room should be isolated in the hosting place and not close to the visitor's rooms.

9. **The hosting place should have a reception room where the**

visiting brother is dealt with, before entering the hosting place, and decide if he is going to stay in it.

10. Public meetings are strictly forbidden in the hosting place.

Security of movement:

First: Security of cars and vehicles

Constant movement of cars between the houses of the brothers and their workplace is a big breach which might lead to discovery of those places if the brother driving was not aware of being watched. It is possible that the car itself, with its occupant, might be a target, therefore:

(TC: several instructions for driving and car security follow; here are a few)

- The brothers driving the cars should check their car daily to make sure it does not contain any foreign material or device.

- All the brothers driving the cars should be armed and should have their weapons license.

- Brothers driving the cars should always be wearing Afghan clothing so their identity cannot be easily discovered.

- Brothers driving the cars should not always follow one path and should not have a constant habit in choosing their way.

Second: security of movement and travel inside Afghanistan

Travel is one of the most important security breaches that we should be careful of because of the long absence from the brothers and facing the dangers of the road.

- It is absolutely forbidden for a person to travel by himself, and it is preferable that the number of travelers be at least three including a trusted Afghan.

- **In rest areas a brother should not show his military ID.**

- The security office should be informed about the travel before the travel, and when you reach your destination you should inform the office for follow up.

(TC: several instructions for mail and communications security are listed, right out of an intelligence personnel book)

Public meetings security:

The danger of public meetings is that it often groups most of the personnel present in Kandahar. If the enemy manages to know and reach the meeting place, he would have a dangerous opportunity and to make him miss this chance we should follow some precautions.

(TC: several instructions concerning public meetings security follow)

End Translation

CHAPTER 11:
THE MASTERMIND OF MOGADISHU

Background

THE CYBER NEWS Service (CNS news) published an article on October 4th, 2004 entitled <u>Exclusive: Saddam Possessed WMD, Had Extensive Terror Ties</u> by Scott Wheeler. The news agency claimed to have received a set of documents from a "senior government official who is not a political appointee." These documents were quickly disregarded by most in the media. Part of the reason is because they were released in an improper fashion with no history of possession to authenticate them. Another reason is because the information they imparted was completely different than anything else the majority of the media was reporting.

The article can be found here:

(http://www.cnsnews.com/ViewSpecialReports.asp?Page=%5CSpecialReports%5Carchive%5C200410%5CSPE20041004a.html)

There are several indicators that these documents are authentic. The first is the fact that they substantially match the content of documents known to have been captured in Iraq and released by the Department of Defense. Those secrets were previously unknown to the public. The original CNS news article presented expert testimony that contributed to the evidence supporting them. One of the authors of this book worked with many of these documents with the Iraqi Survey Group and saw thousands of such documents and has determined that they look consistent with documents captured in Iraq.

Fortunately, another Saddam regime document has been photographed and displayed at the website of a U.S. government agency called USAID. That memorandum is pictured among a group of Iraqis going through reams of captured documents. The photograph of that event is included in an article about the use of official Iraqi documents to identify and locate the victims of the Saddam regime. The USAID photograph is reproduced here for comparison purposes.

Website Caption excerpt: Photo by Thomas Hartwell, May 31, 2003 Volunteers show a secret document that instructs people to create havoc if the Coalition should occupy Iraq at a recently established grass roots Association of Former Prisoners and Missing Persons in Baghdad. The orders

are to destroy documents, buildings and infiltrate and kill religious groups. They are trying to input into computers information from seized prison and other government documents to create a database. Throughout the day queues of people are waiting to search the database for information on missing relatives. USAID-DART plans to help them get better organized and possibly train them on how to properly interview witnesses of atrocities or survivors of massacres.

http://www.usaid.gov/iraq/photogallery/gallery_17/gro8.html

The caption describes a memorandum that sounds remarkably like the *Insurgency Plan* document presented in this book. The document in the photograph resembles the documents used in the CNS article. Here is a scanned electronic copy of one of the CNS documents.

Figure 2. CNS document sample

The USAID photograph and the scanned image from CNS are nearly identical. Both have a spherical emblem in the right upper corner. Both have a linear and taller emblem in the center top portion. Both have three lines of Arabic writing in the upper left corner section. Both have the remnants of a border around the body of the document that appears to have faded with photocopying. Both have handwritten text on a document template, including a formal header.

One hundred percent validation would require identification of the signatures and confirmation by signatories. That is a level of authentication rarely available to private researchers. The authors of this book conclude that the evidence that the CNS documents are authentic vastly outweighs any conjecture that they are not.

Because the authors of this book have made the determination that the CNS documents are authentic based on the evidence available at the time of this writing we include them in the scope of this work. The documents are reproduced here at the generous permission of CNS News.

Narrative

The CNS documents are a series of back and forth correspondence between Saddam Hussein and the Iraqi Intelligence Service. The Top Secret memorandum that began the exchange is an order from Saddam to "hunt the Americans down" in Somalia using our "Arabic or Asian Muslim friends." "Asian Muslim friends" refers to Afghanis and Pakistanis.

That order was dated January 18th, 2003 and it instructed the leader of the *Arabian Bureau-Ba'ath Party* which is apparently a Saddam regime element that deals with people connected to the *global Islamic jihad movement*. The order tells the Arabic Bureau to take the necessary steps for the mission. The document shows the subject had come up as early as December of 1992.

There are several revelations in these documents that we summarize here:

- The IIS revealed contacts and sometime quantifies them with several groups that support the *global Islamic jihad movement.*
  - o Egyptian Islamic Jihad (EIJ and the U.S. based EIG)
  - o Pakistani groups lead by Maulana Fazlur Rahman
  - o Sudanese terror groups and leaders including Othman Taha
  - o Afghani groups including Hekmatyar's
  - o Palestinian groups
- Saddam embarked on a hidden war with the United States in the early 90's.
- Saddam used the EIJ during the first Gulf War.
- Saddam had a bureau dedicated to working with these groups.
- Saddam was behind the attacks on U.S. forces in Somalia at the very least as a contributor.
- Saddam was working with groups strongly tied to the 1993 World Trade Center bombing at the same time as that attack occurred. It should be remembered that a bomb making expert came to the U.S. from Iraq for that attack and fled to Baghdad afterwards.

Broader Context

A U.N. report on the first U.N. mission to Somalia includes this timeline:

Unified Task Force (UNITAF)

On 3 December 1992, the Security Council unanimously adopted resolution 794(1992). The Council welcomed the United States offer to help create a secure environment for the delivery of humanitarian aid in Somalia and authorized, under Chapter VII of the Charter, the use of "all necessary means" to do so. Resolution 794 asked States to provide military forces and to make contributions in cash or kind for the operation. Appropriate mechanisms for coordination between the United Nations and those military forces were also to be established by the Secretary-General and States participating in the operation.

Operation Restore Hope

United States President George Bush responded to Security Council resolution 794 (1992) with a decision on 4 December to initiate **Operation Restore Hope**, under which the United States would assume the unified command of the new operation in accordance with resolution 794(1992). The Secretary-General communicated to President Bush on 8 December his concept of a division of labour between the United Nations and the United States in the following terms: **"The United States has undertaken to take the lead in creating the secure environment which is an inescapable condition for the United Nations to provide humanitarian relief and promote national reconciliation and economic reconstruction, objectives which have from the outset been included in the various Security Council resolutions on Somalia.**

" The first elements of the Unified Task Force (UNITAF) came ashore on the beaches of Mogadishu without opposition on 9 December 1992. On 13 December, United States forces had secured the airfield at Baledogle, and by 16 December they had seized Baidoa.

(http://www.un.org/Depts/DPKO/Missions/unosomi.htm)

The idea of attacking U.S. forces in Somalia came up shortly after the United Nations approved Operation Restore Hope, President Bush's plan to commit more military resources to secure humanitarian relief distribution in Somalia. Saddam's order to "hunt the Americans" was approval of the plan to attack U.S. forces with Islamic terrorist proxies. It is noteworthy that this U.S. mission for the U.N. was ordered by George H.W. Bush, a man Saddam hated for leading the coalition against him in the Gulf War. A few months after this order Saddam sent IIS agents to Kuwait to assassinate him. The order to "hunt the Americans" came just two days before President Clinton assumed office. Was the order a last stab at a hated enemy or a test of the new President?

In response to the order by Saddam to "hunt the Americans" the IIS created a list of terrorist contacts that might do the job of attacking the U.S. forces in Somalia. The IIS endorsed the EIJ (Egyptian Islamic Jihad) which the IIS also called the EIG interchangeably (Egyptian Islamic Group -Egyptian Gama'a al-Islamiyya). The EIJ was a precursor group to al Qaeda. At this time it was allied with Usama bin Laden. Bin Laden would later claim credit for the attack on U.S. forces in Somalia.

It was years after the Battle of Mogadishu before the U.S. government found out Somali warlords had supplied the men for the attack but the training and equipment came from al Qaeda. It was only after al Qaeda rose to prominence and some of its leaders were captured that the intelligence community realized Salafi Islamic terrorists were the actual culprits for instigating the attacks. While investigating the 1998 bombings of two American embassies in Africa, the U.S. Justice Department discovered substantial evidence that bin Laden had been responsible for the Mogadishu attacks. Usama bin Laden has since claimed that it was his fighters who equipped and trained the Somalis.

The U.S. Justice Department indicted Usama bin Laden and al-Qaeda's military commander, Mohammed Atef, in 1998, for conspiring to kill Americans. The indictment included the following references to Somalia and al-Qaeda's training and support to Somali fighters:

> At various times from in or about 1992 until in or about 1993, the defendant USAMA BIN LADEN, working together with members of the fatwah committee of al Qaeda, disseminated fatwahs to other members and associates of al Qaeda that the United States forces stationed in the Horn of Africa, including Somalia, should be attacked;
>
> In or about late 1992 and 1993, the defendant MUHAMMAD ATEF traveled to Somalia on several occasions for the purpose of determining how best to cause violence to the United States and United Nations military forces stationed there and reported back to the defendant USAMA BIN LADEN and other al Qaeda members at USAMA BIN LADENS's facilities located in Khartoum, the Sudan;
>
> Beginning in or about early spring 1993, al Qaeda members, including the defendants MUHAMMAD ATEF, SAIF AL ADEL, ABDULLAH AHMED ABDULLAH, a/k/a "Abu Mohamed el Masry," ... along with "Abu Ubaidah al Banshiri," a co-conspirator not named herein as a defendant, provided military training and assistance to Somali tribes opposed to the United Nations' intervention in Somalia;
>
> On October 3 and 4, 1993, in Mogadishu, Somalia, persons who had been trained by al Qaeda (and by trainers trained by al Qaeda) participated in an attack on United States military personnel serving in Somalia as part of Operation Restore Hope, which attack resulted in the killing of 18 United States Army personnel;

(http://www.fas.org/irp/news/1998/11/98110602_nlt.html)

The indictment identifies Mohammed Atef as the operational chief behind al Qaeda's attacks in Somalia. Mohammed Atef was Ayman al Zawahiri's number two man in the EIJ. In 1993, the EIJ and Usama's followers (not formally announced as al Qaeda yet) were loosely associated at the leadership level.

Mohammed Atef was Zawahiri's liaison between the EIJ and Usama. As such he moved up to become Usama bin Laden's operational commander later. It was Atef who introduced Khalid Sheik Mohammed, the 9/11 mastermind to Usama bin Laden in 1996 most likely at Zawahiri's urging. According to these documents a leader of the EIJ was scheduled to come to Baghdad and meet with the IIS. It is likely that leader was Zawahiri.

Knowing that the IIS was meeting with Zawahiri to contract his EIJ for the attack in Somalia and that his trusted aid Mohammed Atef was working with Usama bin Laden to carry out the attack in Somalia—and that such an attack occurred—it is not to hard to see that Usama and his followers were essentially subcontracted to do the job along with the EIJ. Did Usama bin Laden known he was doing Saddam's bidding? Only Zawahiri had to know.

But the documents show more. The IIS link to the EIJ was via an Islamist in the Sudan named Othman Taha. Taha was closely tied to Usama bin Laden. Since Usama bin Laden was closely tied to two men (Zawahiri and Taha) who were negotiating with the Saddam regime and since he eventually carried out Saddam's orders it is highly likely he knew that the money they received to carry out the mission came from Saddam.

Since this evidence indicates that Zawahiri and UBL were working with the IIS in 1993 and that Zawahiri had done so during the Gulf War are there other signs that they worked for Saddam? Are there other signs of Saddam's hidden war?

The first attack on the World Trade Center on February 26th, 1993 was in the final preparation phase at the time of this order. Abdul Rahman Yasin, the bomb maker for the 1993 attack entered the U.S. in the summer of 1992 from Iraq. Yasin fled to Iraq after being picked up and released in connection with the attack.

Sheik Omar Abdel-Rahman (the Blind Sheik), the leader of the EIG or Egyptian Islamic Group (Egyptian Gama'a al-Islamiyya) was living in the United States acting as the spiritual focal point to the 1993 WTC bomb plot.

Zawahiri's EIJ was closely connected to the EIG. Sheik Omar Abdel-Rahman was close to Zawahiri. The EIG made local U.S. contacts with men who would carry out the 1993 WTC attack. Thus, at the same time Zawahiri was preparing to attack U.S. forces in Somalia, the terrorist group EIG was preparing the way for Ramzi Yousef and Khalid Sheik Mohammed to bomb the World Trade Center. It is too much to be coincidence that the same players were involved in the WTC bombing and Somalia attacks.

There are two reasonable scenarios here. Either the IIS contracted Zawahiri for the 1993 WTC attack and he turned to the EIG to 'subcontract' it since they were already in the United States, or it was a terrorist operation already underway and they asked Saddam for a bomb expert to support it.

There are other indications of coordination. A conspirator in the 1993 WTC bombing named Mohammad Salameh is discussed at the Terrorism Knowledge Base website. (http://www.tkb.org/KeyLeader.jsp?memID=5624)

According to TKB, Salameh—the 1993 WTC plotter who was caught when he went back for the deposit on the cargo truck used in the bombing—was a Palestinian-Jordanian, much like the "returnees from Kuwait". Another Palestinian-Jordanian coconspirator was Nidal Ayyad who traveled to Jordan to get married just months before the 93 attack. Is it a coincidence that these men were from the same Palestinian-Jordanian community that had been kicked out of Kuwait for supporting Saddam? Or is it a sign that the Jordan based Palestinian *"jihad* stream" which had collaborated with the IIS in Kuwait had instructed relatives living in the U.S. to support the Blind Sheik?

What about the masterminds for the 1993 attack: Ramzi Yousef and his uncle KSM? How do they fit in with the hypothesis that Zawahiri was working for the IIS in a hidden war against the US? Although there is no direct evidence that Yousef and KSM worked for Saddam, if it can be shown that pretty much everyone else involved in the 1993 WTC bombing supported Saddam then it is logical to consider that they were working for him.

Perhaps they were recruited by the Maulana Fazlur Rahman or his jihad groups. Yousef and Khalid Sheik Mohammed had Pakistan (Baloch) ethnic identity and had lived in the area that is part of the Maulana's support base. According to Iraq expert Dr. Laurie Mylroie, the Baluchistan area is traditionally tied to support for Saddam (as mutual antagonists to the Iranian Shi'ites) and had been known to work with the IIS during the Iran-Iraq war. The situation she describes is much like the Palestinians who collaborated with the IIS in the Kuwaiti occupation only more direct with some of the Baloch being formal IIS agents. Dr. Mylroie postulates that Yousef and Khalid Sheik Mohammad are likely IIS agents with false identities planted in Kuwait during the Iraqi occupation in 1991.

There are several reasonable theories to where Yousef and KSM came from. But speculation is fruitless until hard evidence becomes available. Because of these documents and the depth of entanglement between the IIS and the *global Islamic jihad movement* revealed here, the authors of this book endorse the theory of Dr. Mylroie because Saddam was connected to the people involved at the time of the bombing and the fact that an Iraqi military bomb maker just happened to show up when needed. The 1993 bombing fits into his *modis operandi* as revealed by the CNS documents.

Another al Qaeda document newly released by the Combating Terrorism Center (CTC) of the United States Military Academy provides an extraordinary new connection to the matter. The al Qaeda document was part of a U.S. Army report on al Qaeda in Africa. That study contends that although al Qaeda managed to train other Islamic fighters in Africa, it did the organization no long term good, as it failed to bend the region to al Qaeda doctrine.

The al Qaeda document is entitled *The Ogaden File: Operation Holding (Al-Msk)*. Its' name refers to a tribal region of Ethiopia extending into Somalia (Ogaden) and 'al-Msk' is an acronym *for the Mission to hold Somalia and Kenya*. The file is a personal log about a group of al Qaeda terrorists sent to Somalia in 1993 to provide military training to local Islamic militants.

The al Qaeda document itself provides a fascinating look at training operations of an expeditionary nature in hostile territory. The log was written by an al Qaeda terrorist named Saif al-Islam al Masri who was known to be a leader of al Qaeda in Somalia and an EIJ leader. He is now in U.S. custody.

Saif writes that on the 20th of January, 1993 he and his men were ordered to drop everything (marriage plans, travel) and report to a man named Abu Hafs in Peshawar, Pakistan. This deployment to Somalia heralded a major escalation of al Qaeda activities in Africa. Abu Hafs is also known as Mohammed Atef. As mentioned previously, Mohammed Atef was the number two man in the EIJ under Ayman al Zawahiri and also part of Usama bin Laden's inner circle. He was included in the 1998 indictment for attacking U.S. forces in Somalia and was considered the number three man in al Qaeda. He was killed by U.S. forces shortly after 9/11.

Saif describes how he and his men were ordered by Atef to go Somalia and set up training camps. The date of Atef's order for them to go to Somalia is very significant because it corresponds with this order by Saddam Hussein to do just that. Mohammed Atef ordered his men to Somalia two days after Saddam's order to use these men in Somalia. This al Qaeda document when combined with the CNS documents provides a sequential timeframe for the events and the human linkages to carry out the order from Saddam to his intelligence service to Ayman al Zawahiri to Mohammed Atef and then to his terror trainers.

This revelation about Mohammed Atef came just days after former CIA Director George Tenet caused a political and media stir with the release of his new book At the Center of the Storm: My Years at the CIA. Tenet devotes a portion of the book to discussing al Qaeda-Saddam ties. In it he writes about the case of Ibn Sheikh al Libi, "a senior military trainer for al-Qa'ida in Afghanistan." Al Libi told his interrogators that "a militant known as Abu Abudullah had told him that...al-Qa'ida leader Mohammed Atef had sent Abu Abdullah to Iraq to seek training in poisons and mustard gas."

Al Libi would later recant his testimony and become a flash point in the debate over pre-war intelligence. Tenet notes the controversy and says it is unclear if al Libi was lying with the initial report or his recantation. Tenet writes, "Another senior al-Qa'ida detainee told us that Mohammed Atef was interested in expanding al-Qa'ida's ties to Iraq, which, in our eyes, added credibility to [al-Libi's initial] reporting."

If we can determine that it is highly likely Saddam was conducting a secret war against the United States then what was Saddam's involvement if any in the 9/11 attacks?

Since Atef was running the Somalia operation ultimately at the behest of Saddam there is every reason to consider it likely to be the same situation may be at play again in 1996 when Mohammed Atef introduced Usama bin Laden to Khalid Sheik Mohammed. It was probably Zawahiri who sent KSM to Atef. KSM would convince UBL to attack the World Trade Center with hijacked planes, a plan that would evolve into the 9/11 attacks. Zawahiri probably also sent Yousef to the EIG to stage for the 93 WTC attack. We know Mohammed Atef came from the EIJ. We know Mohammed Atta the tactical leader for the hijack teams on 9/11 came from the EIJ. However we do not have direct evidence of Saddam being involved in the 9/11 attacks at a level beyond his support to the groups which conducted them.

So where did Yousef and KSM come from?

Our theory: Saddam considered Iraq to be in a state of war with the U.S. continuously after the Gulf War. In 1992 he began to retaliate with a secret war. He set in motion the WTC bomb plot with Yousef and KSM at the core either as formal IIS agents or selected, recruited and trained probably through the Maulana Fazlur Rahman or possibly even Hekmatyar. The IIS picked Zawahiri to provide the operational support for the 93 WTC bombing because of his U.S. based contact, the Blind Sheik. The EIG found local Palestinian-Jordanian men who supported Saddam. Then the IIS sent Yasin to build the bomb and Yousef to liaison and control the project and to act as the 'mujahideen commander' so it wouldn't look like a military operation. At the same time, Zawahiri sent Mohammed Atef to UBL to handle the Somalia contract. The Zawahiri-IIS linkage is made inescapable by this set of documents and the facts surrounding the attacks against the United States beginning after the Gulf War.

And in the middle of this hidden war, President George H.W. Bush presented himself as a target of opportunity by going to Kuwait. Was it just too good an opportunity for Saddam to coordinate through proxies so he used his own military to attempt the plot?

Just as U.S. intelligence missed the connection between the attacks in Somalia and Usama bin Laden for several years it is not unreasonable to determine that they could have missed the involvement of the Saddam regime here as well.

The following is a translation provided by CNS News in its article <u>CNSNews.com Publishes Iraqi Intelligence Docs</u> by David Thibault on October 11th, 2004. It is described by CNS News as a memo from Abid Hamid Mahmud, Saddam Hussein's secretary, to Ali Al-Reech Al-Sheikh, member of Arabian Bureau Ba'ath Party leadership on Jan. 18, 1993.

Translation begins for "Hunt the Americans" document:

(http://www.cnsnews.com/ViewNation.asp?Page=%5CNatio n%5Carchive%5C200410%5CNAT20041011a.html)

In the name of Allah the compassionate the kind

<u>Top secret, personal & urgent</u>

Republic of Iraq

The bureau of presidency

The secretary

Issue # 425/K

Date; Jan.18th, 1993

Rajab 25th.1413 Hijri

Esquire Comrade Ali Al-Reeh Al-Sheikh/a member of
The Arabian Bureau-Ba'ath party leadership.

Subject: instruction

In a continuity with our former book#7184/K on Dec. 20th, 1992, it's decided that the party should move to hunt the Americans who are on Arabian land, especially in Somalia, by using Arabian elements, or Asian (Muslims) or friends.

Take the necessary steps   Stay well for struggle

Signature of the president's secretary

Jan.18th, 1993

Copy to:

The General Director of the intelligence system/

The same purpose mentioned above that concerned your duties

End Translation

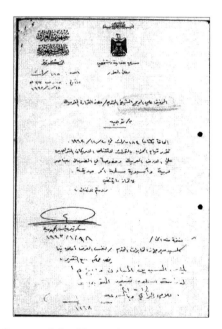

Figure 3: Image of the "hunt the Americans" document

This document was an order to kill U.S. forces in Somalia using jihadist proxies. In reply, the IIS sent to Saddam a list of terrorist organizations that it had contact with. The first page of the list of terrorists groups says it is in response to issue 425/k, which is the issue number of the order to hunt Americans. The documents then details contacts with terror groups by region. As discussed previously, the Maulana's JUI and Hekmatyar's Islamic Party are both mentioned as having good relations with the IIS and both men are mentioned by name. Both translations were shown previously in this work and are not reproduced here. Here is the first page of the terrorist list:

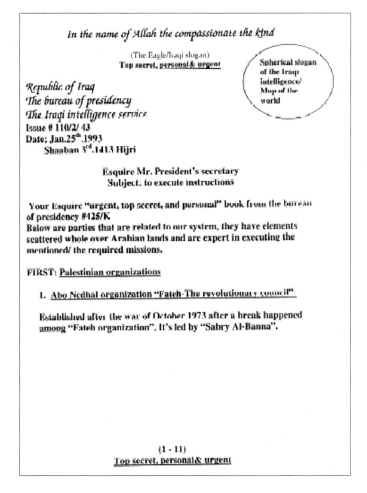

Figure 4: First page of the terrorist contact list

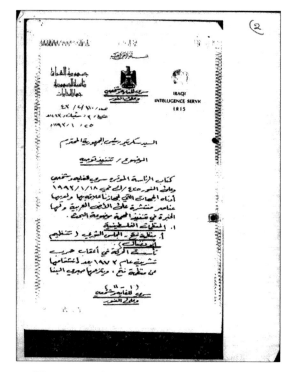

Figure 5: First page of terrorist contact list scanned original

The next document from the terrorist contact list concerns meetings with Sheikh Ali Othman Taha (alternate spelling Osman or Uthman) of the National Islamic Front in Sudan. The NIF provided invaluable support to Usama bin Laden and threw the doors of Sudan open to Islamic terrorists by disregarding visa procedures. The effect of the Islamic extremist influx is still being felt today in the Darfur region of Sudan. In a December 10th, 2001 article from the *Washington Post* entitled Sudan, Newly Helpful, Remains Wary of U.S. by Karl Vick, Ali Othman Taha is described as a frequent companion of Usama bin Laden during his five year stay in Khartoum, Sudan. Othman Taha worked for Dr. Hassan 'Abd Allah al-Turabi leader of the NIF and close UBL confidant. UBL would marry his niece.

Part A of the memo states that the IIS agreed with Othman Taha to work with the EIJ/EIG. The memo mentions working with Sheik Omar Abdel-Rahman at the exact same time he is helping prepare the 1993 WTC attack. The memo also states that the IIS had meet with a representative of the EIJ during the Gulf War and reminded Saddam of his part in the planned Egyptian coup. Part B of the memo states that the IIS wants to use the displaced mujahideen who fought in Afghanistan who are located in Somalia, Sudan, and Egypt. These would be primarily Zawahiri's and bin Laden's men.

The document is dated a week after Saddam ordered the IIS to attack U.S. forces via mujahideen proxies.

Begin translation for EIJ contact request:

In the name of Allah the compassionate the kind

<u>Top secret, personal & urgent</u>

Republic of Iraq

The bureau of presidency

The Iraqi intelligence service

Issue # 110/2/ 43

Date; Jan. 25th,1993

Shaaban 3rd.1413 Hijri

Recently, our system met Sheikh Ali Othman Taha the vice chairman of the National Islamic Front in Sudan, we agreed with him on the following:

A) Re opening of the relationship with "Al-Jehad al-Islamy" organization in Egypt, also known as "Al-Jama'at al-Islameya/ The Islamic groups" which was found by an Egyptian (Mohammed Abdel Salam Faraj) and currently led by Dr. Omar Abdel Rahman, the organization is considered as the most violent in Egypt, they assassinated "Anwar Sadat" & "Refa'at Al-Mahjoob," who was the chairman of people's council in Egypt.

A meeting had already been conducted with a representative from the organization on Dec. 14th, 1990. We agreed on a plan to move against Egyptian regime by doing martyr operations on conditions that we should secure the finance, training and equipments.

B) B- To use the Islamist Arab elements that were fighting in Afghanistan and got no place to station in, who physically are present in Somalia, Sudan and Egypt.

We are expecting the visit of Sheikh Ali Othman who should visit Iraq soon, we shall discuss the above mentioned (A&B); we shall explore their abilities and estimate the results.

End Translation

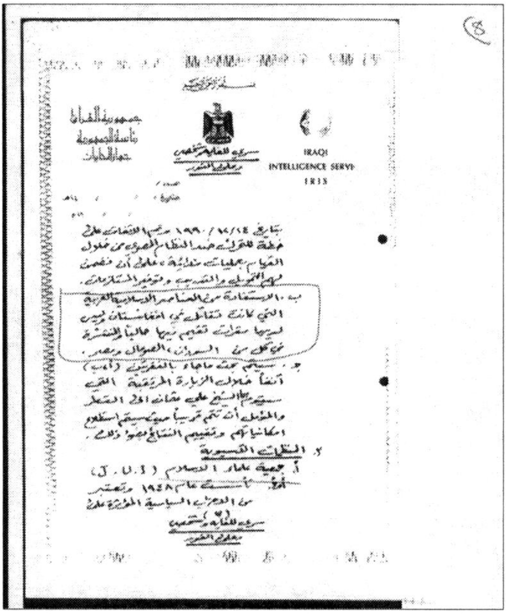

Figure 6: Page one of the EIJ document

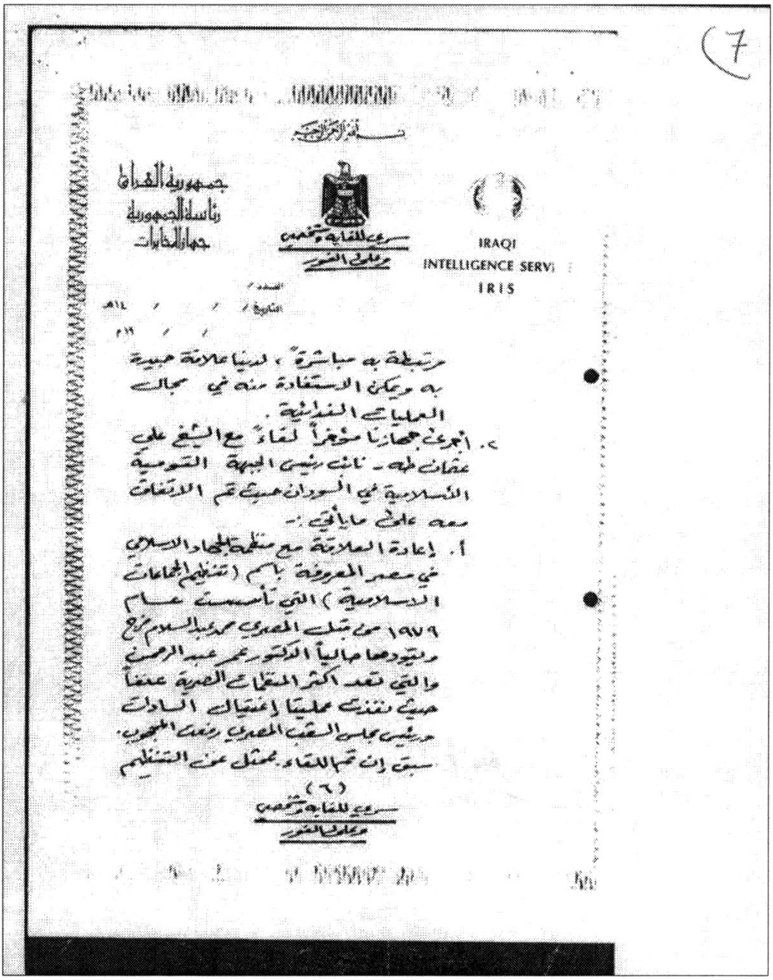

بسم الله الرحمن الرحيم

جمهورية العراق
رئاسة الجمهورية
جهاز المخابرات

سري للغاية وشخصي
ويفتح باليد

IRAQI
INTELLIGENCE SERVI
IRIS

العدد /
التاريخ / / ١٤١هـ
/ / ١٩م

مرتبطة به مباشرة ، لدينا علاقة جيدة
به ويمكن الاستفادة منه في مجال
العمليات الفدائية .
٢. أجرى جهازنا مؤخراً لقاءً مع الشيخ علي
عثمان طه - نائب رئيس الجبهة القومية
الإسلامية في السودان حيث تم الاتفاق
معه على ما يأتي :-
أ. إعادة العلاقة مع منظمة الجهاد الإسلامي
في مصر المعروفة باسم (تنظيم الجماعات
الإسلامية) التي تأسست عام
١٩٧٩ من قبل المصري محمد عبد السلام فرج
ويتزعمها حالياً الدكتور عمر عبد الرحمن
والتي تعد أكثر المنظمات المصرية عنفاً
حيث نفذت عملياً اغتيال السادات
ورئيس مجلس الشعب المصري رفعت المحجوب.
سبق أن تم اللقاء بممثل عن التنظيم
(٦)
سري للغاية وشخصي
ويفتح باليد

Figure 7: Page two of the EIJ document

The terrorist contact list also mentions a relationship to the JUP which is another one of Maulana Fazlur Rahman's groups that authorized the 1998 *fatwa*. The memo claims that one of the clerics from these groups conducted operations for Iraq during the Gulf War. That page is seen here:

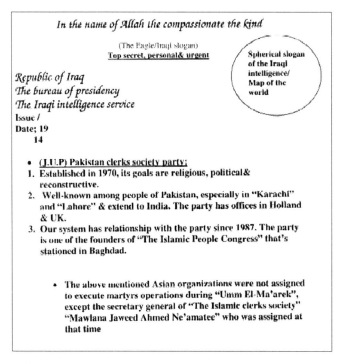

Figure 8: Memorandum concerning the Pakistani terror group JUP

Figure 9: Scanned copy of the original JUP memorandum

Saddam Hussein responded with this document (confirmed by the matching issue number 110/2/43) and tells the IIS that he did not think they had agreed to overthrow the Egyptian government. Saddam approves the use of mujahideen to attack U.S. forces in Somalia. These are Zawahiri's and UBL's forces. Part B adds that they should use Hekmatyar's forces as well.

Saddam is telling the IIS to use the Arab elements of the Afghan mujahideen in the Sudan. Since the coordination is coming from Taha in Sudan, a frequent friend of Usama bin Laden who was in Sudan and who was also an Arab mujahideen in Afghanistan, the situation is clear. Saddam was looking to contract out the EIJ and Usama bin Laden to attack U.S. soldiers in Somalia. They did in fact train and equip the forces that attacked the U.S. army rangers at the Battle of Mogadishu.

Begin translation of Saddam's response to IIS request to work with the EIJ and Arab mujahideen:

<u>Top secret, personal and urgent</u>

Republic of Iraq

The Bureau of the Presidency

The Secretary

Issue # 828/K

Date: Feb. 8th, 1993

Sha'aban 17th. 1412 Hijri

Esquire the Director of the Intelligence system

Subject: to execute instructions

Mr. President "May Allah save him review the content of your book # 110/2/43 on Jan. 25th, 1993. He ordered the following:

1. THE SECOND- A

I think we did not instruct against the Egyptian regime.

2. THE SECOND- B

Yes and he should concentrate on Somalia

His Excellency agreed to assign the Afghan Islamist Party to the mentioned mission.

Signed

The President's Secretary

February 8th, 1993

End Translation

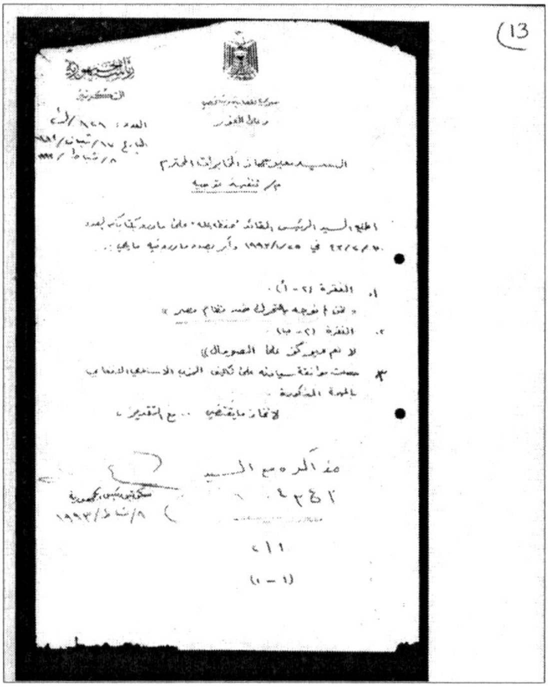

Figure 10: Scanned original of Saddam memo replying to terrorist list

On March 11th of 1993 the IIS sent a memorandum acknowledging that Saddam ordered funds for the issue 828/k, support to Arab mujahideen to attack U.S. soldiers in Somalia; in other words he authorized the payment of Zawahiri and Hekmatyar. The IIS also tells them that Ali Othman Taha in Sudan, Usama bin Laden's friend, is going to send one of the leaders of the EIJ to Baghdad to meet with Saddam. It is highly likely that this leader of the EIJ is Ayman al Zawahiri (or possibly Mohammed Atef) since the al Qaeda letter *The Status of Jihad* confirms that Zawahiri went to Iraq. According to page two of the memo, the IIS tried to delay the meeting but Taha insisted. The IIS recommended that the meeting proceed and the EIJ leader should fly on a Sudanese plane used for shipping meat to maintain secrecy.

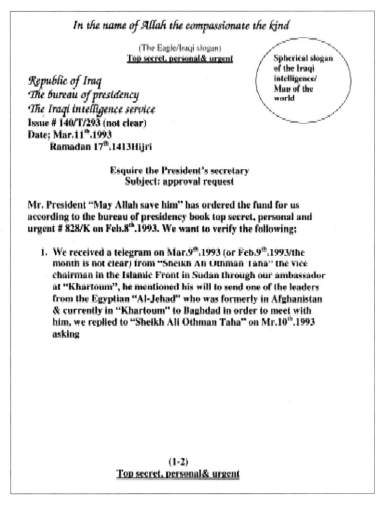

In the name of Allah the compassionate the kind

(The Eagle/Iraqi slogan)
Top secret, personal& urgent

Spherical slogan of the Iraqi intelligence/ Map of the world

Republic of Iraq
The bureau of presidency
The Iraqi intelligence service
Issue # 140/T/293 (not clear)
Date; Mar.11th.1993
Ramadan 17th.1413Hijri

Esquire the President's secretary
Subject: approval request

Mr. President "May Allah save him" has ordered the fund for us according to the bureau of presidency book top secret, personal and urgent # 828/K on Feb.8th.1993. We want to verify the following:

1. We received a telegram on Mar.9th.1993 (or Feb.9th.1993/the month is not clear) from "Sheikh Ali Othman Taha" the vice chairman in the Islamic Front in Sudan through our ambassador at "Khartoum", he mentioned his will to send one of the leaders from the Egyptian "Al-Jehad" who was formerly in Afghanistan & currently in "Khartoum" to Baghdad in order to meet with him, we replied to "Sheikh Ali Othman Taha" on Mr.10th.1993 asking

(1-2)
Top secret, personal& urgent

Figure 11: Meeting with the EIJ page one

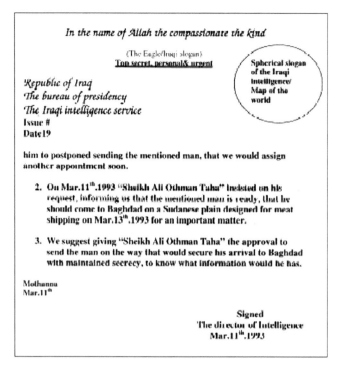

In the name of Allah the compassionate the kind

(The Eagle/Iraqi slogan)
Top secret, personal& urgent

Spherical slogan
of the Iraqi
intelligence/
Map of the
world

Republic of Iraq
The bureau of presidency
The Iraqi intelligence service
Issue #
Date19

him to postponed sending the mentioned man, that we would assign
another appointment soon.

2. On Mar.11ᵗʰ.1993 "Sheikh Ali Othman Taha" Insisted on his
request, informing us that the mentioned man is ready, that he
should come to Baghdad on a Sudanese plain designed for meat
shipping on Mar.13ᵗʰ.1993 for an important matter.

3. We suggest giving "Sheikh Ali Othman Taha" the approval to
send the man on the way that would secure his arrival to Baghdad
with maintained secrecy, to know what information would he has.

Mothanna
Mar.11ᵗʰ

Signed
The director of Intelligence
Mar.11ᵗʰ.1993

Figure 12: Meeting with the EIJ page two

Figure 13: Scanned original of the meeting with EIJ page one

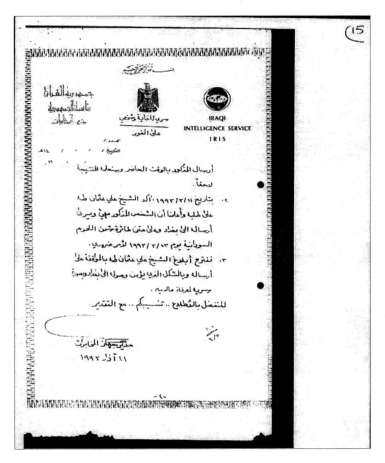

Figure 14: Scanned original of the meeting with EIJ page 2

In the February 8th, 1993 memo, Saddam told the IIS he didn't remember authorizing support for the EIJ against the Egyptian government. On March 16th, 1993 Saddam sent another memo to the IIS telling them that he needed a response concerning the issue of the EIJ support against the Egyptian government. The IIS added a note at the bottom of that March 16th document explaining they had made the agreement in 1990. This is demonstrated by the fact that issue number 828/k is located on both documents.

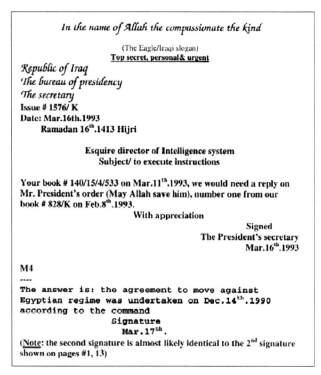

Figure 15: IIS reminding Saddam that they agreed to help the EIJ in 1990.

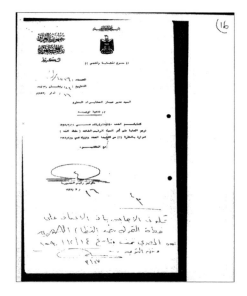

*Figure 16: Scanned original of IIS reminding Saddam
of his support to EIJ in 1990.*

On March 18th of 1993 the IIS sent a memorandum to Saddam to further explain the agreement made with the EIJ/EIG. The IIS says that on December 24th, 1990, the IIS agreed to support the EIG/EIJ against the Egyptian government. The IIS says this was related to Egyptian involvement in the coalition to remove Saddam's army from Kuwait. Saddam was using militant Islamic Egyptian opposition groups to attack the Egyptian government during the Gulf War. The IIS says the aid ended after the cease-fire stopped the fighting in 1991. It appears that the previous letters did not make clear that the operation had ended and Saddam was concerned that the coup attempt was still ongoing.

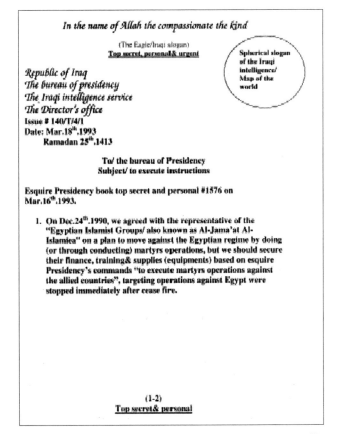

Figure 17: Further explanation of the 1990 agreement Page 1.

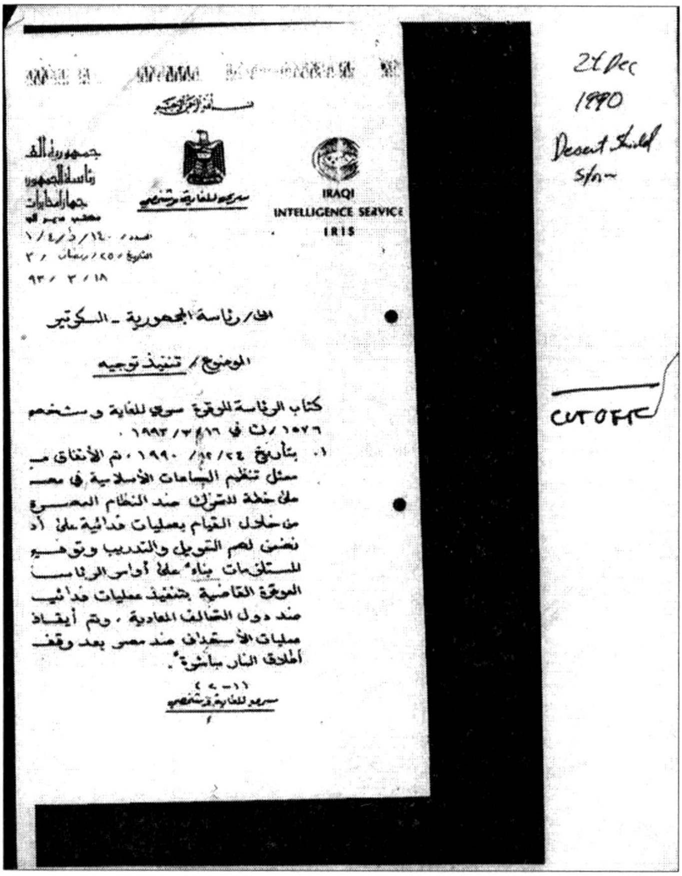

Figure 18: Scanned original of the explanation document.

A second page to that memorandum sums up the correspondence between the IIS and Saddam concerning the issue since the IIS sent the initial request to meet with the EIJ in February, 2003. It refers to the original request and then to an order by Saddam on March 11th, 1993 (not included) to provide financial support only to the mujahideen for attacks in Somalia. The order limited the aid to financial support probably excluding the use of Iraqi weapons and Iraqi military. It orders the IIS to maintain intelligence activities concerning the issue in Africa (Somalia.)

In the name of Allah the compassionate the kind

(The Eagle/Iraqi slogan)
Top secret, personal & urgent

Spherical slogan of the Iraqi intelligence/ Map of the world

Republic of Iraq
The bureau of presidency
The Iraqi intelligence service
The Director's office
Issue /
Date:

2. Our suggestion to meet (to bring) the representative of the
"Islamist Groups" in Iraq ... (unclear sentence/margin) our top
secret, personal & urgent book #4/533 on Mar.11th.1993 came with
accordance of Mr. President (May Allah save him) "no way other
than financial helps due to the absence of... (unclear
word/margin) for the time being, the intelligence activities should
be active & present inside Arabian countries or at the territories of
Arabian lands", we received this esquire book top secret and
personal, # 1681/K on Mar.25th.1992.

For your kind review... with appreciation

Khadhaaar
Mar.18th.

Signed
The director of Intelligence
Mar.18th.1993

Mohammed
Mar.18th.

-2-
Top secret & personal

Figure 19: Further explanation of the 1990 agreement Page 2.

Figure 20: Scanned original of the second page of the detailed explanation.

The report concludes with a memorandum to provide the names of those Arab volunteers who were trained in the "martyr's camp" for the Gulf War.

This list of names is solid evidence that Saddam Hussein had trained Arab volunteers from outside Iraq. This is crucial to the debate over Salman Pak. Salman Pak is a training camp in Iraq which some have claimed was used to train Arab terrorists. After the war a debate ensued of this allegation with doubters claiming it was merely used to train Iraqi anti-terror forces. These documents provide solid evidence that the Saddam regime had engaged in terror training in Iraq at a previous time so it is a bit silly to claim he would not have done so at Salman Pak because he "opposed Islamic terrorists".

CHAPTER 12:
COURTING USAMA BIN LADEN

A S REPORTED BY ABC news, the *New York Sun*, the *Weekly Standard* and others, a document captured in Iraq and posted at the Department of Defense website demonstrates that the Saddam regime wanted to work with Usama bin Laden.

This memorandum details relationships with Saudi Arabian opposition groups. Included among them is Usama bin Laden. The memorandum mentions meetings with bin Laden in Sudan aimed at establishing good relations. Usama requested from Iraq that it broadcast the teachings of a Saudi cleric. The IIS indicates it did so. Usama also requested direct cooperation from Saddam's regime for action against foreign forces (American) in Saudi Arabia. Considering that the CNS documents make it clear they had cooperated against American forces in Somalia and that the operation was successful, it should come as no surprise that Usama bin Laden would request continued assistance from Saddam against U.S. forces in his homeland. The meetings with bin Laden were coordinated via Ibrahim al Sanusi. He was recently known to be the Assistant Secretary of the Popular Arab and Islamic Congress (PAIC) in Sudan. The PAIC had a large hand in influencing the Sudanese government to allow their country to become a terrorist safe haven.

Hassan al Turabi, leader of the National Islamic Front in Sudan, created the PAIC as a means to bring in Islamic extremists such as Usama bin Laden and their associated Islamic financiers. This included the Saddam regime. The Sudanese government, sympathetic to Islamists but strong armed by the Islamic jihad movement, enjoyed the financial benefits of becoming important to more wealthy governments like Iraq. Therefore, while the IIS was negotiating through Ali Othman Taha of the National Islamic Front in 1993, it was setting the stage for later contacts through al Sanusi, a Turabi confidant of the NIF. It should be noted that the CNS documents claimed Taha was arranging meetings between the IIS and Egyptian opposition (EIJ), which is an offshoot of the Muslim Brotherhood of Egypt. The NIF as well is an offshoot of the Muslim Brotherhood.

The section on Usama bin Laden concludes by noting that contact with Usama has been maintained via the NIF but with his relocation to Afghanistan, the IIS is seeking a closer contact. Usama relocated to Afghanistan in 1996 to the Kandahar area just as the Taliban was securing southern Afghanistan. Thus, local contacts would have had to continue through the Taliban and its associates like Maulana Fazlur Rahman.

The following translation was originally provided by Dr. Laurie Mylroie and Ayad Rahim at the website of *The American Spectator* and is reproduced here by their generous permission.

(http://www.spectator.org/dsp_article.asp?art_id=9612)

Begin Translation for ISGZ-2004-009247

In the name of God, the compassionate, the merciful

Subject: The Saudi opposition and achieving relations with it

1. The Committee for the Defense of Legitimate Rights

An organization opposed to the Saudi regime, established

in Riyadh on date 3/5/1993, led by the Saudi Dr. Muhammad Abdullah al-Mas'ari. Its headquarters are in London. We moved to find a connection with it by the following:

A. On 10/9/1994, we ensured a contact with Dr. Ibrahim al-Sanusi, deputy secretary general of the Sudanese National Islamic Front, to achieve a meeting for us with a representative of al-Mas'ari, called Muhammad Shihat al-Deeb, an Egyptian national. This was done, and the meeting was attended by our ambassador (the representative of the agency) in Khartoum and by Dr. Ibrahim al-Sanusi. Al-Mas'ari's representative proposed joint cooperation and coordination with Iraq and the possibility of putting in place a working apparatus and program with his movement, as he also presented their work plan and the necessary requirements.

B. In light of the above meeting, it was agreed that Dr. Ibrahim al-Sanusi would make a visit to London, and he would meet the Saudi oppositionist Muhammad al-Mas'ari in order to become directly acquainted with the reality of their position about establishing a relationship with Iraq. The honorable sir director of the agency, on the date 6/10/1994, was shown the results of the meeting (exhibit 2).

C. Al-Sanusi left for London and carried out the meeting with al-Mas'ari in the month of October 1994. Al-Sanusi asked for, in the light of this meeting, a visit to Iraq to present the ideas with which al-Mas'ari deputized him. The respected leadership was informed of this, referenced by our report 2656 of 14/111994 (exhibit 3).

D. Dr. Ibrahim al-Sanusi visited Iraq on 12/12/1994, and he was met by the master Uday Saddam Husayn, in the presence of the honorable sir director of the agency. They discussed with him in detail the issue of the Saudi opposition and how to establish a relationship with it and studied the recommendations that al-Sanusi proposed on behalf of al-Mas'ari. The respected leadership was notified of the details of the meeting by our report 782 of 17/12/1994 (exhibit 4).

E. The approval of the respected leadership came, referenced by its report 137 of 111/1995, on replaying transmission of the Saudi opposition's program over our broadcast directed towards Saudi Arabia (exhibit 5).

F. For the purpose of ensuring a permanent relationship with Muhammad al-Mas'ari, work was carried out with another channel, whose leanings are exemplified by the Saudi oppositionist Ahmad Khidhayyir al-Zahrani (a Saudi diplomat in the Saudi embassy in America, who requested political asylum from America; his request was denied, and he headed to London).

G. The respected leadership requested in its report 1025 on 18/3/1995 an explanation of the opinion in the matter of what appeared in the telegram of our embassy in London regarding the request of the diplomat Ahmad al-Zahrani for political asylum to Iraq after the American authorities refused to give him this right.

H. The response to the respected leadership came in our report 502 on 22/3/1995 with our information on the named and our recommendation for approval on granting him and his family the right of political asylum in Iraq.

I. A comprehensive plan was put in place to bring the named to Iraq in coordination with the foreign ministry and our station in Khartoum, as he and his family were granted Iraqi travel passports in pseudonyms from our embassy in Khartoum. He reached Iraq on the date 21/4/1995, and more than one meeting was carried out with him to gain information on the Saudi opposition.

J. A plan was put in place with him for finding a framework for Iraq to have a relationship with Muhammad al-Mas'ari's group, so there was more than one phone contact between him and al-Mas'ari. Two conversations were documented, the last of them, on 11/1/1997. We were assured of the contact with Muhammad al-Mas'ari and Dr. Saad al-Faqih (one of the Saudi oppositionists), both residing in Britain.

K. Muhammad al-Mas'ari expressed in his two phone conversations with al-Zahrani his intention to visit Iraq in the near future, as the matter of his political asylum in Britain is not settled until now, and he can't leave Britain in this light. We are thus following up this issue to achieve the goal of establishing the nucleus for the Saudi opposition in the country and use our relationship with him as it serves our intelligence goals.

2. The Reform and Advice Committee

Led by the Saudi, Usama bin Ladin, who belongs to a wealthy Saudi family whose roots go back to the Hadhramout and which is linked by a very close relationship with the ruling family in Saudi Arabia. He is one of the leaders of the Afghan Arabs who volunteered for the jihad in Afghanistan. After the expulsion of the Soviets, he moved to reside in Sudan, in the year 1992, after the arrival of the Islamists to power in Sudan.

Because of his position in opposition to the ruling Saudi family, because of the foreign presence there [in Saudi Arabia], the Saudi authorities issued a decision to withdraw his Saudi citizenship. We moved toward this committee through the following:

A. During the visit of the Sudanese Dr. Ibrahim al-Sanusi to Iraq and his meeting with Mr. Uday Saddam Husayn on the date 13/12/1994 and in the presence of the honorable sir head of the agency, he indicated that the oppositionist Usama bin Ladin, who resides in the Sudan and who had reservations and fears of being accused by his enemies that he has become an agent of Iraq, is prepared to meet with him in Sudan. (A report was made of the results of the meeting to the respected leadership, referenced in our report 782 on 17/12/1994.)

B. The approval of the respected leadership was given to the meeting with the oppositionist Usama bin Ladin by the agency, referenced by its report 138 on 11/1/1995 (exhibit 6). The meeting was carried out with him by the former sir D.G.D. in Sudan in the presence of the Sudanese Ibrahim al-Sanusi on 19/2/1995. A discussion of his organization was carried out, and he requested the broadcast of the speeches of Shaykh Salman al-Awdah (who has influence in Saudi Arabia and the outside, as he is a well-known and influential religious personage), and to make a special program for them through the broadcaster directed inside the country and carrying out joint operations against the foreign forces in the Land of Hijaz (the respected leadership was informed of the details of the meeting, with reference of our report 370 on 4/3/1995 exhibit 7).

C. The approval of the Leader Mr. President, God preserve him, was given on making a special program for them through the directed broadcaster and we leave the development of the relationship and cooperation between the two sides to what is open before it, in dialogue and agreement by way of other cooperation. The Sudanese side was informed of the approval of the above respected leadership, by the representative of the honorable sir director of the agency, our ambassador in Khartoum.

D. Because of the recent conditions in Sudan and its being accused of supporting and embracing terrorism, they agreed with the Saudi oppositionist Usama bin Ladin to leave Sudan to other parts. So he left Khartoum in July 1996, and information indicates that he is present in Afghanistan at the present time.

The relationship with him continues to be through the Sudanese side, and we are working at the present time to activate this relationship through a new channel in the light of the headquarters of his current whereabouts.

3. Union of the People of the Peninsula Organization

A. In the year 1993, a relationship was made with the Saudi oppositionist Abdul Karim al-Qahtani, who currently resides in Yemen and who belongs to the above union.

B. He is currently managed by our station in Sana'a. The report on the subject was made to the respected leadership, reference 524 on 26/3/1995 to accept one of his sons in the Iraqi universities. Approval was given to that in their report 1752 on 9/5/1995. He visited Iraq a number of times and we met with him. His last visit to Iraq was in August 1996.

The relationship with him continues still, and it is fruitful for the Saudi opposition to use his relationships inside and outside Saudi Arabia for our purposes.

4. Saudi Hizbullah

A. A number of meetings were held between the representative of the honorable director of the agency, our ambassador in Yemen in the year 1993 with the leader of the Yemeni Hizbullah (Abdullah Ajineh), who expressed his willingness to carry out a secret meeting in Yemen between the honorable sir representative and some of the leaders of Saudi Hizbullah.

B. Because of the suspicions and signs that indicate Ajineh has a relationship with Iranian intelligence, the honorable sir representative was directed to work with the aforementioned with caution and to listen to what he proposes only, taking into consideration that the aforementioned would, with the encouragement of Iranian intelligence, reveal our inclinations towards the Saudi opposition and, from that, relay it to the Saudi side.

5. We carried out a number of attempts in 1993 with each of our stations operating in New Delhi and Islamabad to establish contacts with the Islamic opposition inside Saudi Arabia through our sources in these fields. They, in turn, did not yield any results, because of the financial situation of the Muslim scholars in these countries, who suffer from poverty and material want, which pushes them into the laps of Saudi Arabia, which has increased its movements in these countries.

6. We have attempted to contact the Saudi oppositionist the former diplomat in the United Nations Muhammad Abdullah al-Khalawi, who requested the right of political asylum in America. So our station in New York moved on him, but we have not reached any results until now.

7. The approval of the honorable sir head of the agency was given on 6/10/1994 for our ambassador in Sana'a (the representative of the agency) to coordinate with the Yemeni side with regards to achieving a meeting for us with the Saudi opposition, although the follow-up with the Yemeni side has not yielded any tangible results, because the Yemeni side did not keep the promise it gave, for reasons unknown to us.

PART TWO:
THE INTRIGUE OF SADDAM

CHAPTER 13:
FOREIGN CONTACTS AND INFLUENCE

Background

A DOCUMENT RELEASED BY the Pentagon through the Foreign Military Studies Office provides a glimpse at how the Iraqi Intelligence Service (IIS) attempted to influence foreign governments and the United Nations. The document is a collection of memorandums spanning from 1998 to 2001. It talks about contacts and influence by region, including the United States, which is part of what the IIS calls the "fourth international." It gives some hint of the spying apparatus Saddam Hussein implemented around the world.

The memorandums provide further evidence of the corruption of the United Nations Oil-For-Food program including a specific reference to paying Russians who would support Iraq at the UN. Another significant item from the translation is a reference to ten spies who worked to get technology for Iraq from U.N. Special Committees.

The IIS clearly indicates that they use oil shares to engender Russian support at the U.N. Security Council. Perhaps this explains Russian President Putin's remarks at the G8 summit at which he remarked sarcastically about America's attempt to build a democracy in Iraq. The Iraq war denied Putin access to back room deals with murderous tyrants to violate U.N. sanctions for profit. The evidence here is supported by another government provided translation of a tape recording made of a meeting between Saddam and his regime leaders. One of Saddam's officials recorded on the tape stated:

> "We have succeeded in a few of the U.N. paragraphs (BIOT: referring to the paragraphs of U.N. resolutions stating the conditions Iraq must meet to remove the sanctions) we have won Russia. ahhh...we have convinced Russia by way of generous accounts"- ISGQ-2003-M0004667

Another interesting item from the IIS file is the stated attempt to recruit Americans who are in a position to influence political leaders. The memorandum reads "...action was taken with some nongovernmental organizations and through them on some parliament members and government officials to let them voice their opposition to the Iraqi embargo, as happened lately in the American field." While the document does not state any names, there is an obvious example of this strategy in the public record. The *Seattle Weekly* reports on the indictment of Susan Lindauer in an article entitled From 'Spy' to Psychotic published February 15th, 2006:

> In a letter written to her second cousin, White House Chief of Staff Andrew Card, two months after Sept. 11, 2001, Lindauer made no secret about her activism or her emotional mission to aid Iraqi citizens. The letter, a copy of which she gave to basement tenant Fields, is apparently one of at least two she sent or gave to Card in 2001 and 2003.

The indictment of Lindauer describes several meetings with Iraqi intelligence agents who convinced her to act as an undisclosed agent for Iraq. She used her family connection to a White House Chief of Staff to attempt to influence policy at the behest of Iraqi intelligence, according to the indictment.

There are multiple examples that can be found of American human rights groups and peace activist groups that protested American policy and were in contact with the Saddam regime. According to this document, some of them were under the influence of the Saddam regime. This document shows that some of the U.S. based left-wing groups that opposed U.S. actions in Iraq were barely more than shills for Saddam Hussein.

Narrative

These memorandums provide evidence of a covert program by the Saddam regime to corrupt the U.N. process and use private citizens and activist groups to influence the U.S. government.

The memos are a mix of handwritten and printed pages with and without Iraqi government letterhead. Due to the length of the document, some sections are marked "Gist," which is the translator's summery of content instead of a direct transcription. This is an original work of our translator Sammi. The original document writer uses a term "constructed work" that we are not familiar with. Our best guess is that it is a reference to a specific and secret plan.

Translator's comments:

- A term which would be literally translated as "constructed work" is used to describe the modus operandi of the intelligence network.
- The areas covered by the IIS are divided into "internationals:" First, second, third and fourth. The fourth interna-

tional covers Europe and the US.

- The IIS activity covers many countries in the Middle East, and their contacts reach the US, Canada, Europe and Russia.
- Other documents contain a paragraph mentioning that Iraq is buying off opposition parties in Russia.
- The following translations and gist are from a report describing the situation in the fourth international. This report is handwritten. It covers pages 81 to 87 out of 239 pages.

Begin Translation for CMPC-2003-000331

The Fourth International

The method of "constructed work" will be adopted in the field of the fourth international.

A. Western Europe:

1. The "constructed work" method will be used in Great Britain through our sources in Ireland and Spain. (2 cases) (translator's notes: A case is a source or person)

2. We have contacted one of our friends in Sweden to collect information about the USA and Holland. (1 case)

3. Use one of the operating sources in Greece to move into the American arena.

B. The two Americas:

A number of sources operating in Cuba, Mexico and Canada were recruited and sent to work in the USA (3 cases).

C. Eastern Europe:

1. A Russian was recruited to work on both Israel and Iran (1 case).

2. A Croatian was sent to work on Slovenia (1 case).

3. We proceeded to recruit several different nationalities to Romania (3 cases).

D. Asia and non-Arab Africa:

We proceeded to recruit several different nationalities for Iran, Israel, Afghanistan, Africa, Lebanon, Jordan, and the Gulf to work according to "constructed work". (11 cases).

E. Scientific Intelligence section:

Several sources from different nationalities were sent to some scientific institutions, the U.N. and the Special Committee to acquire advanced scientific and technical information and also to transfer technology to Iraq (10 cases).

Translation of Page 24

Republic of Iraq

Office of the Presidency

Intelligence Service

Top secret and Urgent

2-5-2000

Mr. M. M 714

Re your memo 2467 on 30-4-2000

1) Your memo's instructions were coupled with the directives of Mr. Director General concerning the plans of the different directives of our "International" for the year 2000. We have focused our actions towards Saudi Arabia and Kuwait because those 2 countries are particular. According to our memo 12/3/4/23 dated 19-1-2000 we have instructed our operating stations in Jakarta, Kuala Lumpur, Viet Nam, China, Tokyo, Islamabad and new Delhi to look for new and trusted sources from Far East Asian nationals and convince them to work inside Saudi Arabia and Kuwait in addition to choosing some of our sources working in the Arab area to push them to work inside Saudi Arabia and Kuwait.

(Translator's note: Millions of Far East Asian nationals work in the Gulf countries)

2) Our stations were instructed to invest in the Iraqis working in their fields (translator's notes: probably Iraqis working abroad) in a way which benefits our scope of work. This follows the directives of Mr. the President leader may God protect him and guide him in this matter. The number of Iraqis with skills which were contacted in 1999 numbered 44.

Please review

Respects.

Gist of Page 80

It is a printed report, about a Lebanese, on an official paper. Someone added a note saying "In the future those memos should be handwritten and I think that there are directives from the presidency about this matter". The word "Re'assa" in Arabic means presidency so this directive could be coming straight from the presidency of the country (Saddam) or some highly placed official (presidency of an important agency). (BIOT: before PCs it was common practice to hand write a memo and have a clerk type it on official stationary.)

Gist of Pages 82-87

Next are several instructions for recruiting and the report discusses some of the problems being faced and the intent to start "illegal stations" (probably undercover stations). The potential of using the Iraqi expatriate population is also discussed. The sixth annual expatriate conference was used to renew the contacts. Iraqi businessmen are also mentioned as potential technology transfer factors.

Translation of Page 87

17. The work was as follows:

A. The fourth international (the U.S. district) has connections and friends in most of its countries that are "moved" in the required directions to continuously influence the decision makers in the target countries. In many of our operating areas this effort bared fruit in letting the Iraqi cause be known, to affect the domestic public opinion and the political decisions of those countries.

B. In some countries action was taken with some non governmental organizations and through them on some parliament members and government officials to let them voice their opposition to the Iraqi embargo, as happened lately in the "American field" (Translator's note: USA)

Gist of Page 107

An excerpt from a report (12-16-1999) of a meeting between the Director of Intelligence with the fourth international staff:

1. The purpose from establishing companies should be an intelligence return and not material profit.
2. Establish contact with the Islamic Center in London and the (Shiite) Najafi center in Syria.
3. The USA section should focus on people with influence to strengthen the relations with them because most of the existing relations are of the business type.

Gist of Page 207/239

The section's needs for research with M10:

The section coordinated with M10 to identify the nature of the research which is beneficial to the concerned sections. Among them is a report about the help provided by Iraq to the Russian parties of opposition through the oil "shares" (coupons) and the extent of their influence on the making of the Russian political decision regarding the lifting of the sanctions on Iraq. Another memo requested reports about the presidential elections in Poland and Hungary, and the intelligence services in Poland and Hungary to strengthen existing information. (BIOT: M10 is the Directorate of Studies and Research, part of the IIS)

End Translation

CHAPTER 14:
ANONYMOUS SOURCE DESCRIBES IRAQI ACTIVITY BEFORE THE WAR

A MONG THE CAPTURED documents are items of interest that are not verifiable in content. They make interesting reading but do not necessarily add to our understanding of Saddam's support to Islamic terrorism.

Sammi provides a partial translation of a notebook that appears to be from an Iraqi connected with the former Special Security Organization, or SSO. The Center for Non-Proliferation Studies describes the SSO as follows:

> "The key unit in the deployment of such weapons is Al-Amn al-Khas (Special Security Organization, referred to as the SSO), which was created during the Iran-Iraq War to serve as a super-secret organization and emerged as the most powerful agency in the security apparatus. It emerged from within al-Amn al-'Amm in 1982 to provide bodyguards to the President after a failed assassination attempt on Saddam. There are an estimated 5,000 members in this organization mostly from Saddam's hometown of Tikrit."

This document is given less creditability as it is anonymously written and can't be linked to other documents via content. But it does give some interesting insight to the role that Syria and Russia played with Iraq as an arms provider. Other released documents detail Russian assistance to Iraq even as coalition forces were staging to attack the Saddam regime.

Translator's notes:

1. Document CMPC-2003-000878 is a note book made of 60 pages.

2. It is handwritten.

3. The Foreign Military Studies Office website describes it as information on SSO (Special Security Organization) ISS (Iraqi Secret Service) and assistant to "Chemical Ali"

4. Whoever wrote it was close to the ruling circle and could have been an assistant to someone.

5. In many pages he is critical of the clan of Saddam and the many people around him who benefited from their positions.

6. The notes are written after the removal of Saddam Hussein from power. Pages 53-54-55 are hand written in English and it looks as if the author wanted to give this information to an American officer as an anonymous source. Apparently he changed his mind because the pages are still in the note book.

Translation begins for CMPC-2003-000878

Page 34

Body armor from Russia: They were ordered following a request from the Special Republican Guards (13,000) protective vests from Russia. They were delivered to the headquarters of Qusai Saddam Hussein, in total, eight days before the start of the war. Three Russian experts came along. The deal was funded by one of the rich people of Al Kut (180 Kms South of Baghdad). Each one was bought for $250 and sold to Qusai Saddam Hussain for $600 and they were introduced through Syria after being packaged with Swedish made jackets in an effort to not embarrass Syria and fool the U.S. intelligence. The U.S. intelligence was able to uncover the operation. One of its specifications is that (unclear) (unclear) the American rifle M16A2 with the very high initial velocity and the piercing bullet from only a distance of 5 meters. And from the ammo of the American MG machine gun of medium caliber 7.62 from the same distance.

Gist of Page 36

He mentions the Russian T-72 tank in the republican guards units. Apparently their engines suffered terribly in the desert during the Iraq-Iran war.

Gist of Page 37

The commanders of the Republican Guards complained of their inability to move. In 1998 during operation Desert Fox the best brigade was only able to move 6 tanks out of 21 and only for 1,200 meters. The capability of the new Russian made tanks includes fire power, movement and armor protection. Suddenly new engines appeared that were imported from Russia. Republican guards units were equipped with 70 engines for every operational brigade. The engines were also shipped from Syria. That happened one month before the start of the war.

Gist of Page 38

The notes explain how Sebaaoui (Saddam's half brother) escaped to Syria.

Gist of Page 39

The notes explain how Saddam used the Oil for Food Program to reinforce his status by buying the loyalty of his supporters.

Translation of Page 42-43

Emptying Saddam's palaces of all the expensive items. When

the Anglo-American forces entered one of Saddam's palaces in Basra everybody here saw this event on TV. The strange thing is that the palace was completely empty save from some chairs, one table and a bed in a room. Where did the furniture go? What about the other palaces especially in Baghdad, (unclear) next to Baiji, Mosul and Al Anbar. Three months before the war the news was coming about trucks loaded with very expensive items (all the world saw faucets made of gold). There was a talk about trucks moving those riches to Syria. Someone who works at al Walid center told me that once he saw 35 private trucks (trailer) that crossed the border to Syria.

Gist of Page 44-45

The notes explain how Saddam used gifts to buy loyalty.

Translation of Page 46-47

Saddam's crocodile pets.

One day in 1998 I was passing (unclear) which is situated at the other side of the Tigris river facing Al Ouja and I passed by one of my friends who is a police officer. When I asked him how he was doing he laughed and said that the most courageous man will not be able to operate the water pump on the river, to irrigate his crops, because 6 crocodiles escaped from Saddam's palace. At that time I was going to Kirkuk for 2 days and when I came back he told me that there were 6 Africans looking for the crocodiles and they were able to catch them but he was afraid from those crocodiles having laid their eggs on the banks of the river.

When I asked another friend of mine in the Tikrit police force, who was a friend of the driver of First lady Sajida wife of Saddam, about the truth of the crocodiles' story and why does Saddam own them he said that he enjoys watching them when he is sitting by the side of (unclear) while drinking his luxurious whisky and feeding them meat and live birds.

Translation of Page 48-49

The Iraqi regime used to always declare that the U.N. and USA is preventing access to medicine. And I have the document which says that 3 Swedish companies with excellent ties to Iraq for more than 30 years are selling very good quality pharmaceutical products to the Iraqi ministry of health. Those companies do not sell drugs to third parties (triangle deals) (Translator's note: triangle deals is written in English in the original text) made of high ranking Iraqis. Those Iraqis want to buy those drugs from the Swedes and sell them to the Iraqi governments at many times the real price. Those respectable companies refuse those dirty dealings and appeal the Iraqi government to directly deal with it in a clean manner. They refuse to deal with third parties to protect their reputation.

End Translation

CHAPTER 15:
RUSSIAN SCIENTISTS IN IRAQ HIDE FROM UN

Background

IN THE PERIOD leading up to the U.S. invasion of Iraq, there was widespread concern—if not a general consensus—that Iraq was pursuing weapons programs that had been specifically prohibited by U.N. resolution. One such program was Iraq's long-range missile program. UN Security Council Resolution 687 had limited the range of Saddam's missiles to 150 kilometers, while allowing development of short-range missiles for defensive purposes.

A pre-war CIA report focuses on evidence that Saddam's missile program was continuing, despite international sanctions, with the aid of scientists and equipment from abroad:

> Iraq managed to rebuild and expand its missile development infrastructure under sanctions. Iraqi intermediaries sought production technology, machine tools, and raw materials, in violation of the arms embargo. UNMOVIC reported that Iraq illegally imported 380 SA-2/Volga engines. These were the same engines used in the al-Samoud 2 SRBM, and some were imported as recently as December 2002 — when UNMOVIC inspectors were already in Iraq....

Baghdad would not have been able to complete this facility without technical and material assistance from abroad. In August 1995, Iraq was caught trying to acquire sensitive ballistic missile guidance components, including gyroscopes originally used in Russian strategic nuclear submarine-launched ballistic missiles, which demonstrated that Baghdad had pursued proscribed, advanced, long-range missile technology for some time. Iraqi officials admitted that, despite international prohibitions, they had received a similar shipment earlier that year. (*Unclassified Report to Congress on the Acquisition of Technology Relating to Weapons of Mass Destruction and Advanced Conventional Munitions*, December 31, 2002.)

> The CIA report was confirmed in March 2003 — just days before the start of the war — by news reports that Saddam was now dismantling his missile program:
>
> Saddam Hussein made a last-ditch attempt to avoid military conflict with America and Britain last night when he began destruction of his al-Samoud 2 missile system and allowed two military scientists to be interviewed by U.N. weapons inspectors
>
> [**The Guardian,** March 2. 2003].

The role of Russian engineers in developing Iraq's long-range ballistic missile program has since been publicly reported. "Iraqis who were involved in the missile work told American investigators that the technicians had not been working for the Russian government, but for a private company," and that they had worked on the program "both in Moscow and in Baghdad" (James Risen, "Russian Engineers Reportedly Gave Missile Aid to Iraq," *New York Times,* March 5th, 2004).

Iraqi Intelligence Report

Figure 21. HARMONY No. CMPC-2003-000776 (page 1) [1]

Highlights

This document, evidently captured shortly after the start of the Iraq war (March 2003), is a handwritten Iraqi intelligence report describing the unannounced inspection visits to Iraqi laboratories carried out by the IAEA inspection team on December 15, 2002.

The most revealing detail is the statement that foreign experts (from Turkey and Russia) had to be hidden from the inspection team, with a demand for official guidance as to how to handle a "face-to-face" encounter, should one occur.

The same report also mentions the inspectors' complaint that their luggage had been broken into while at the hotel (as previous inspectors had also discovered).

The entire four-page document, with translation, appears at the end of this chapter.

1

Narrative

Several U.N. inspection teams visited sites within Iraq on the same date as this Saddam regime memorandum (UNMOVIC IAEA Press Statement on Inspection Activities in Iraq 15 December 2002). This document evidently refers to the International Atomic Energy Agency (IAEA) inspection teams which visited Al Maarik, Kadessiya and Badr.

According to the IAEA, Al Maarik was a facility focused on civil and military manufacturing. Prior to 1991, Al Maarik was involved in Iraq's Electromagnetic Isotope Separation program, which produced weapons grade uranium. Kadessiya was a military engineering facility, and Badr focused on Iraq's centrifuge program prior to 1991. In 2002, Badr was supposedly only a general engineering facility. In the past, however, Badr had been used as a nuclear development facility for electromagnetic isotope separation, a crucial component in the development of nuclear weapons when applied to turn natural uranium into depleted or enriched uranium.

Badr was the last destination of the day for the IAEA inspection team. The team had arrived at Kadessiya at 1152hrs, and it began its inspection at Badr at 1300hrs. This gave the Iraqi intelligence unit just over an hour to prepare Badr for inspection, notably by hiding Turkish and Russian scientists:

> When we visited Badr company **there were Turkish and Russian experts at the site and they had to hide away from the inspectors**. We demand your [General Director of the Office of National Supervision: translator's note] instructions for what to do in case there is a face to face between the agency's inspectors and the experts. [Harmony No. CMPC-2003-000776: emphasis added.]

The broader context

The document clearly demonstrates that the Iraqi government had some sort of program in operation that had to be concealed from U.N. inspectors — a program in which foreign assistance played a role. It suggests, moreover, that great importance was attached to this covert program. At a time when Saddam was campaigning for the removal of U.N. sanctions, he was nevertheless willing to risk that these foreign scientists would be discovered by inspection teams.

What exactly was the operation that was pursued at such a risk? The pre-war CIA report cited above indicates that foreign scientists were involved with developing prohibited missiles. A focus on long-range missiles is also confirmed by a 2003 report of the Iraq Survey Group:

> Detainees and co-operative sources indicate that beginning in 2000 Saddam ordered the development of ballistic missiles with ranges of at least 400km and up to 1000km and that measures to conceal these projects from UNMOVIC were initiated in late-2002, ahead of the arrival of inspectors.
>
> [Statement of David Kay, head of the Iraq Survey Group (ISG), October 2, 2003]
>
> [http://www.globalsecurity.org/intell/library/congress/2003_hr/david_kay_10022003.htm]

The statement goes on to discuss the intended use of these missiles for delivery of unconventional weapons:

> One cooperative source has said that he suspected that the new large-diameter solid-propellant missile was intended to have a CW-filled

warhead, but no detainee has admitted any actual knowledge of plans for unconventional warheads for any current or planned ballistic missile. The suspicion expressed by the one source about a CW warhead was based on his assessment of the unavailability of nuclear warheads and potential survivability problems of biological warfare agent in ballistic missile warheads. This is an area of great interest and we are seeking additional information on warhead designs. [Ibid.]

Further documentation may provide definitive evidence regarding the covert program underway at Badr, but it seems likely that it was related to the long-range missile production discussed in the CIA and ISG reports.

The question remains, however, as to why this covert program was worth the risk of discovery. If the program was related to long-range missile production, the answer is suggested by the terms of the U.N. resolution itself, which limited Iraq to 150-kilometer short-range ballistic missiles. Such short-range missiles could provide defense against neighboring countries, but they would be ineffective against Israel. The intent of the U.N. measure was precisely to prevent Saddam from launching missiles into Israel, as he had done during the Gulf War.

Those SCUD missile attacks on Israel had served no tactical military purpose; Israel was not a member of the US-led coalition. Saddam's intention was clearly to provoke Israel into launching a retaliatory response — and thereby to unify the Arab World on the side of Iraq.

The long-range missile program being pursued in 2002 was almost certainly intended for a similar attack on Israel. But in view of the failure of this provocative tactic in the Gulf War, the new missile program was apparently designed for the delivery of *un-*

conventional warheads, as indicated by the ISG report cited above.

What was the logic behind this escalation? Even if Israel should respond to an Iraqi missile strike, a conventional retaliation for a conventional attack would not necessarily realign Middle East alliances. If, however, Saddam put chemical warheads on those missiles, we can imagine an entirely different scenario. If Saddam were to use chemical warheads against Israel, it is not hard to imagine that Israel might respond with an unconventional strike. Any unconventional assault on an Arab/Muslim country would be likely to provoke millions of Muslims to take up arms against Israel. It is reasonable to imagine that Arab militaries would attack Israel as well. This would be a war of disastrous proportions, a worldwide holy war.

General Sada, in his book *Saddam's Secrets,* recalls an occasion when he had to talk Saddam out of a chemical weapons attack on Israel, his hated adversary. Israel had of course bombed Iraq's nuclear reactor in 1981, which destroyed billions of dollars worth of Iraqi nuclear equipment and crippled Saddam's program to develop nuclear weapons.

This, then, is one plausible scenario to explain why those missiles were so important to Saddam—he may have intended to use them on Israel. In that scenario, the United States would confront a strategic nightmare—support for Israel would mean taking on a large portion of the world—and the difficulties we currently face in Iraq and Afghanistan would be magnified to encompass a war with nearly every Muslim or Arab nation. Such a war could be extremely difficult to win by conventional means, and it might ultimately lead to the destruction of Israel and the weakening of the United States.

In another of the captured documents, Saddam himself can

be heard endorsing this strategy. Harmony no. ISGQ-2003-M0006893 is a discussion about lifting the U.N. sanctions and the imminent threat of war with the US, transcribed and translated from an audiotape of a meeting between Saddam and his council. Saddam reproaches his council that Iraq has no WMD—eliciting this response from one member: "We don't need it." Saddam's response: "If they would've come and attacked Baghdad, don't you think we'd have needed it to send one to Israel?"

Jihad against Israel has been a theme of Saddam's speeches for several years, as reported, for example, by the BBC:

> On Tuesday he was seen on television banging his fist on the table in anger, criticizing Arabs for not doing enough in response to Israeli killings in the Palestinian territories. . . . Iraq has also been calling for a holy war to liberate Jerusalem from Israeli control. President Saddam Hussein has said Iraq did not need to wait for sanctions to be lifted before striking Israel. The United States says it closely monitors Iraq for any signs of military activity, but United Nations inspectors looking for Iraq's alleged weapons of mass destruction have not been in the country for nearly two years now (BBC Report, October 4th, 2000).

Clearly, Jihad was on Saddam's mind. And that is at the core of a strategic shift in Saddam's planning, related to the focus on long-range missiles. Throughout the 80s and early 90s, Saddam portrayed himself as an Arab leader. This strategy proved futile when many Arab nations turned against him in the Gulf War. But Islamic Jihad had meanwhile emerged as a revitalized strategy, due to the success of the Mujihadeen in Afghanistan. Jihadist organizations were now pursuing truly international operations on an unprecedented scale. Terrorist organizations that had previously targeted primarily their own nation's governments now began to focus on Israel and the U.S. as the primary enemy.

Did Saddam realize that support for his strategy would not be found in Arab governments, but would instead be found in Islamic Jihad? Did he decide to ignite holy war? This is an unpopular idea among many in the intelligence community, but it is consistent with the pattern of Iraq's involvement with and support for terrorist organizations, as revealed in other captured documents.

Chemical weapons

Did Saddam in fact have chemical weapons to use against Israel? The claim has often been made that Iraq ceased production of WMD in 1991. This view is countered by Rolf Ekeus, the chief of the U.N. inspections operation (Interview with Jim Lehrer on PBS's show NewsHour, September 22, 2003):

ROLF EKEUS: . . . the son-in-law of Saddam Hussein who defected at some stage and returned and was killed by Saddam, he told me during the debriefings in Amman in '95 that they had taken the decision not to produce during the prevailing circumstances, any new biological, chemical weapons—but instead develop the quality to...

JIM LEHRER: The capability to do it?

ROLF EKEUS: Precisely, the engineers, process specialists and so on.

JIM LEHRER: So back...

ROLF EKEUS: And quality. Small batches of production to develop quality.

[http://www.pbs.org/newshour/bb/middle_east/july-dec03/ekeus_9-22.html]

In this statement, which is generally overlooked by the media, Mr. Ekeus acknowledged that in the mid 1990s, Saddam was still *producing* (rather than stockpiling) WMD—that is, retaining the "capability" to produce such weapons at least in small amounts. Whether you make a gallon of VX or ten thousand, you have to have the resources to create VX. What would be the point of small-scale production of WMD? For a state such as Iraq, it doesn't seem to be a very effective option for national defense. If Saddam wanted to just bluff that he had WMDs, as some have suggested, he wouldn't need to actually make them. Whether or not Saddam had hidden caches of WMD in Iraq just prior to the invasion, the actual production of a limited quantity in a short amount of time was clearly within Iraqi capabilities.

A PBS report in October of 2004 cites testimony of Charles Duelfer (who succeeded David Kay as head of ISG) as follows:

> Iraq continued to work on missile delivery systems in the wake of the Gulf War. While it is clear that Saddam wanted a long-range missile, there was little work done on warheads. It is apparent that he drew the line at that point, so long as sanctions remained. However, while the development of ballistic missile delivery systems is time consuming, if and when Saddam decided to place a non-conventional warhead on the missile, this could be done quite quickly.
>
> [http://www.pbs.org/newshour/bb/middle_east/july-dec04/wmd_10-7.html]

Whether Saddam had WMD on hand, had safeguarded a cache in the possession of Syria, or planned to produce new batches "just in time," it seems clear that the intention was to develop an operational, long-range delivery capability for unconventional warheads. In spite of the pressure of U.N. sanctions, Saddam took the risk of maintaining a banned missile program.

Why would Saddam have taken such an unnecessary risk if he did not plan to use those missiles with chemical warheads on Israel? He could have chosen to bluff if his intention was to merely threaten Israel. If he had not built those missiles, he might well have succeeded in getting the sanctions lifted. But he did build them, and by handing them over to the U.N.—just days before the war and after four months of inspections—he ultimately sealed his own fate. This unnecessary risk was a gambler's strategy, part of an overall scheme in which Saddam would win it all or lose it all by igniting holy war.

Conclusion

Several significant points are beyond dispute.

• Within a few days of the start of Operation Iraqi Freedom, the government of Iraq was still involved with the development of prohibited weapons (long-range missiles).

• The CIA was correct in this aspect of its pre-war analysis, relating to Iraq's non-compliance with U.N. resolutions.

• Even though the U.N. teams inspected the location containing part of this secret program, essential elements were successfully concealed and went undetected.

• Russian companies closely tied to the Russian government were violating resolutions of the U.N. Security Council—of which Russia is a permanent member.

The captured document provides some important evidence to help fill in the picture of Iraq's illegal activities. It confirms the active role of Iraqi intelligence in monitoring the activities of the U.N. inspections teams and "preparing" the sites for inspection. It documents the collaboration of Turkish and Russian scientists in Iraqi operations. And, significantly, even though this secret document discusses a situation clearly involving prohibited items, it does not refer specifically to those items. Evidently, Iraq routinely kept references of prohibited items out of its own documents, adding to the difficulty of detecting these secret programs even now, in retrospect.

The role of Russian engineering firms is especially noteworthy, given the strength of the Russian government's opposition to the U.S. position on the enforcement of U.N. sanctions. It is extremely unlikely that such assistance was conducted out of view of the Russian government. Essentially, the Putin government was playing a double game— trusted member of the U.N. Security Council by day and covert partner in Iraq's prohibited weapons program at night.

Although this document alone provides no direct evidence of a broader scheme by Saddam Hussein to destabilize the region, the secret program must have had a deadly serious purpose, important enough to justify the great risk it created for Iraq's chances of lifting the sanctions. Viewed in a geopolitical context, these details are consistent with the theory that Saddam was developing an arsenal for a WMD attack on Israel, particularly with the intention of sparking a much broader war.

IRAQI INTELLIGENCE REPORT ON VISIT OF IAEA TEAM

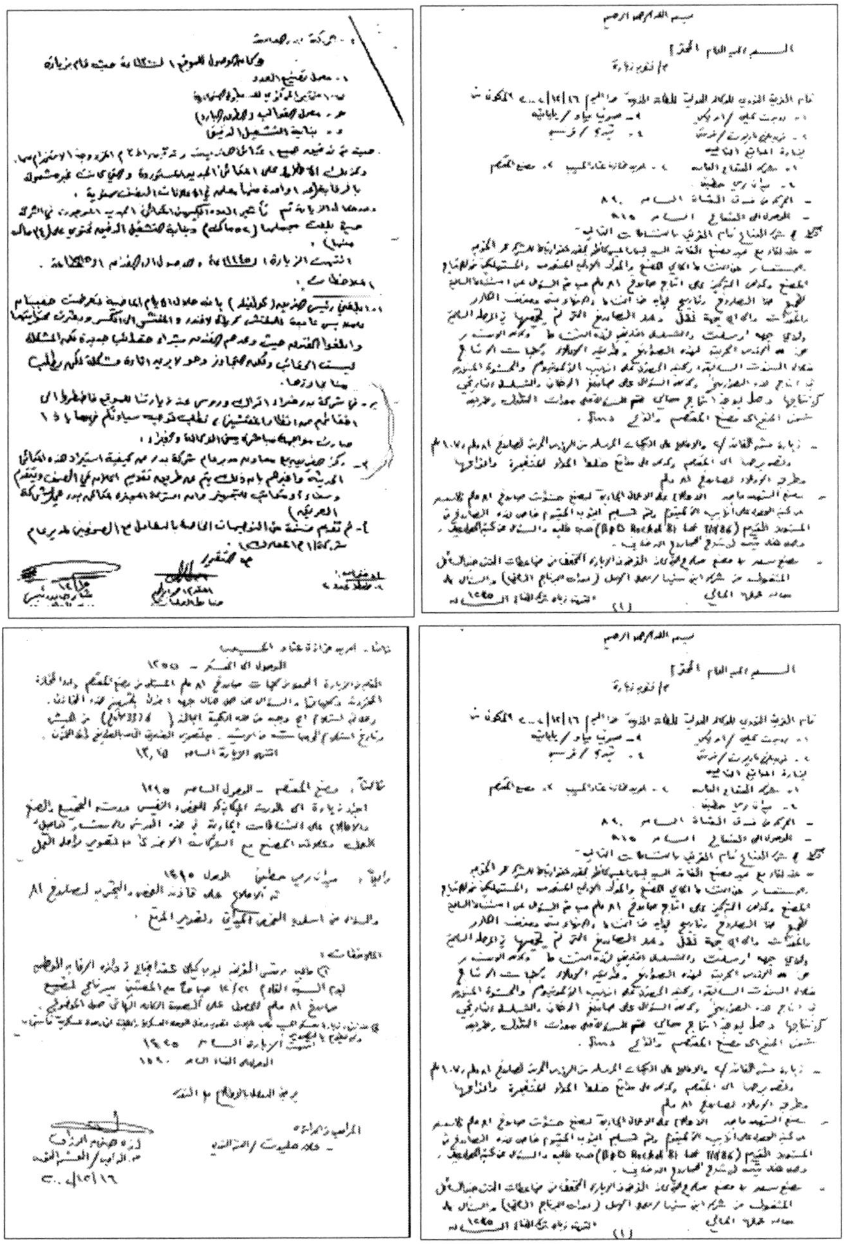

Figure 22: INTSUM (HARMONY No. CMPC-2003-000776),
complete document
Document dated 15 December 2002 (captured 2003)

INTSUM (DOCUMENT HARMONY NO. CMPC-2003-000776)
DOCUMENT DATED 15 DECEMBER 2002 CAPTURED 2003
UNCLASSIFIED DOCUMENT TRANSLATION FOLLOWS.

Mr. General Director of the Office of National Supervision

Subject: **Visit of the IAEA team**

A team of the IAEA did a SURPRISE visit today, on the 15th of December 2002, to

1) Oumm Al Maarek Company (Mother of all battles Company)

2) Al Qadessia Company

3) Badr Company

The agency's team consisted of two cars and 6 members:

1- Philip Coalfield, team leader, English

2- Greg Lavender, English

3- Thomas Moriati, English

4- Franck (family name unclear), American

5- Roy (or Ron) (family name unclear), American

6- Kenneth Phyllis, Ecuadorian

They left Al Qanat hotel at 8:25 and here follows what time they reached the companies and what they did:

1) Oumm Al Maarek company:

The team arrived at 8:55 and did the following

1- Met with the director's assistant (liaison member) and inquired about all the new buildings (after 1998) and their activities. Then focused on all the mechanical operations done by the company for the 81 millimeter (mm) rocket.

2- Visit the sites containing the manufacturing machines and the steps involved in the production of the 81 mm rocket. They also requested technical drawings for the rocket (copy enclosed with the report).

3- General tour in the factory and checking of the machines, especially the ones imported after 1998 and making a list of equipment present in the Central lab of measurement. The inspection finished at 11:45 and they headed to Al Qadessia.

2) Al Qadessia company:

The team arrived at 11:52 and from the gate one of the cars left towards the hotel with 3 inspectors: Coalfield, Franck and Phyllis.

1- They visited the company's factories and its shops, checked its machineries and made sure the machineries present corresponded to the agency's lists and checked the newly imported machinery (type CNC, 5 pieces) which is not covered by the inspection scope. The visit ended at 12:55 and all headed to Badr company.

3) Badr company:

Team arrived at 13:00 and visited:

1- Machinery production factory

2- Shaping factory (Cold method)

3- Central laboratory for quality control

4- Building of precision manufacturing

All the old machinery was inspected along with the seals of the double purpose machinery. They also inspected the newly imported machinery, which were not included in the supervision program (except one disclosed in the biannual report).

During this visit signs were put on a large number of new machinery. They totaled 52 and in the building of precision manufacturing 34.

Inspection visit ended at 14:45 and hotel arrival was at 15:15.

Remarks:

1- I was informed by the team leader (Coalfield) that during the past days **two clothing suitcases belonging to inspector Greg Lavender and the inspector (probably Coalfield: translator's note) were broken into** and their contents dispersed. They informed the hotel who promised to buy them new ones. But for the inspector the problem is not with the suitcases but the infraction and he does not want to make a problem but requests that this infraction be stopped.

2- When we visited Badr company there were **Turkish and Russian experts at the site and they had to hide away from the inspectors.** We demand your (General Director of the Office of National Supervision: translator's note) instructions for what to do in case there is a face to face between the agency's inspectors and the experts.

3- During his meeting with the general director of Badr company the team focused on how the new machinery is being imported. The director told them that it is advertised in the newspaper and middlemen or equipment agencies apply for the bid. He also told them that the equipment agency for Badr company is Al Ariqa company.

4- A copy of the special instructions for dealing with journalists was given to the director of Oumm Al Maarek company.

Respectfully,

Enclosed: 2 copies of technical drawing (Most probably for the 81mm rocket)

1st signature: Major Ahmad Ibrahim Operations officer

2nd signature: [Not clear].

END TRANSLATION

Translator's notes:

• Document CMPC-2003-000776 is made of two reports each one made of two pages, dated 15th December 2002 and 16th December 2002.

• The first report dated 15th December 2002 is translated here.

• This memo is hand written which made it difficult to read the names of the American inspectors.

CHAPTER 16:
SADDAM'S ANTHRAX ATTACK WARNING

Background

T HE VOLUME OF documentary evidence revealed here indicates Saddam Hussein did work with Islamic terrorists despite his claim that they were a threat to his regime. This realization could lead to the detection of another Saddam technique. Saddam was, after all, called the "master manipulator" by many observers. It seems to have been typical of Saddam to claim to be the victim of his own strategies. But this is perhaps not the strategy of a "master manipulator," since it is common for criminals to claim innocence as the victim of someone else's plot.

An example of this technique can be seen in the matter of Depleted Uranium (DU). While there is no question that DU is a radioactive substance and that when significant quantities are internalized it can be dangerous, instances such as these are very rare. For the most part, the contact with Depleted Uranium from spent munitions on a conventional battlefield would be very minimal.

An environmental impact study conducted by the International Atomic Energy Agency (IAEA) on the use by American forces of Depleted Uranium in Kosovo determined that DU munitions have "negligible environmental impact." In one instance, the researchers measured the radioactivity surrounding a penetration hole with a DU shell inside. Inside the hole, minute amounts of radioactivity were detected. Outside the hole, levels were the same as the surrounding environment. Despite this scientific research, the Saddam regime continually claimed that DU was causing wide spread health problems in Iraq.

Many health experts attribute these problems to Saddam's own widespread use of chemical weapons in Iraq. To put it succinctly, Saddam used chemical weapons on battlefields that would later be used to grow food for major Iraqi cities. But in order to deny his culpability, he needed something to blame the health crises on. This became the source of the "DU controversy" as Saddam supporters and anti-American groups picked up on his claims. As for DU, it is called *Depleted* Uranium for a reason. While it is radioactive, it is much less radioactive than what one would normally think of for a radioactive substance. Casual contact would not create a nation wide health emergency, as evidenced by the IAEA study, unlike using chemical weapons on one's crops.

Keeping in mind that Saddam liked to portray himself as the victim of his own strategies to maintain deniability and blame the horrors he created on others, whether it be the use of chemical weapons or Islamic terrorism, another document captured in Iraq can be very suggestive.

Narrative

The day before the anthrax attacks of September, 2001 started in the United States, the Saddam regime sent out a security alert of an impending WMD attack on its own government. According to the memorandum, Saddam's office issued a security alert on September 17th, 2001. The first envelopes used in the U.S. as part of the American anthrax attack were postmarked September 18th, 2001.

Saddam's alert consisted of a warning that "agents" who were instructed by their "Iranian masters" were going to submit personal paperwork to Iraqi government offices that they called "poisonous papers." While the memo does not state the nature of the poison, it would seem to mirror the distribution through documents that occurred in the US.

While the evidence presented here is not conclusive, it raises some interesting questions. There are a few different scenarios that could explain why Saddam was sending out this alert the day before a similar attack occurred in the United States.

One theory would be to take the memos at face value. Perhaps the Iraqi government actually picked up information that the Iranians were planning this attack. In that case, it raises the level of suspicion that the Iranians were possibly involved with the attack on the United States. If this was the case, and Iran was plotting an anthrax attack on Iraq, this document could make the case for intervention in Iran that much stronger. However, CIA reports from that period make no mention of Iran having active biological production; the reports do, however, mention some dual use technologies.

On the other hand it could have been a ploy by Saddam, who is well known to have had biological weapons in stockpile during the 90's, to turn his enemies against each other by blaming one for his own actions. If Saddam had knowledge of the impending attacks in the US, he might have written the memo believing that U.S. intelligence would pick it up and be more suspicious of Iranian complicity in the anthrax attack. He might have believed this would deflect the suspicion from Iraq as a fellow victim and place it on Iran. While it may sound a bit naïve for him to believe this might work, there are other references to his use of similar tactics. A March, 2006 White House press release demonstrates how Saddam routinely pitted enemies against each other:

> To Prevent Iraq's Different Groups From Coming Together To Challenge His Regime, Saddam Undertook A Deliberate Strategy Of Maintaining Power By Dividing The Iraqi People:
>
> He brutally repressed different Iraqi communities and pitted them against one another. By displacing communities and dividing Iraqis, Saddam sought to establish himself as the only force that could hold the country together.
>
> (http://www.whitehouse.gov/news/releases/2006/03/20060329-5.html)

It is worth noting that according to Iranian state run media, two of its newspapers received anthrax mailings in December of 2001. This could also have been a ploy by the Iranians to deflect suspicion, but in this case it occurred after the American anthrax attack—a key factor.

Of course, this alert may be just one instance of numerous security alerts that just happened to fall on a date that makes it appear suspiciously like there is a relationship between it and the U.S. anthrax attack. We may never know what initiated this security alert, but the coincidental time and mechanism of attack certainly warrants consideration.

Broader Context

The *Washington Post,* in an article entitled FBI Is Casting A Wider Net in Anthrax Attacks authored by Allan Lengel and Joby Warrick and published September 25, 2006, made clear that the predominant "lone U.S. scientist with a grudge" theory promulgated by the media was not the FBI's sole theory. The article also explained that much of what the public was told about the anthrax attack by the media was wrong.

The article explained that the Anthrax used in the 9/18 attack was not so sophisticated as to have been made in a premier bioweapons facility. The rumored advanced additives indicating an extremely sophisticated source of origin were not present. But the anthrax does show the expertise of a trained professional with access to modest laboratory facilities. In fact, the new characterization matches remarkably close to what would have been found in Iraq's anthrax program in the mid 80's; a high level program a decade or two behind the cutting edge, but still very significant.

Saddam's anthrax program was characterized by the ISG final report in its Key Findings. Bold font added for ease of reference:

The Biological Warfare (BW) program was born of the Iraqi Intelligence Service (IIS) and this service retained its connections with the program either directly or indirectly throughout its existence.

• The IIS provided the BW program with security and participated in biological research, probably for its own purposes, from the beginning of Iraq's BW effort in the early 1970s until the final days of Saddam Husayn's Regime.

In 1991, Saddam Husayn regarded BW as an integral element of his arsenal of WMD weapons, and would have used it if the need arose.

• At a meeting of the Iraqi leadership immediately prior to the Gulf war in 1991, Saddam Husayn personally authorized the use of BW weapons against Israel, Saudi Arabia and U.S. forces. Although the exact nature of the circumstances that would trigger use was not spelled out, they would appear to be a threat to the leadership itself or the U.S. resorting to **"unconventional harmful types of weapons."**

• Saddam envisaged all-out use. For example, all Israeli cities were to be struck and all the BW weapons at his disposal were to be used. Saddam specified that the **"many years"** agents, presumably anthrax spores, were to be employed against his foes.

ISG judges that Iraq's actions between 1991 and 1996 demonstrate that the state intended to preserve its BW capability and return to a steady, methodical progress toward a mature BW program when and if the opportunity arose.

• ISG assesses that in 1991, Iraq clung to the objective of gaining war-winning weapons with the strategic intention of achieving the ability to project its power over much of the Middle East and beyond. Biological weapons were part of that plan. With an eye to the future and aiming to preserve some measure of its BW capability, Baghdad in the years immediately after Desert Storm sought to save what it could of its BW infrastructure and covertly continue BW research, hide evidence of that and earlier efforts, and dispose of its existing weapons stocks.

• From 1992 to 1994, Iraq greatly expanded the capability of its Al Hakam facility. Indigenously produced 5 cubic meter fermentors were installed, electrical and water utilities were expanded, and massive new construction to house its desired 50 cubic meter fermentors were completed.

• With the economy at rock bottom in late 1995, ISG judges that Baghdad abandoned its existing BW program in the belief that it constituted a potential embarrassment, whose discovery would undercut Baghdad's ability to reach its overarching goal of obtaining relief from U.N. sanctions.

In practical terms, with the destruction of the Al Hakam fa-

cility, Iraq abandoned its ambition to obtain advanced BW weapons quickly. ISG found no direct evidence that Iraq, after 1996, had plans for a new BW program or was conducting BW-specific work for military purposes.

Indeed, from the mid-1990s, despite evidence of continuing interest in nuclear and chemical weapons, there appears to be a complete absence of discussion or even interest in BW at the Presidential level.

Iraq would have faced great difficulty in re-establishing an effective BW agent production capability. Nevertheless, after 1996 Iraq still had a significant dual-use capability—some declared—readily useful for BW if the Regime chose to use it to pursue a BW program. Moreover, Iraq still possessed its most important BW asset, the scientific know-how of its BW cadre.

• Any attempt to create a new BW program after 1996 would have encountered a range of major hurdles. The years following Desert Storm wrought a steady degradation of Iraq's industrial base: new equipment and spare parts for existing machinery became difficult and expensive to obtain, standards of maintenance declined, staff could not receive training abroad, and foreign technical assistance was almost impossible to get. Additionally, Iraq's infrastructure and public utilities were crumbling. New large projects, particularly if they required special foreign equipment and expertise, would attract international attention. U.N. monitoring of dual-use facilities up to the end of 1998, made their use for clandestine purpose complicated and risk laden.

Depending on its scale, Iraq could have re-established an elementary BW program within a few weeks to a few months of a decision to do so, but ISG discovered no indications that the Regime was pursuing such a course.

• In spite of the difficulties noted above, a BW capability is technically the easiest WMD to attain. Although equipment and facilities were destroyed under U.N. supervision in 1996, Iraq retained technical BW know how through the scientists that were involved in the former program. ISG has also identified civilian facilities

and equipment in Iraq that have dual-use application that could be used for the production of agent.

ISG judges that in 1991 and 1992, Iraq appears to have destroyed its undeclared stocks of BW weapons and probably destroyed remaining holdings of bulk BW agent. However ISG lacks evidence to document complete destruction. Iraq retained some BW-related seed stocks until their discovery after Operation Iraqi Freedom (OIF).

• After the passage of U.N. Security Council Resolution (UNSCR) 687 in April 1991, Iraqi leaders decided not to declare the offensive BW program and in consequence ordered all evidence of the program erased. Iraq declared that BW program personnel sanitized the facilities and destroyed the weapons and their contents.

• Iraq declared the possession of 157 aerial bombs and 25 missile warheads containing BW agent. ISG assesses that the evidence for the original number of bombs is uncertain. ISG judges that Iraq clandestinely destroyed at least 132 bombs and 25 missiles. ISG continued the efforts of the U.N. at the destruction site but found no remnants of further weapons. This leaves the possibility that the fragments of up to 25 bombs may remain undiscovered. Of these, any that escaped destruction would probably now only contain degraded agent.

• **ISG** does not have a clear account of bulk agent destruction. Official Iraqi sources and BW personnel. state that Al Hakam staff destroyed stocks of bulk agent in mid 1991. However, the same personnel admit concealing details of the movement and destruction of bulk BW agent in the first half of 1991. Iraq continued to present information known to be untrue to the U.N. up to OIF. Those involved did not reveal this until several months after the conflict.

• Dr. Rihab Rashid Taha Al 'Azzawi, head of the bacterial program claims she retained BW seed stocks until early 1992 when she destroyed them. ISG has not found a means of verifying this. Some seed stocks were retained by another Iraqi official until 2003 when they were recovered by ISG.

And:

The IIS had a series of laboratories that conducted biological work including research into BW agents for assassination purposes until the mid-1990s. ISG has not been able to establish the scope and nature of the work at these laboratories or determine whether any of the work was related to military development of BW agent.

• The security services operated a series of laboratories in the Baghdad area. Iraq should have declared these facilities and their equipment to the UN, but they did not. Neither the U.N. Special Commission (UN-SCOM) nor the U.N. Monitoring, Verification, and Inspection Commission (UNMOVIC) were aware of their existence or inspected them.

• Some of the laboratories possessed equipment capable of supporting research into BW agents for military purposes, but ISG does not know whether this occurred although there is no evidence of it. The laboratories were probably the successors of the Al Salman facility, located three kilometers south of Salman Pak, which was destroyed in 1991, and they carried on many of the same activities, including forensic work.

• Under the aegis of the intelligence service, a secretive team developed assassination instruments using poisons or toxins for the Iraqi state. A small group of scientists, doctors and technicians conducted secret experiments on human beings, resulting in their deaths. The aim was probably the development of poisons, including ricin and aflatoxin to eliminate or debilitate the Regime's opponents. It appears that testing on humans continued until the mid 1990s. There is no evidence to link these tests with the development of BW agents for military use.

(https://www.cia.gov/cia/reports/iraq_wmd_2004/Comp_Report_Key_Findings.pdf)

The report tells us that the Iraqi bioweapons program was born of, and remained tied to, the Iraqi Intelligence Service; this is the same group that practically boasts of its links to the *global Islamic jihad movement* in its own documents. The ISG report tells us Saddam valued his bioweapons and would have used them if he felt the need.

As of 1996, the BW programs were considered important, and Saddam wanted to restart large-scale production, but he couldn't because of sanctions. Then the report tells us that "Depending on its scale, Iraq could have re-established an elementary BW program within a few weeks to a few months of a decision to do so, but ISG discovered no indications that the Regime was pursuing such a course." In other words, a small-scale program of a few batches of anthrax, not for military production, but low quality for a terror attack, was easily within the capability of Iraq at anytime, especially in the years proceeding 9/11 when the inspectors were not allowed in Iraq. No such secret program after the mid 90's has been detected.

How could the Saddam regime produce anthrax in secret? The report also tells us "The IIS had a series of laboratories that conducted biological work including research into BW agents for assassination purposes until the mid-1990s." Secret laboratories that the U.N. knew nothing about and were *never inspected*. Secret labs that were used for small–scale production, particularly for the amounts that would be used in an assassination attempt, is a level of production that would be nearly impossible to detect and would be easily kept hidden, especially if the people involved had incentive to keep the secret. The report also notes the shortcomings of interrogations:

> Nonetheless, the interview process had several shortcomings. Detainees were very concerned about their fate and therefore would not be willing to implicate themselves in sensitive matters of interest such as WMD, in light of looming prosecutions. Debriefers noted the use of passive interrogation resistance techniques collectively by a large number of detainees to avoid their involvement or knowledge of sensitive issues; place blame or knowledge with individuals who were not in a position to contradict the detainee's statements, such as deceased individuals or individuals who were not in custody or who had fled the country; and provide debriefers with previously known information. However, the reader should keep in mind the Arab proverb: "Even a liar tells many truths."
>
> Some former Regime officials, such as 'Ali Hasan Al Majid Al Tikriti (Chemical 'Ali), never gave substantial information, despite speaking colorfully and at length. He never discussed actions, which would implicate him in a crime. Moreover, for some aspects of the Regime's WMD strategy, like the role of the Military Industrialization Commission (MIC), analysts could only speak with a few senior-level officials, which limited ISG's assessment to the perspectives of these individuals. (Ibid)

It is clear that there are secret aspects of Saddam's WMD activities that may never be known. In the grand scheme of things, a few kilograms of military grade anthrax would not be difficult to produce in the secret labs of a regime with the expertise. We have seen documentary evidence that the IIS has had sustained high-level contacts and agreements with Islamic terrorist leaders that were involved in recruiting, training and harboring al-Qaeda and the Taliban. Six days after the 9/11 attacks, the Saddam regime warns of an impending WMD attack using poison papers. The very next day a "poison paper attack" begins in the US. According to the ISG report, he had hidden bioweapons labs.

Saddam had the hidden facilities and the scientists to create the anthrax powder, and he had plenty of opportunity through his IIS contacts with the *global Islamic jihad movement* to provide anthrax to al-Qaeda for the American anthrax attack. Now we have motive, opportunity, and potential evidence of prior knowledge. But did Saddam have the intent? Saddam did gas tens of thousands of his own people; intent to use a WMD on his enemies doesn't take a great deal of imagination. In fact the ISG report also tells us:

> Saddam envisaged all-out use. For example, all Israeli cities were to be struck and all the BW weapons at his disposal were to be used. Saddam specified that the "many years" agents, presumably anthrax spores, were to be employed against his foes. [Ibid]

As described by the ISG final report, Saddam had the intent during a 1991 meeting to use anthrax on his enemies. But his intent didn't end there. A government-provided translation of a tape recording released through the Foreign Military Studies Office held this revelation. In an undated meeting with his regime leaders, held in the late 90s judging by the discussion of a stalemate in U.N. sanctions and chemical weapons accountability, Saddam told his cabinet as he reflected on the Gulf War, "too bad, if I knew that the war would stop, we would've fire[d] those on Israel." (ISGQ-2003-M0004244-2) Saddam was telling his leaders that if he knew the Americans were not going to depose him, he would have fired chemical missiles at Israel.

And what he envisioned for Israel, he envisioned for the US, as there was no distinction in his mind between the two, (or within the minds of his jihadist accomplices) as demonstrated by his own public speeches. In a July 20th, 1998 National Day Speech, Saddam stated that the White House was "the creator of the requirements for Zionist occupation, aggression, and expansion against the Arabs." In other words, the United States created Israel, making the U.S. culpable in Israeli actions. If Saddam had the intent to use WMD against Israel, it would be correct to think he would do the same to the US.

Despite all this, we must acknowledge that there is to date no public evidence tying the anthrax attack with the 9/11 attacks or Islamic terrorists. There may be no direct evidence yet, but there is an interesting indicator that many people are still unaware of to this day.

Ramzi Yousef, who orchestrated the 1993 WTC attack, is the nephew of Khalid Sheik Mohammed, the plotter of the 9/11 attack. When Ramzi Yousef built the bomb used in the 1993 attack under the guidance of his uncle, it had two components—a conventional high explosives element and an unconventional poison gas element. According to Iraq expert Dr Laurie Mylroie, the bomb was designed to release a cloud of cyanide gas upon the survivors of the explosion. But the gas was destroyed in the explosion itself.

Clearly, for the dual conventional/unconventional attack to be effective, it required separation of time and space. Was the lesson of the failed chemical attack remembered for the subsequent attack on 9/11? It really only makes sense that given the failure of the first WMD attack that KSM would have learned to separate the conventional/unconventional elements of the attack. This is exactly what happened on 9/11 and the subsequent Anthrax attack. An explosive attack occurred and within a week the WMD attack occurred.

If we grant our terrorist mastermind the ability to learn from past mistakes, yet keep the desire for a similar attack in a grander fashion, you get an attack scenario that mirrors what actually happened. This is not solid evidence, but it is a very interesting indicator that perhaps we should not be so quick to eliminate a connection between the anthrax attack and 9/11 in the same way some experts dismissed a connection between Saddam Hussein and Islamic terrorists. Neither should we eliminate the possibility that this anthrax was produced by the Saddam regime for their terrorist accomplices, especially after we discover evidence that may indicate prior knowledge of the anthrax attack.

Our finding is that there is still substantial reason to investigate if the anthrax attack was part of the 9/11 attack. If that is actually the case, the Saddam regime would be the most likely originator of the anthrax. There is no information available to the public (that we are aware of) that excludes the possibility. Of course, it must be noted, our determinations are made upon publicly available information. Investigating agencies undoubtedly have undisclosed information. It is our sincere hope that such undisclosed information is not tainted by unfounded assumptions over the inaccessibility of Islamic terrorists to anthrax or even to support from the Saddam regime.

The original is in Arabic and our translator "Sammi" provides an original English translation below. The memorandum has two pages with what appear to be official letterhead and stamps.

Begin Translation for CMPC-2003-006051

In the name of Allah the Merciful

Republic of Iraq

Presidency of the Republic

The Secretary

Top secret and personal

Number: K/9320

Date: 17 September 2001

To: Respected Director of the Intelligence Service

Respected Director of the General Military Intelligence

Respected Director of General Security

Subject: Information

We have received information saying that agents, following instructions from their Iranian masters have instructed their followers to go to official and semi-official government offices to follow up on paper work. They were instructed to submit personal files containing poisonous papers that were specially prepared to target the officials and the important places in the security, (translator's comment: Ba'ath) party, and administrative offices in all the provinces of the country.

Please be informed and respond as needed.

With respects.

Colonel

Dr. Abd Hamid Khattab

Secretary of the President of the Republic

16 September 2001

Translation of second memo

Republic of Iraq

Presidency of the Republic

Intelligence Service

Top secret and personal

Announcement

Date: 19 September 2001

Number: 4637

Respected Assistant Director of the Operations of Intelligence.

Enclosed is a photocopy of the letter of the Presidency of the Republic-Secretary 9320 on 17 September 2001, regarding information about targeting the officials through submitting forms containing poisonous papers.

Please review...With respects

Enclosed: Letter

Signed by; M.M 1

18th September 2001

Copy to:

Respected Mr. M. A. M 4

Respected Mr. M. A. M 5

Enclosed copy of the mentioned letter

Respected Mr. M. M 40

With respects.

Respected Mr. M. M 6

Respected Mr. M. M 16

End Translation

CHAPTER 17:
SADDAM'S NUCLEAR TEST?

Background

ON FEBRUARY 25ᵀᴴ of 2001, the *Sunday Times* ran the article Saddam's Bomb by Gwynne Roberts. Roberts tells of a meeting with a man in Iraq who told him of a secret underground nuclear test Iraq had conducted in the late 90's. To be sure, the plot of the story sounds highly improbable. But the man, who called himself Leone, left descriptions and drawings of the nuclear device which he claimed was tested in Iraq.

Roberts then investigated the claims and came away with significant supporting evidence to key elements of Leone's story from Iraq and from various nuclear experts. The bomb itself was described as practical but not of a typical design usually pointed to by faux nuclear scientists. A nuclear weapons design expert stated that the Iraqi "should be taken seriously because he was obviously competent." Leone claimed that he had participated in a successful nuclear test performed in the Rezzaza Lake area of southern Iraq in 1989. Leone claimed that the test was conducted underground in a massive tunnel that reached under the lake. The benefit of conducting a secret small-scale nuclear test under a lake would be the ability of the water to absorb some of the energy and reduce the intensity of the seismic signature. He said that creating the tunnel required workers who were later murdered to keep it a secret:

> The tunnel and the entrance were huge and the manpower needed to block it up massive. Leone had told me that thousands of political prisoners worked on the tunnel after a presidential amnesty.
>
> "They were well fed and lived in comfortable caravans. In return, they worked hard. But none of them came out of it alive," he said. "Many were contaminated with radioactive waste. Friends working for Iraqi security who were guarding them said they were buried in caves nearby. The Iraqi regime hoped the secret of the Rezzaza lake test would die with them. "Hussein Kamel gave the order to kill these people . . . I was disgusted by it and it's one of he major reasons I fled.

Leone's story includes mass graves filled with bodies contaminated by radioactivity. One of the captured Saddam regime documents, CMPC-2003-015757, included a copy of the Roberts' article in English. The Saddam regime was aware of the article.

Another captured document appears to contain some startling revelations related to the Roberts story. That document was originally identified and translated at the *Free Republic* website. It is a memorandum dated February 7, of 2001. It appears to predate the Roberts article by two weeks. If the memo does predate the article, this could be due to the vagaries of publishing and assigning dates. It could also mean someone became aware of the article and notified the regime just before it came out. Whatever the case, the timing is very close together and there are a myriad of reasons to deduce the Saddam regime was responding to the Roberts article in their memorandum.

Narrative

The memorandum is from Iraqi intelligence. It is written to

the "Director of the Fourth Directorate." Leone tells Mr. Roberts that the nuclear weapons development group in charge of the test was called "Group Four." This may be just a coincidence, but it would be one of several in this case. Iraqi intelligence tells the Fourth Directorate "No information is available about the Mass Graves in the Southern Region."

It appears from this statement that the Fourth Directorate has asked the IIS what it knows about mass graves in southern Iraq, where Lake Rezzaza is located. The IIS responds that it doesn't know anything about them. Then the IIS recommends a course of action. It wants the graves located and the bodies investigated. It also lays out a propaganda plan. The propaganda is another indication that they are responding to the Roberts story. It sounds very much like a plan for damage control and spin.

The first directive from the memorandum is to inspect the bodies for nuclear contamination. This is a stunning revelation. The IIS considers it possible that these bodies may have been contaminated by radiation. This directive relates the memorandum almost directly to the mass graves contaminated with radiation described by Leone in the Roberts article. If the IIS had no reason to believe the article might be true, there would be no reason to test for radiation.

The memorandum then directs the Iraqi investigators to determine if the bodies were buried alive and thus suffocated. This is important because if the evidence shows they were buried alive, the regime could not counter that Coalition forces slaughtered them during the Gulf War, which was the basis of the propaganda plan outlined in the document. The absence of bullet wounds and other such wounds would discredit their story if international investigators inspected the bodies. The directive says to determine if they are military personnel or civilians. The IIS also wants to know if there are tombstones that carry the names of the victims. Then the directive tells the investigators to determine how easy it would be for others to find these graves.

The memorandum concludes by outlining a media strategy. They do not want the discovery of mass graves to be reported in Iraq, of course. They want to leak the story to the international media that while making a search for missing coalition soldiers (thus portraying themselves as helpful), they discovered these mass graves. They want to give the impression that the graves are related to the Gulf War and they are victims of the US. This would make sense, since the Saddam regime claimed Depleted Uranium was the cause of a health emergency in Iraq to cover for its own use of chemical weapons. This would account for radiation on the bodies in their propaganda. Of course, they want to preclude the discovery of these graves, but in their view, since Roberts is writing about them, the international community probably already knows where they are. Thus, the regime needs a good cover story.

It is difficult to determine if this memorandum was written from the perspective of already knowing the location of the graves but having no concrete prior knowledge of them , or knowing absolutely nothing of the graves at all. It is worth noting that the directives do not include orders to locate the graves, to confirm the graves exist, or to perform another similar act. This could be an oversight, but it seems like it the first task would have been to order that the graves be located, specifically if they didn't already know their location.

Now look at the "observations." None of those actually say "confirm the graves exist" or something similar. If they weren't sure they existed or believed they didn't exist, that should be the first point. Another indicator is the fact that they planned to control the story. If the graves didn't exist, why did they need a cover story?

There is also the simple strategy of hiding the mass graves in plain site. The directive concerning tombstones may indicate that if they put grave markers up, the burial site is now a cemetery and is no longer a "mass grave." No mystery there, it is just a cemetery. Then if the story breaks and gains traction, they run some investigative reporters out to show them it is nothing but a well- known cemetery, while stating that the source was lying.

Broader Context

All these are techniques well established under the regime of the Master Manipulator, Saddam Hussein. While the evidence is not conclusive, it in fact raises more questions than it answers; however, it is an indicator that the Saddam regime was spooked by Leone's story. Now the case must be made that they may have reacted with fear merely because of the ramifications of such a story even if it is false. But on the other hand, would those radiation detectors be needed if there was no truth in Leone's story about mass graves contaminated by radiation?

Of course, beyond the question of whether or not Leone's story is true, is the question of could it be true? Could the Iraqis have detonated a nuclear weapon without the world knowing? Leone's story meets heavy resistance because of an incorrect impression that it couldn't have happened without us detecting it. Roberts deals with the question in his article:

Officials at the International Seismic Centre near Newbury said detecting an event of this size—about 2.7 on the Richter scale—would be "extremely difficult" in this region. especially if it had been decoupled (BIOT: a process for reducing seismic signature), as Leone claimed.

I visited Sulaymaniyah's local seismic station. It is 640km from the Rezzaza site, and its director confirmed that its range was limited. "Whether we would pick up an event 100 to 200km away would depend on its magnitude," he explained. "If it's really big, we would record it. If it's small, then we may miss it."

Records from 1989 showed no trace of an event on September 19, but a map of Iraq's main earthquake zones provided a potential clue. The Rezzaza region is virtually earthquake-free, but the map showed one exception—a tremor marked by a red circle on the southwestern shore of the lake, close to Leone's test site. Nobody at the seismic station knew when this tremor occurred, except that it was after 1985 and before 1991.

Roberts' findings are validated elsewhere. During the Cold War, most of us (around back then) labored under the misconception that American satellite and seismic technology was so powerful and omnipresent, that we would know it if a mouse squeaked under the Soviet Secretary General's chair. Not so say six men who held the position of United States Secretary of Defense. A *Washington Times* article entitled Former Defense Chiefs Oppose Pact from October of 1999 is a letter from those six men to Congress, protesting a proposed arms control agreement. They write:

"Finally, it is impossible to verify a ban that extends to very low yields. The likelihood of cheating is high. "Trust but verify" should remain our guide. Tests with yields below 1 kiloton can both go undetected and be militarily useful to the testing state. Furthermore, a significantly larger explosion can go undetected — or mistaken for a conventional explosion used for mining or an earthquake — if the test is "decoupled."

Decoupling involves conducting the test in a large underground cavity and has been shown to dampen an explosion's seismic signature by a factor of up to 70. The United States demonstrated this capability in 1966 in two tests conducted in salt domes at Chilton, Miss"

Respectfully,

James R. Schlesinger, Richard B. Cheney, Frank C. Carlucci, Caspar W. Weinberger, Donald H. Rumsfeld and Melvin R. Laird"

These six former SecDefs are describing a situation that mirrored what Leone reported. Of course, none of this is proof that such an event took place. The International Atomic Energy Agency (IAEA) has denied that it happened. But the reaction of the Saddam regime to this story should pique the interest. Something about the story involving radiation and mass graves seems to have hit close to the mark, judging by the reaction.

This article from the *New York Times* entitled <u>Document Reveals 1987 Bomb Test by Iraq</u> by William Broad and dated April 29, 2001 provides an alternate explanation. It is a well- founded report about an Iraqi document that details the testing of a nuclear or "dirty bomb." Such a device does not create a nuclear explosion but instead spreads radiation. According to the document, the dirty bomb functioned, though some experts state not as well as the memo writer tries to insinuate. It does offer a theory for why the regime was concerned about radioactive mass graves. It could be possible this weapon functioned and contaminated local towns. The fact that the test occurred is not in dispute based upon the Saddam regime document. Apparently, the *New York Times* at one time found Iraqi documents a credible source. The *Times* only began an effort to de-legitimize Iraqi documentation when they became inconvenient to the Democratic leadership political positions on the Iraq War and the Bush Administration.

The memorandum also includes a recommendation to work with CNN to control the spin of this story. There is a basis for this statement in the writings of Eason Jordan, a former CNN chief news executive who admitted that CNN reported Saddam's propaganda to maintain access in Iraq. His article entitled The News We Kept to Ourselves from April 11th, 2003 detailed many instances in which the Cable News Network sat on a story of an atrocity. Jordan states that the news network even failed to report a threat by Saddam's son to kill a foreign leader. No wonder the IIS turned to them to carry their propaganda! The network had become hardly more than Saddam's personal mouthpiece.

The following is an original translation done by "Sammi".

Begin translation for ISGQ-2004-00224003

The Republic of Iraq
The Intelligence Service

Date: 7/2/2001

No 1687

In the Name of God the Merciful the Most Compassionate
Secret

To: the Director of the Fourth Directorate
Subject: Your letter secret and immediate numbered B 264 on 2/4/2001

1. No information is available about the Mass Graves in the Southern Region.

2. We want to do the following:

- Inspect the graves to confirm the existence of nuclear radiation.
- Were they buried alive and thus suffocated?
- Are they military personnel or civilians?
- Are there tombstones that carry the names of the martyrs?
- Identify evidence of the graves and the possibility of them being found.

3. We believe it should not be spoken about by Iraqi media so the Iraqi public will not comment on it and it will remain an international story, and we should work on the following tasks for now:

Leak the news through reliable sources, news agencies and satellite stations. Claim that there is confusion within the Coalition forces about the existence of mass graves civilians and military personnel in the southern Iraq.

Claim the activity is a serious attempt to search for soldiers from the Coalition forces via the media.

Ask some of the friendly countries with good technology to find these graves, their media will ask to participate. In case the graves are discovered their media will be able to influence the internationally and foreign media to sway international opinion against the countries that did this. (BIOT: Putting the blame on the US)

Do not dig up these graves. Work with CNN and give them priority on this subject because it can influence the international discussion more than Iraqi media. (BIOT: CNN can spin for us if we work with them.

End Translation

CHAPTER 18:
SADDAM'S MILLENNIUM PLOT

THE IIS AGENT'S notebook contained startling revelations about the company Saddam was keeping with Islamic terrorist leaders. It also holds some mysteries. A few pages from the notebook reveal some type of secret activity involving the royal family of the United Arab Emirates. It starts off with a conversation between Saddam Hussein and a foreign VIP. The conversation makes clear that during 1999 Saddam was involved in some secret dealing with the UAE King. At this time, UAE princes were hanging out with Usama bin Laden while falcon hunting in Afghanistan. Saddam mentions Iraq will not attack the UAE if it attacks any other nation.

Translation for ISGP-2003-0001412 follows:

Page 62

Master: —1990- Would you please allow me to contact the Minister in order to invite him and whoever will be with him for lunch?

'Ala' Al-Qaysi

The director: we want to meet and talk

Our master: if the kings invaded a village, they destroy it. What is happening in Saudi Arabia? there is an issue (TC: Possibly "Remark".)

["Our master" appears to be Saddam based on the following conversation. He appears to be asking someone familiar with the Saudi Arabian royal family about internal politics.]

1. Deep disagreement between the rulers of Saudi. When I visited Mr. President **[Saddam Hussein]** in 1990 before you entered Kuwait, I told Mr. President that the Saudis will fight you, as Sheikh Zayd told me. He told me Saddam is brave, cruel, and a hero, but the price for princes and sultans is discrepant.

[The foreign dignitary has answered that there is trouble within the House of Saud. The visitor has conversations with *Sheik Zayed bin Sultan Al Nahyan* who was President (and king) of the UAE from 1971-2004. To refer to Saddam as cruel even in third person indicates this person has high stature.]

The director: Have you recently met Sheikh Zayd?

[This seems to be the director of the IIS asking Saddam a question.]

Our master: yes, in the past time I met him.

The director ordered to bear the expenses of their residence at Al-Rashid

The Organization's Director ordered to bear the expenses of their residence at Al- Rashid The director: Tomorrow, I will call 'Ala' Al-Samirra'I and follow up the issue tomorrow morning.

Page 61

Tomorrow, I will call the office of Mr. Taha and Mr. 'Uday **[probably Taha Yassin Ramadan, Saddam's VP and Uday Hussein, Saddam's son]** to discuss the issue. At 11 am, I will phone the Minister of Information and Culture Dr. Hasan 'Ala' Al-Samirra'I, Abu Dhabi; Khalid Khamis Batti Al-Rumaythi Secretary [female] General Manager Booking / car Car 17 17 Seri Lankan Official in Charge Tahsin, Protocol Director Master of Ceremonies Guaranteed to take

[We believe this is the notebook author writing a reminder to himself]

Page 60

...our master (unintelligible)

1. UAE

As we discussed with you and the head of the organization.

He is authorized by Mr. Zayd Bin Sultan. He arranges everything and is authorized to sign on his behalf—

If good relations exist with Iraq, Iraq will not attack UAE if it attacks any other country.

Now, the American and the Iranians conspire against us.

We work with Iraq. We sent a lot of authorizations [or medicine]. Here is the speech of Mr. Khamis Al-Rumaythi, Office Manager

[The notation here runs together, but we have separated it based on what makes sense in a back and forth conversation. The visitor has told Saddam that the King of UAE is sending a representative who has the full authorization of the King. In response, Saddam tells the visitor that the UAE will be immune from Iraqi supported attacks. The visitor then pledges cooperation and names the person who represents the King, Khamis al Rumaithi. His son will be visiting with Saddam's officials. The translation of "here is the speech" probably means "here is the letter" from the representative, because that just makes more sense.]

Page 59

I went twice to Abu Dhabi **(in UAE, location of Zayed)** and stayed in his palace ... and he agreed to work secretly with Iraq .. he was an official appointed by the President. I invited him, he came to my house in the presence of their embassy official at Dacca **(a city in Bangladesh)**, along with another person. However, I convened three times with him; he agreed to place the matter in his son's name. As for him, he would work with the president in favor of Iraq without conditions.

[The visitor has now revealed he has a house in Bangladesh. He visited the King's palace in UAE where he met with a man (probably UAE royalty) who agreed to have his son deal with the issue (the issue still goes unstated in the document). The man support's Saddam. The father is Khamis al Rumaithi.]

D4: It is a political issue: is there any new political issue? he always calls for the necessity to talk with Iraq... but when the GCC meets, he signs all resolutions without objection.

[D4 may be the head of the 4th Directorate of the Iraqi Intelligence Service or Secret Service. This organization was the unit that performed foreign infiltration; the spies. The GCC is a Persian Gulf nations league (Gulf Cooperation Council) and D4 is saying that the UAE king talks of support but then votes against Iraq at the GCC council.

As described on the Federation of American Scientists website:

Directorate 4. Secret Service

The Secret Service Directorate is located inside the headquarters complex of the *Mukhabarat*. Its activities take place both in Iraq and abroad, with agents of D4 infiltrated into Iraqi Government departments, the Baath Party, associations, unions and organisations, Iraqi embassies and the opposition. In addition, the Secret Service receives intelligence from the Al Hadi Project, responsible for SIGINT. The Directorate includes a number of offices specialising in the collection against a specific country or region, including offices for Southern Asia, Turkey, Iran, America (North and South), Europe, Arab states, Africa and the former Soviet Union. D4 works in co-ordination with D3, D5, D9, D12, D14, D18. The current Director of D4 is Maj.

Gen. Abdul Aziz Al Qurtan, and the Assistant Director of D4 is Brig. Mohammed Yasin Al Shammari, from Mosul.] http://www. fas.org/irp/world/iraq/mukhabarat/org.htm

But did Al-Rumaythi show anything new?

[An alternate spelling is "Al Rumaithi", a family name that seems to be part of the ruling class or one of the royal families in UAE, comes up in conjunction with several individuals who are ministry and military leaders.]

A recommendation from AL-Rumaythi.

Our master: I asked two things of him: he should be serious; Iraq's embargo is unfair. I asked him that he should talk in the GCC, *(Gulf Cooperation Council- nation league of Arabian Peninsula)* he should be serious and not only talk. He phoned us at 9 am and 2 pm and informed me that he talked with...

[Saddam has apparently spoken with the elder al Rumaithi or perhaps he has shifted to speaking about the UAE king.]

Page 58

The officials agree...and at 2 o'clock, I will give you the answer. We do not want to meet anyone at Amman's quarter lest we would be discovered. You know that meeting individuals outside Iraq is not on our favor or theirs. We can provide requested accommodations within Iraqi territory only.

[This appears to be Saddam stating that the meeting with the son of Khamis al Rumaithi, the UAE V.I.P., who has the Kings authority is requested to be held in Amman, Jordan. Saddam opposes and wants the meeting in Iraq.]

In public, Qatar is not against you, however, they fear the American pressure. This person talks and Sheikh Zayd listens. Sheikh Zayd told me that he informed the brothers—and he would rather keep his identity unknown.

[The visitor appears to explain that King Zayed has a relationship with "the brothers" common jihadist parlance for mujahideen. And whatever they are up to, Zayed wants it a secret]

I even refused to pay compensations for the American army. In my opinion, this would be good for you. The Saudis wanted $10 million dollars from him for a loan and other expenses. Disagreement arose between him and Prince 'Abdallah. You notice next to every university a small camp as they especially fear the female professor.

[The reference is to Abdullah bin Abdul Aziz al-Saud now King of Saudi Arabia. It is not clear what is being said here but one interpretation might be that King Zayed is in disagreement with the Saudis. The visitor says he (himself) refused to pay compensations for the American Army. This might be a reference to a host nation of U.S. forces paying a portion of the costs. If so, it is likely that the visitor is UAE royalty since the UAE hosted U.S. forces at the time. Of course, the same could be said for Saudi Arabia, Qatar, Kuwait, and Bahrain. The conversation has turned to Islamic extremism in the comment about "the female professor".]

Page 57

(Unintelligible)

our master: Ibn Al-Rumaythi when he comes to Baghdad, does he have any ideas or he intends to come for trade?

[Saddam wants to know what the son of Khamis al Rumaithi has to offer.]

He says: M4: According to your understanding of the issue, his son does not have any political ideas, we need to consider this issue. Can we meet Khamis [or Khays] directly?

Is it better to meet him in the UAE, outside the UAE or Amman? Inform them that the Presidency Office…

Also in Amman … Jordanians gather the intelligence.

[M4 was an IIS directorate that, among other things, spied on the U.N. and procured banned items such as WMD related materials.]

I want a secret meeting with Al-Rumaythi to talk with him. We prefer to hold this meeting in Morocco or Tunisia. First allow his son to come for trade. We have certain ideas, if we meet Al-Rumaythi to send some religious Arabs who possess a national and Islamic background to form a group. I will talk directly to him about this issue to form an Islamic group who will talk with Sheikh Zayd.

[It looks like the M4 director wants to send Islamists to talk to king Zayed. He doesn't say why or what for.]

Our master: In my opinion, you will succeed

D4: How will you arrange the meeting with Khamis, by phone or by person?

Our master: it is not neither safe for you nor for them. So we would proceed on this approach, depending on God.

Page 56

…(unintelligible: unintelligible): It is important to meet with him face to face to converse. Maybe it is better the delay his son's visit to Baghdad, you can talk to him from Daka. **[We believe the translator meant Dacca because of the previous reference to meetings there.]** The meeting will be in the beginning of the seventh month, as I am busy this and the next month (unintelligible): this meeting is secret, but will he notify Sheikh Zayd? yes, hence the approval of Sheikh Zayd is required to allow him leave the country.

Page 55

510 + 515 will be our guests

small suit + daughter [or son]

+ international phone calls

Baha' Al-Din

He furnished the communications system that uses satellite frequency to make international calls as a present, along with a 5 hours subscription. This device would be used by our organization for emergency purposes, considering the possibility that it could be located...

[Some wealthy visitor has provided the IIS with satellite communications equipment as a gift]

Page 54

Ask Mr. Khidr about the work range. Then ask about the Mercy Speech of (unintelligible) Sudanese Sheikh Yasin 'Umar Al-Imam in (unintelligible) (TC: Possibly Lura.) (unintelligible) Hassan Al-Turabi

[According to a U.N. document, Yassin Omar al- Imam is identified as a long time National Islamic Front militant in Sudan. The NIF is a Sudanese spin off of the Muslim Brotherhood in Egypt, the origin (of splinter groups) of much of the world's Islamic terrorism. Turabi is the NIF leader and strongly associated with Usama bin Laden. Turabi orchestrated at least one face –to face meeting between UBL and the IIS in 1995. His NIF also orchestrated meetings between al Zawahiri and the IIS when Saddam was looking to contract a hit on the U.S. forces in Somalia in 1993. The evidence is strong that Turabi is a "friendly" and not a target of the IIS]

1. considered like their master 'Umar 72 years Arab Afghani Mujahidins Zahir (unintelligible) 8863883 'Abd-al-Samad, Foreign 5432987 3 12/5

[This appears to be contact info for or a note about Sudanese

based Mujahideen (like the NIF).]

END

What can we learn from this translation?

1. The Saddam regime was looking for political support from the UAE. Nothing nefarious there.
2. Saddam pledged immunity from attacks to the UAE.
3. The UAE King was sponsoring "the brothers" and did not want it to be known.
4. Saddam wants to send "religious men" to meet with the King.
5. The UAE didn't want to go to Baghdad and preferred Jordan.
6. Saddam believed Iraq was safer and was worried about Jordanian intelligence.
7. These meetings took place in early 1999 with the secret meeting in Jordan planned for the summer of 1999.
8. They mention trade and politics in passing but no serious discussion of the meeting agenda.
9. Saddam had an idea he wanted to run by the King.
10. The IIS agent then switches to notes about Islamic terrorists.
11. At this same time, the Saddam regime was meeting with several leaders of the *global Islamic jihad movement.*

So what were these secret meetings with the UAE royalty in Jordan during 1999 involving "the brothers" and "religious men" possibly about? The notebook doesn't say, but there is some context to ponder.

Let's look at what else was happening in 1999. In November of 1999, Jordanian intelligence broke up a bombing plot by al Qaeda. The plot involved the release of poisonous chemicals. It was possibly the first attack in a sequence of events that would become known as the Millennium Plot.

Global Security.org has this summation of the Millennium Plot:

On December 31, 1999, an Algerian/Jordanian terrorist cell with co-operation from Al-Qaeda planned to execute two thwarted terrorist attacks. One an attack on Los Angeles International Airport, and the other on biblical sites in the Middle East and a hotel in Amman Jordan. In late 1998 two Palestinians, Raed Hijazi and Abu Hoshar settled on a plan to attack multiple targets throughout the middle east. They would first attack four targets: the SAS Radisson Hotel in downtown Amman, the border crossings from Jordan into Israel, and two Christian holy sites, at a time when all these locations were likely to be thronged with American and other tourists. Next, they would target a local airport and other religious and cultural sites. Hijazi and Abu Hoshar cased the intended targets and sent reports to Abu Zubaydah, a longtime ally of Osama Bin-Ladin, who approved their plan.

[http://www.globalsecurity.org/security/ops/millenium-plot.htm]

Global Security.org reference:

Final Report of the 9-11 Commission National Commission on Terrorist Attacks upon the United States 22 Jul 2004

CBS News tells us more about the plot:

Other suspects told their interrogators about a safe house in a refugee camp in the outskirts of Amman. Police stormed the house and found hidden under a sofa five two-way radios wired as detonators. When they ripped the floor open, they discovered canisters, 70 of them, leaking and highly toxic.

"If these chemicals had been mixed and manufactured well, they would have resulted in very dangerous explosives, enough to bring a huge explosion. These chemicals were even just dangerous to breathe." says Obeidat.

[http://www.cbsnews.com/stories/2001/10/03/60II/main313398.shtml]

Jordanian intelligence found the chemical weapons in a Palestinian-Jordanian refugee camp where the "returnees from Kuwait" settled after supporting Saddam during the occupation of Kuwait. Hijazi and Hoshar are both Palestinian.

A few weeks later, an al Qaeda operative named Ahmed Ressam would be caught sneaking bomb materials across the Canadian border near Seattle. Ressam operated as an al Qaeda member but from an Algerian terror cell that was a splinter group from the Islamic militant group the FIS. The FIS had pledged to fight for Saddam during the Gulf War.

The bombing of the *U.S.S. Cole* would follow in October of 2000. In fact, the attacks of 9/11 could be considered as the capstone event of the "Millennium Plot", although delayed (the original planning began in 1996).

Was Al Qaeda alone in the millennium plot or was it a joint operation with the Saddam regime? We should look at these attacks as something other than individual plots and see them for what they truly were; a direct assault on Christianity at a significant event on the Christian calendar, 2000 years of Jesus Christ. One planned site for the attack was near a river in Jordan at which tradition says John the Baptist baptized Jesus Christ. But were the attacks motivated by another purpose as well?

It is well known that King Hussein of Jordan ran afoul of the international community by supporting Saddam in the first Gulf War. Jordan's populace was heavily numbered with Palestinians who favored Saddam because of his support for the Palestinian cause. Subsequently, Jordan was punished by economic sanctions from many nations. Within a few years King Hussein would come to realize his error and move Jordan into agreements with Israel and would speak out against Saddam. This change of position had to hit Saddam as a betrayal by one of his few remaining supporters. Jordan would be added to his enemies list.

In November of 1999, Saddam's cronies were meeting with the Defense Minister of the Taliban, terror statesman Maulana Fazlur Rahman, Fazlur Rahman Khalil of the Taliban and al Qaeda, and Gulbidden Hekmatyar, an al Qaeda affiliate and terror camp operator.

In February of 1999, King Zayed's sons and other UAE royalty were in Afghanistan hunting falcons with bin Laden. We know a significant portion of the 9/11 money was transferred through the UAE. We also know some of the support personnel for the 9/11 attacks were located in the UAE.

So are all these things, all these meetings and events, interrelated? Is there a reason why two Arab regimes that were dealing directly with al Qaeda and the Taliban were holding secret meetings with them and each other just prior to the kick off of the millennium plot? Is this why Saddam promised not to attack the UAE if he attacked any other country? Was he in fact planning attacks on another country—Jordan and the U.S?

Two documents published at the Captain's Quarters blog of Ed Morrissey provide startling evidence when put into this context.

The following are original translations done by "Sammi" of the same source document posted on the CQ blog.

Translation follows for ISGZ-2004-018948:

In the name of God the most merciful

the most compassionate

Respectful Sir in charge of Fedayeen Saddam

My respects and regards, Sir:

In reference to your Excellency's orders dated May 20-25th, 1999 to start planning to perform special operations to include assassinations and bombings for the centers and the landmarks in London, Iran and other areas and to coordinate with the IIS for supplies, accommodations, and target selection. Also, I would like to show all the orders we have received from you with the explanations during the first and the second meetings with your Excellency to achieve the goal. (BIOT: In military parlance this might be a "brief back' which means you tell the commander what he just told you so that he knows you got it all.)

1- Code name of the special operations is Blessed July.

2- The duties will be divided into two branches which are:

    a. Bombings

    b. Assassinations

3- Tasks

    a. Select (50) fedayeen martyrs according to required specifications.

    b. Train them at the intelligence school to prepare them for the required duties.

4- After passing the tests they will be selected for the targets as follows:

    a. First: The first ten will work in the European field (London).

    b. Second: The second ten will be working in the Iranian field.

   c. Third: The third ten will be working in the self ruled area (BIOT: This is probably a reference to the Kurdish north.)

5- After passing the final test the fedayeens will be sent as undercover passengers to his region to prepare and to acquire from and coordinate with the Intelligence Apparatus and Mr.'Aiath.

6- After completion of step five above, the final plans for execution and are to be supervised by the Fedayeen Commander as per his orders.

7- Revisions of the plan, according to orders will be presented to the IIS Director as follows:

   a. The plan will be submitted to the Director for final comments.

   b. His changes will be made and the plan re-written.

   c. The final plan, including the execution timing should be written in two copies. One copy for senior officials and the other copy to be kept with the operations team until the orders are issued.

8- General subjects

   a. The execution order in Jordan is cancelled.

   b. The traitors must be followed (movements, residences, activities) in all locations during the operation.

   c. Possible addition of the Lebanese region. (BIOT: Adding Lebanon to the target set.)

   d. Reminders to use suicide pills if they are captured in Europe.

   e. Any problems

END Translation

This memo shows that Saddam was planning attacks in London to occur as part of a "blessed July" plot. Since the document was signed in May of 1999, and the martyrs had yet to be trained, it makes sense that these attacks were meant for the July of 2000 or later. Is this evidence of Saddam's own millennium plot? Notice that Saddam had canceled an operation in Jordan and ordered the "traitors" followed. It is quite possible the IIS had detected a spy and canceled the plot. The al Qaeda plot in Jordan was busted up a few months later. Very interesting coincidence. Where they the same plot?

It is also interesting to note that in July of 2005, London actually did became the target of a series of bombings. It was indeed a blessed July for the jihadists. The bombers were Brits of Pakistani ethnicity and had met with jihadists in Pakistan. At the trial of the men responsible for the failed attacks of July 25th, 2005 the prosecution showed a video of Ayman Al Zawahiri. In the video, he claimed that the men who perpetrated the July 7th bombings had been to a jihadist camp in Pakistan. These men had been trained by the same terrorists that were clearly tied to Saddam and later carried out an operation similar to that planned by Saddam. If one takes in to account that it is a hallmark of al Qaeda plans that they take some time to develop, it is quite possible that the London bombings first began as a coordinated millennium plot between the IIS and Zawahiri and that the plans finally manifested in July of 2005. Of course, the 2005 attacks were so far removed from the original plans they might be considered an independent operation, but the hand of Saddam is unmistakable with the revelation of this document.

This captured document more directly links the Saddam plot to the millennium plot.

Begin Translation for CMPC-2003-005935

In the Name of God the Most Merciful the Most Compassionate

The Presidency of the Republic

The Director of the Intelligence Service

Subject: Project Plan

Below are tasks for the plan for the year 2000 and the expenses for it in the year 2000 budget:

2. Prepare an armored brief case to protect the VIPs in 180 days.

3. Study the Epoxy currently used to prepare the explosives and the possibility of finding another type that will not affect the explosive.

4. Research for material that will increase the intensity of the explosive.

5. Prepare theoretical and applied training lessons on the explosives in 120 days.

6. Training of the Arab Fedayeen for the year 2000 plan.

7. Establish tournaments specialized in the explosives 30 days.

Please review and give guidance.

Signature...

Khaled Ibrahim Ismail

Senior Chemist

22/11/99

END Translation

In late 1999, Saddam is training "Arab Fedayeen" (codeword for non-Iraqi fighters trained in Iraq; Iraqis were called "Fedayeen Saddam") for "the plan of the year 2000" involving briefcase bombs. These documents together are strong evidence that Saddam had in place his own millennium plot that involved the West, Iran and Jordan which mirrors what Al Qaeda was doing at the time.

But does this mean that Saddam and al Qaeda were working together? Or is it simply coincidence that both had a plot that involved the West and Jordan at the same time? Is it a coincidence that Iraq and the UAE were planning a meeting in secret in Jordan shortly before the WMD plot on Amman? Is it a coincidence that in 2004, Jordanian intelligence busted up another al Qaeda WMD bomb plot in which the bomber claimed to have been trained in Iraq a full year before Saddam was toppled? Why did Saddam want to send "religious men" to the UAE to represent his supposedly secular regime? Exactly what Iraqi attacks was Saddam talking about?

Is it a coincidence that the U.S. anthrax attack occurred a week after 9/11 and the day after Saddam issued an alert for an impending "poison paper attack" in Iraq? Is it a coincidence that both the Saddam regime and the UAE kingdom were making deals with major leaders of the global Islamic jihad movement at this time? Is it a coincidence that Zawahiri was contracted by the IIS to attack U.S. forces in Somalia, that he also had close ties to the 93 WTC bombers including a bomb-maker who came from and fled back to Iraq, and now claims to know the bombers in the London "Blessed July" operation?

Or, are all these things glimpses of a plan by Saddam Hussein to use Islamic jihadists against the United States just as the CIA used them against the Soviets? In fact, such a plan might be viewed by Saddam as poetic justice.

CHAPTER 19:
IMPLICATIONS OF SADDAM'S SUPPORT TO ISLAMIC TERRORISM

THE IIS NOTEBOOK, CNS documents, and other relevant documents enhance the historical perspective of the Saddam regime in relation to the *global Islamic jihad movement*. They show that for many years the Saddam regime had good relations with significant leaders of Islamic jihad from Afghanistan, Pakistan, Egypt, Sudan, Algeria and Saudi Arabia. The records show that Saddam Hussein was an opportunist who plied money into jihad centric nationalistic opposition forces. These terror groups needed support to carry on their missions against their home country governments and their attacks mutually supported Saddam's objectives. If Saddam provided support to Usama bin Laden, the EIJ, the Maulana, Hekmatyar, al-Qaeda, Palestinian jihad streams and the Taliban, does that imply he was culpable in the spread of Islamic terrorism? Does that mean he was partially responsible for the 93 WTC attack, the Millennium Plot, the London bombings, the American Anthrax attacks, and 9/11?

The prospect of a Saddam regime providing support to Islamic terrorism is a fundamental reason for the war in Iraq. Democratic leaders have expressed the opinion that his general support to terrorism was not *casus belli* for war against Saddam. Indeed, some have expressed the opinion that nothing less than direct culpability for 9/11 specifically can justify the invasion. While this work does not provide absolute proof of direct culpability regarding 9/11, the knowledge provided by these captured documents can lead to a reexamination of the information already in the public domain. It tells us that at a very minimum Saddam put into place, supported, and assisted Islamic terrorism that would lead to 9/11. Even absent his intelligence service and funding, the London attacks still took place. Those attacks demonstrate that even without Saddam's direct support and knowledge of mission details his influence can still be felt.

The reporting available on the Maulana Fazlur Rahman demonstrates his leadership of the *global Islamic jihad movement*. The Pakistani organizations that make up the Islamic jihad-centric political parties allied under the MMA, the Muttahida Majlis-e-Amal or the United Action Front, are restated here for ease of reference. The Maulana is the Secretary General of the MMA. Global Security.org states that "MMA is an alliance composed of 4 powerful religious parties: Jamaat Islami (JI), Jamiat Ulema-e-Islam (F), Jamiat Ulema-e-Islam (S), and Jamiat Ulema-e-Pakistan (N)." Jammat Islami is known alternately as Jamaat-e-Islami or sometimes JeI or JEI.

A March 8th, 2004 report prepared for the U.S. Congress concerning international terrorism in South Asia indicates that the JUI, under the leadership of Maulana Fazlur Rahman was training al-Qaeda affiliated terrorists:

Madrassas and Pakistan Islamists.

A notable development in September 2003 was the arrest by Pakistani security forces of 19 Indonesian and Malaysian nationals at a Karachi madrassa (Islamic school). The men are suspected of running a sleeper cell of the Jemaah Islamiyah (JI) terrorist network in what would be the first indication that JI, a group linked to Al Qaeda, is operating in Pakistan. Among the approximately 10,000 madrassas in Pakistan are some that have been implicated in teaching militant anti-Western, anti-American, and anti-Hindu values. Many of these madrassas are financed and operated by Pakistani Islamist political parties such as Jamaat-e-Ulema Islam (JUI, closely linked to the Taliban), as well as by multiple unknown foreign entities. While President Musharraf has in the past pledged to crack down on the more extremist madrassas in his country, there is little concrete evidence that he has done so.

The Muttahida Majlis-e-Amal (MMA) –– a coalition of six Islamist opposition parties –– holds about 20% of Pakistan's National Assembly seats, while also controlling the provincial assembly in the North West Frontier Province (NWFP) and leading a coalition in the provincial assembly of Baluchistan. Pakistan's Islamists, including the leadership of some of their legal political parties, are notable for their virulent expressions of anti-American sentiment; they have at times called for "jihad" against what they view as the existential threat to Pakistani sovereignty that alliance with Washington entails.

K. Alan Kronstadt, Coordinator
Analyst in Asian Affairs
Foreign Affairs, Defense, and Trade Division
Bruce Vaughn
Analyst in Southeast and South Asian Affairs
Foreign Affairs, Defense, and Trade Division
[http://terrorisme.net/pdf/2004_terrorisminsouthasia.pdf]

The JUI is providing training in madrassas to Jemaah Islamiyah terrorists. The Jemaah Islamiyah is closely linked to Usama bin Laden and al-Qaeda and to Khalid Sheikh Mohammed, the mastermind behind 9/11. It also carried out the horrendous Bali bombings. Please note that the JI referred to in the report is the Jemaah Islamiyah of South East Asia, which has sent its fighters to the madrassas in Pakistan and is different from the Jamaat Islami (JI) indigenous to Pakistan under the MMA. The JI of SE Asia is overtly militant while the JI of Pakistan attempts to maintain political legitimacy. The Maulana continues to train al Qaeda terrorists even though Saddam's money no longer supports them. His legacy remains even though he was hanged shortly before the time of this writing.

A September of 2006 release by the Director of National Intelligence entitled <u>Detainee Biographies</u> provides the names and specific information about high-level terrorism detainees kept in U.S. detention facilities. One of them is described as having obtained safe houses for al-Qaeda leadership in Pakistan. This brings up a direct connection between the Maulana and 9/11. His political groups harbored the 9/11 ringleaders.

NAME

'Ali 'Abd al-'Aziz 'Ali

KEY ALIAS(ES)

'Ammar al-Baluchi

AFFILIATION

Al-Qa'ida

NATIONALITY

Baluchi born and raised in Kuwait

Pakistan-based al-Qa'ida operative 'Ammar al-Baluchi is a member of an extended family of extremists that has spawned such notorious terrorists as his detained uncle and 11 September mastermind Khalid

Shaykh Muhammad (KSM) and cousin and incarcerated World Trade Center bomber Ramzi Yousef. 'Ammar served as a key lieutenant for KSM during the operation on rr September and subsequently assisted his uncle on various plots against the United States and United Kingdom.

'Ammar, who is 29 years old, spent most of his teen years in Iran before moving to the United Arab Emirates (UAE) to work as a computer programmer in Dubai in 1998. Even before this move, he was gradually being influenced by his extremist relatives to become involved in terrorism: his chief mentor was Ramzi Yousef, who taught him in the early 1990s in Iran about the importance of war against the West. 'Ammar volunteered his services to KSM in 1997, and during 2000-2001 played an important role helping facilitate the operation on 11 September by transferring money to US-based operatives and acting as a travel facilitator to hijackers transiting the UAE on their way from Pakistan to the United States.

After the collapse of the Taliban in Afghanistan in late 2001. 'Ammar assisted KSM in organizing the movement of al-Qa'ida operatives and their families to safehouses in Pakistan. KSM also directed him at the forefront of planning for a variety of terrorist plots against the West, including:

• In late 2001 in Afghanistan, KSM directed 'Ammar to be the communications intermediary between al-Qa'ida and "shoe bombers" Richard Reid and Saajid Badat, in early 2002 in Pakistan. 'Ammar helped KSM prepare operatives for travel to the United States, ostensibly to carry out attacks.

• During 2002-2003 'Ammar also worked with KSM to prepare Majid Khan and others for travel to the United States to conduct terrorist operations. 'Ammar also sent Khan in late 2002 to Thailand to deliver $50,000 to finance plotting by Jemaah Islamiya leader Hambali against U.S. and Israeli targets in Southeast Asia.

- From late 2002. 'Ammar began plotting to carry out simultane-
ous attacks in Karachi against the U.S. Consulate. Western residences,
and Westerners at the local airport. After KSM's detention. 'Ammar
assumed responsibility for the plot to carry out hijacking attacks from
Heathrow Airport but decided to delay that plot until after the bombings in Karachi occurred. He was within days of completing prepara-
tions for the Karachi plot when he was captured.

- In 2002. 'Ammar directed Aafia Siddiqui — a US-educated neu-
roscientist and al-Qa'ida facilitator — to travel to the United States
to prepare paperwork to ease Majid Khan's deployment to the United
States.

'Ammar married Siddiqui shortly before his detention.

(http://www.dni.gov/announcements/content/DetaineeBiographies.
pdf)

Ammar al-Baluchi is an al-Qaeda operative, directly involved
in 9/11 via his uncle KSM who planned 9/11. After the U.S. invasion of Afghanistan, he helped to relocate key al-Qaeda members to safe houses in Pakistan. He did so with the assistance of
the Maulana's political parties. These safe houses were often the
homes of MMA members. Khalid Sheikh Muhammad himself
was captured at the home of a member of a Jamaat Islami (JI)
in Pakistan. Again, the JI is a powerful member of the MMA, of
which the Maulana is the General Secretary.

According to CBS News in an article entitled Mass Of Clues At
Terror Suspect's Home dated March 3rd, 2003:

Authorities recovered a huge amount of information about al Qaeda at the house in Pakistan where Mohammed and two others were arrested early Saturday. a senior law enforcement official said Monday.

Recovered at the home in Rawalpindi were computers, disks, cell phones and documents. Authorities believe the materials will provide names, locations and potential terrorist plots of al-Qaeda cells in the United States and around the world.

Khalid Sheikh Muhammad wasn't just passing through; judging by the reports the home contained a significant amount of his equipment and thus was most likely a base of operations as well as a safe house. This implies a significant commitment on the part of his hosts.

The *Christian Science Monitor* noticed the links between al-Qaeda and the Maulana's groups in a March 6th, 2003 article entitled Al Qaeda-Pakistani ties deepen by Gretchen Peters about the capture of KSM:

Officials here are quick to brag that local security forces nabbed Khalid Sheik Mohammed, along with another senior Al Qaeda leader, on their own. What they aren't crowing about is that Mr. Mohammed's arrest exposes a link between Al Qaeda and Pakistan's largest Islamic political party, Jamaat-e Islami.

The emerging connection highlights the political risks the Pakistani government faces as it hunts Al Qaeda leaders. It also implies a greater order of difficulty in rooting them out if thousands of Jamaat party members are willing to harbor terrorists in their homes.

Ahmed Abdul Qadoos, a Jamaat party member, was arrested alongside the two Al Qaeda terrorists. They had been holed up in the home of his mother, Farzana Qadoos, who is an elected district counselor for the conservative Islamic party.

Her residence, where the three men were arrested, is just five minutes from Army headquarters in this twin city to the nation's capital, and tucked in a guarded community that's home to top military officials. Officials say Mohammed had been coming and going from the home, apparently with little notice.

The party has also been implicated in other recent terror arrests. A Jamaat member was in the Karachi apartment where police found Al Qaeda leader Ramzi Binalshibh, and a doctor arrested in Lahore several months back for Al Qaeda ties was also linked to the party.

That's an uncomfortable fact for Pakistan, since Jamaat is a leading member in a coalition of hard-line Islamic parties that won control of two of Pakistan's four provinces in November elections and commands a sizable block in the National Assembly.

(http://www.csmonitor.com/2003/0306/p01s04-wosc.html)

Note that the *Christian Science Monitor* identified another significant al-Qaeda leader, Ramzi bin al Shibh (who was supposed to be a 9/11 hijacker but couldn't get a visa), was also captured with a JI member in Pakistan. Continuing with the article:

But senior officials here are starting to admit that they are finding growing links between the Jamaat and Al Qaeda terrorists on the run. "All of the activists and terrorists who have been apprehended in recent months have had links to the Jamaat-e-Islami, whether we have arrested them in Lahore or here or Karachi...." says Pakistan's Interior Minister Makhdoom Faisel Saleh Hayat. "They have been harboring them."

Pakistan's religious parties themselves are a reflection of official ties to terrorism here—which Mr. Musharraf insists have been severed since Sept. 11, 2001. Past administrations here nurtured and funded extremists groups both to wreak havoc in Kashmir, the neighboring state which both India and Pakistan claim, and also during the Soviet occupation of Afghanistan, when the CIA and Britain's MI6 funded the mujahideen to fight a holy war against the communist invaders.

Some of that extremism took root here. Though the fundamentalist parties in the past had more success organizing street protests than getting into Parliament, a five-party coalition of Islamic parties, known as the United Front, made stunning gains in last October's election, and now commands the third-largest block in the National Assembly. [Ibid]

Again, the United Front is the MMA of which the Maulana is the General Secretary. Back to the article:

Jamaat is the largest and most popular party in the group. It had focused most of its attention on Kashmir, not Afghanistan or the Taliban. But yesterday, a spokesman for the party told Reuters that Al Qaeda's third-in-command was "a hero to Islam."

"The Jamaat has never condemned 9/11, and denies that Al Qaeda is a terrorist organization. This is a group that believes 9/11 was carried out by Jews in America," says Ahmed Rashid, a Pakistani author on terror issues. "The really scary thing is that this is also the most moderate Islamic party in Pakistan." [Ibid]

The third-in-command "hero" mentioned in the article is Khalid Sheikh Muhammad, plotter of 9/11. Note that this expert states the JI has never condemned 9/11, signaling their support of it. Back to the article:

Some have even more direct links to terror. Many Front leaders run religious schools that sent young Pakistanis to fight alongside the Taliban and Al Qaeda in Afghanistan. The man who owns the Islamic

school where so-called "American Taliban" John Walker Lindh studied,
for example, is now a United Front senator.

As members of Parliament, these fundamentalist leaders enjoy immunity, though experts say they would have little access to sensitive
information about the hunt for terrorists here or the political power to
change Mr. Musharraf's policy to support the U.S. war on terror. [Ibid]

The senator referred to in the article is Maulana Fazlur Rahman, who was a leading member of the Pakistani Parliament and
represented the MMA at the time of this article. Considering that
Fazlur Rahman Khalil, leader of the HUM, a subgroup of the JUI
(the Maulana's core political group), and Shaykh Mir Hamzah, the
Leader of the JUP (under the Maulana's guidance), both signed
the 1998 *fatwa,* it would seem that the relationship between the
Islamic jihad-centric political parties of the MMA and al-Qaeda
is nothing new. However, the relationship only began to manifest
itself openly when al-Qaeda leaders needed safe houses after the
U.S. invaded Afghanistan and the Pakistani government began to
cooperate against al-Qaeda.

The *Christian Science Monitor* mentioned that Ramzi Bin al
Shibh was also found with a Jamaat Islami member. Ramzi is currently a U.S. detainee. Here is his detainee biography:

NAME

Ramzi Bin al-Shibh
KEY ALIAS[ES]
Abu Ubaydah, 'Umnr Muhammad 'Abdallah Ba' Amar

AFFILIATION

Al-Qa'ida

NATIONALITY

Yemeni

Ramzi Bin al-Shibh, a key facilitator for the attacks on 11 September 2001, was a lead operative — until his capture in 2002 — in the post-11 September plot conceived of by 11 September mastermind Khalid Shaykh Muhammad (KSM) to hijack aircraft and crash them into Heathrow Airport in the United Kingdom.

Bin al-Shibh was born in 1972 in southern Yemen. He noted that he was religious from the age of 12 and fought briefly in Yemen's civil war in 1994. After two attempts to immigrate to the United States failed, Bin al-Shibh traveled to Germany, where he applied for political asylum under an assumed name and as a Sudanese citizen. Denied his request for asylum in January 1996, he left Germany and returned to Yemen, where he applied for a visa in his true name. In December 1997, he returned to Germany, where he became a student. In Hamburg, he met hijackers Muhammad Atta, Marwan al-Shebhi, and Ziad Jarrah.

Bin al-Shibh, Atta, al-Shebhi, and Jarrah traveled to Afghanistan in 1999. In Afghanistan, the four men met Usama Bin Ladin, pledged their loyally to him, and readily accepted Bin Ladin's proposal to martyr themselves in an operation against the United States. Bin al-Shibh was slated to be one or the 11 September hijacker pilots. He and Atta traveled to Karachi, where they met with KSM.

• After returning to Germany in early 2000, Bin al-Shibh obtained a new passport but was unable to obtain a U.S. visa, despite four attempts. Bin al-Shibh said that in late 2000 he tried to convince a U.S. citizen in San Diego via e-mail to marry him to gain entry into the United States, but Atta convinced him to abandon the idea. During the eight months before the attacks, Bin al-Shibh was the primary communications intermediary between the hijackers in the United States and al-Qa'ida's leadership in Afghanistan and Pakistan. He relayed orders from al-Qa'ida senior operatives to Atta via e-mail or phone, and he met with Atta in Germany in January 2001 and in Spain in July 2001 for in-depth briefings from Atta on the progress of the plot. He also made travel plans to the United States for some of the 11 September terrorists and facilitated the transfer of money to the 11 September terrorists, including convicted terrorist Zacharias Moussaoui. After learning from Atta in late August 2001 of the date of the hijacking attacks, Bin al Shibh passed the information to KSM.

• A week before the 11 September attacks, Bin al-Shibh left Germany and arrived in Afghanistan three or four days after the attacks. In late 2001, he fled Afghanistan after the collapse of the Taliban and began working with KSM in Karachi on follow-on plots against the West, particularly the Heathrow plot. He was tasked by KSM to recruit operatives in Saudi Arabia for an attack on Heathrow Airport, and, as of his capture Bin al-Shibh had identified four operatives for the operation.

Ramzi was an essential member of the 9/11 plot who later turned up under the safeguard of the Maulana, just as KSM did. Is this a coincidence? Or is it evidence that the Maulana was providing significant support to the 9/11 plot? If the Maulana was directly involved does that qualify Saddam's support to the Maulana as support for 9/11?

Terrorism journalist B Rahman wrote the following in an article entitled JAMAAT-E-ISLAMI, HIZBUL MUJAHIDEEN & AL QAEDA for the *South Asian Analysis Group* on May 29th, 2003:

US intelligence officers posted in Pakistan have reportedly been making detailed enquiries into the likely links of the Jamaat-e-Islami

(JEI) of Pakistan headed by Qazi Hussain Ahmed with Al Qaeda of Osama bin Laden. These enquiries are reported to have been started following the arrest of Khalid Sheikh Mohammad, supposedly No. 3 in Al Qaeda, in March from the house of a women's wing leader of the JEI at Rawalpindi in an area where many serving and retired officers of the Pakistan Army live.

2. Earlier this year, two other suspected cadres of Al Qaeda were arrested from the house of another JEI member in Karachi. These arrests have given rise to a suspicion that JEI office-bearers and cadres not only in the North-West Frontier Province (NWFP) and Balochistan, but also in other parts of Pakistan have been helping the surviving members of Al Qaeda who crossed over into Pakistan from Afghanistan in the beginning of last year.

3. After the arrest of Khalid Sheikh Mohammad and his handing over to the USA's Federal Bureau of Investigation (FBI), Pakistan's Inter-Services Intelligence (ISI) had organised separate briefings for foreign and Pakistani journalists at the ISI headquarters. At those briefings, in response to questions about any links between the JEI and Al Qaeda, Maj. Gen. Rashid Quereshi, who was then the media spokesman of President Pervez Musharraf, had claimed that the fact that some Al Qaeda members were arrested from the houses of individual JEI members did not mean that the JEI as an organisation was having links with Al Qaeda.

4. However, the U.S. intelligence officers, who have been interrogating Khalid Sheikh Mohammad at a place outside Pakistan, do not appear to be convinced that this was just the rogue actions of some individual members of the JEI, of which the JEI leaders were not aware. Their concerns over possible links between the JEI and Al Qaeda have been heightened by the newly-established links of the Hizbe Islami (HI) of Gulbuddin Heckmatyar with Al Qaeda and the Taliban to harass the American troops in Afghanistan.

5. Of all the Islamic fundamentalist parties of Pakistan, the JEI had been the closest to the HI and had maintained contacts with Gulbuddin even when he and his associates were living in Iran with the knowledge of the Iranian Government. After 9/11, Teheran, under pressure from the US, expelled them from Iranian territory. They were welcomed in Pakistani territory by the JEI and sympathetic serving and retired officers of the ISI and given shelter in the border areas.

[http://www.saag.org/papers7/paper699.html]

Here again it is reported that the JI is under suspicion for involvement with al-Qaeda, with a twist. According to B Rahman, a well regarded terrorism researcher, the JEI (Jammaat-e-Islami is alternate for JI, same group) has a long standing relationship with the HI (Hizbe Islami) or Islamic Party, led by Hekmatyar who was also supported by the IIS and probably involved with the Somalia operation. Hekmatyar, a terror camp operator, and the Maulana, a leader of the umbrella group MMA, are all deeply tied to al-Qaeda and each other.

Another report from the *Christian Science Monitor* provides significant evidence that the Maulana was complicit in the 9/11 attacks. The report entitled <u>Al Qaeda planning next phase</u> by Mashall Lutfullah is dated December 28th, of 2001, just weeks after the U.S. invasion of Afghanistan. Mashall reports on a meeting with "Qari Ahmadullah, the Taliban's chief of intelligence and a top negotiator for Taliban leader Mullah Mohammad Omar." Mashall sets the stage for his interview:

The owner of the house, Malik Gulmarjan, warmly welcomes us, guiding us to his guesthouse near the entrance at the main gate of the compound. Three men armed with Kalashnikovs are seated on the floor, offering afternoon prayers. Pictures of Osama bin Laden and Mullah Fazal Rehman, the leader of Jamiat-ul-Ulema-e-Islam (JUI), Pakistan's largest and most influential religious party, hang on the walls. (http://www.csmonitor.com/2001/1228/p4s1-wosc.html)

The residence of the Taliban intelligence chief is adorned with pictures of Usama bin Laden and the Maulana. The article continues with a question about Usama bin Laden's reported death:

"That is baseless, absolutely baseless," Ahmadullah says. "Osama is alive, healthy, and safe. Last night our friends in Urozgan informed me by phone that he had met Osama somewhere near the border, and he said Osama was safe. He is always in close contact with Mullah Omar. (Ibid)

And Ahmadullah's details his own escape:

"It was really difficult to come into Pakistan," Ahmadullah continues. "But the cordial cooperation of our tribal Muslim brethren helped us come here. They even offered their own residential compounds to us to stay for a while, may Allah reward them in paradise!" (Ibid)

And who are these Muslim brethren he describes who helped the Taliban out of Afghanistan and gave them safe haven? He doesn't say specifically, but Mashall provides a strong clue:

Somewhere around 3:15 p.m., some tribal chiefs and several religious scholars from JUI come into the guesthouse. After they exchange greetings, Ahmadullah very politely asks the reporter to leave. "If you don't mind, please leave the room with our friends here. I have an important meeting with these people." (Ibid)

The JUI appears to have directly aided in the escape of Taliban and al-Qaeda operatives from Afghanistan. Unless we are to believe that the relationship between the MMA and its subgroups, al-Qaeda and the Taliban manifested itself shortly after the Taliban and al-Qaeda were on the run following the 9/11 attacks, it stands to reason they were involved at some level beforehand, just as they provided Usama bin Laden the 'religious authority' to wage war on America in 1998.

Steve Coll, author of *Ghost Wars*, a Pulitzer Prize winning narrative of al-Qaeda, the Taliban, and Afghanistan, provides further evidence of the collaboration between the Maulana's parties and Usama bin Laden directly:

> According to Badeeb, [a Saudi intelligence official] on bin Laden's first trip to Pakistan he brought donations to the Lahore offices of Jammaat-e-Islami, Zia's political shock force. Jamaat was the Pakistani offshoot of the Muslims Brotherhood...

Coll provides testimony that indicates Usama bin Laden himself was directly tied to the JI, the most powerful member of the MMA. He was paying them off to establish himself as a high roller in the Afghani jihad in the mid 80's. This provides an interesting indicator of just why these groups provided bin Laden his 'religious authority' for the 1998 *fatwa*—not just ideology but cold, hard cash. It also presents a precedent for Saddam Hussein—pay off the Maulana's groups and he might get their "religious authority" in the form of a religious edict calling for the end of U.N. sanctions.

There are other indications that cash is a sure way to buy oneself entry into the good graces of the Maulana. Noted Pakistani expert Mary Anne Weaver stated in an online interview with PBS's news show Frontline in November of 2002:

> ...Maulana Fazlur Rahman who, according to a spokesman from the Afghan Ministry of Defense, in the spring of this year, was instrumental in getting Osama bin Laden across the border, out of Afghanistan and into Pakistan; who considers Osama bin Laden to be the greatest jihadi who ever lived; who counts Mullah Mohammed Omar as one of his closest friends; who won, for all intents and purposes, a landslide in the Northwest Frontier Province, and even in the cities of Pakistan, with his viscerally anti-American platform; a man who, along with Mullah Omar, also counts the Libyan leader, Colonel Qaddafi, as one of his closest friends; who has been variously said by Western intelligence organizations to have been funded over the years by Libya, by Saudi Arabia, by Iran.
>
> (http://www.pbs.org/wgbh/pages/frontline/shows/search/etc/weaver.html)

If the Maulana was taking funding from another supposedly secular regime in Libya and a Shi'ite regime in Iran, there is every reason to believe he would take support from the Saddam regime especially when one of its own documents tells us so.

Another article from the *Asian Times* written by By Syed Saleem Shahzad and carried on October 15, 2002 entitled Elections Throw Pakistan's Iran, Iraq Ties in Focus, is one of the few public articles to directly link Maulana Fazlur Rahman to Saddam before the release of these documents:

> As far as Iraq is concerned, Saddam Hussein has traditionally focused his attention on the "nuisance" groups within Pakistan, rather

than deal with the government itself. Maulana Samiul Haq and Maulana Fazalur Rehman, the leaders of their own factions in the Jamiat-i-Ulema-i-Islam and members of the MMA, have very special relations with Iraq. Both have on many occasions been official guests of the Iraqi government. And Maulana Shah Ahmed Noorani also has close relations with Saddam. These men are reported to already have had private meetings with the Iraq ambassador to Pakistan. Further, the Iraqi government has contributed generously to many of the Islamic seminaries operated by these Pakistani religious leaders. Recently, at a graduation ceremony at Daralulom Akora Khatack (where Taliban leader Mullah Omar received his education), the Iraq ambassador was the chief guest.

[http://www.gvnews.net/html/DailyNews/alert2523.html]

According to this report, Ahmed Noorani, a former leader of the JUP, one of the groups that authorized the 1998 *fatwa*, was a close friend of Saddam as well. The article claims that the Saddam regime made generous contributions to the Islamic seminaries, or madrassas, run by these groups. It also notes the place of importance held by the Iraqi ambassador at a madrassa ceremony in Akora Khatack. As discussed previously, many of these groups and madrassas trained Taliban and al-Qaeda fighters.

An article from the *South Asia Intelligence Review* written by Ajai Sahni and carried November 27th, 2002 entitled Pakistan's New Government 'Takes Charge,' mentions Akora Khatack and also describes the bonds that tie the Maulana's groups and Islamic terrorism:

The leaders of the MMA are now "repackaging" themselves as democrats and parliamentarians, and it is crucial that the current avatar of the MMA as a democratic political party is not allowed to cloud

336

the history of its many constituent members, including several of its most prominent elected representatives, many of whom comprise the frontline of the terrorist leadership in Pakistan, and have direct linkages with Osama bin Laden, al-Qaeda and the Taliban. The most significant of these are the MMA's prime ministerial candidate, Fazlur Rehman of the JuI-Fazlur, Maulana Sami ul-Haq of the Jamaat-e-Ulema-e-Islam (Sami-ul-Haq faction) and Maulana Azam Tariq of the Sipah-e-Sahaba Pakistan (SSP).

Fazlur Rehman is generally believed to be a "supporter" of the Taliban. He—with Sami ul-Haq—was their creator and remained intimately linked with both Mullah Omar and bin Laden throughout the period of the Taliban regime in Afghanistan, and he spearheaded street demonstrations in Pakistan, vociferously protesting the American campaign in Afghanistan after September 11. He is also the creator of the banned terrorist organization Harkat-ul-Mujahideen (HuM, earlier called Harkat-ul-Ansar) and is closely linked with the activities of the Harkat ul-Jihad-i-Islami (HuJI), and the Jaish-e-Mohammed (JeM). HuM and HuJI are active in India, Bangladesh, Chechnya, the Arakan areas of Myanmar and southern Philippines, while the JeM is currently active only in India.

Sami ul-Haq, who heads his own faction of the JuI, runs the Haqqani madrassa (religious school) at Akora Khattak, which produced much of the Taliban leadership. Haq was the principal advisor to Mullah Omar and was closely associated with bin Laden.

(http://www.borrull.org/e/noticia.php?id=11652)

The interlinking of the Maulana's groups, al-Qaeda, and the Saddam regime has been demonstrated in Saddam's documents. With the least bit of reasoning and research we can find common cause (anti-Americanism and money) among these groups. While such linkage may not establish direct involvement in 9/11, it demonstrates an apparent alliance between the Saddam regime, the Maulana and his Pakistani groups, the Taliban and al-Qaeda. If Saddam was providing significant financial support to the Maulana, which is quite likely, such money was no doubt finding its way into al-Qaeda support operations.

We only need listen to the Islamic extremist's own words when they tell us they support Saddam Hussein to know the regime was more than capable of succeeding at its attempts to garner the support of Islamic extremists. Thus, there is no reason to believe that the Saddam regime could not have been providing direct support to al-Qaeda as well. When history judges whether or not Saddam had a hand in 9/11, it would do well to look at his ties to the Maulana as well as al-Qaeda.

The truly disturbing fact here is that while the documents and the specific evidences in them are new, what the evidence tells us isn't. After the start of OIF, the Democratic leadership de-linked Saddam from Islamic terrorism. They were backed by a few career intelligence professionals who had made names for themselves by providing new theories on Islamic fundamentalism after the 1993 WTC attack.

These officials began to de-link Sunni extremist terrorism from state sponsorship after the 1993 WTC attack to explain the 'new breed' of independent acting terrorist. The rise of Usama bin Laden seemed to fall right into the mold created around Ramzi Yousef in 1993 of an independently operating group of Islamic extremists who were too pious to work with Arab regimes which were not religious enough except for the Taliban. There have been public allegations that the "new breed of terrorist" was a theoretical cop-out to avoid having to respond against nations that backed terror. In other words, the new terrorism theory was not based on evidence but on political theory.

The irony here is that this supposed terrorist transformation happened within a few years of the end of the U.S. government effort to fund Islamic militants in the war against the Soviets. Before the WTC attack, they were taking state money (American, Saudi, Pakistani, anybody who offered) hand over fist. Practically the next day, it was theorized Sunni extremists wouldn't dream of taking money or aid from state sponsors, according to these officials.

However, in light of the new evidence, there is a much simpler explanation than the hypothesis that Sunni extremism transformed overnight. Support from state sponsors began flowing through third party arrangements to make it difficult to detect. Lack of detection was misinterpreted as lack of support. For instance, the a-Qaeda letter about the state of jihad mentions that Qadaffi of Libya built the jihadists a hospital. It is highly likely that the hospital was built through donations to legitimate nongovernmental groups like the Red Crescent. Al Zawahiri himself was a surgeon to the mujahideen at a Red Crescent hospital.

This is not to say that the Red Crescent organization is supporting terrorism. But it is a demonstration of how the state sponsorship to terrorism can work through third parties. This allows both sides to maintain deniability and to maintain their ideological credentials while working towards a common goal.

But this de-linking of Sunni extremism by certain CIA officials was not a government-wide phenomenon. The U.S. attorney's office in New York must have missed the memo because it linked al-Qaeda to Iraq in its indictment of Usama bin Laden. It said that Iraq was cooperating with weapons development with al-Qaeda. Though unstated, the obvious implication is WMD development. This is the exact scenario that the Bush Administration and Congress used to justify the use of force in Iraq in October of 2002—that Saddam might give WMD to terrorists.

UNITED STATES DISTRICT COURT

SOUTHERN DISTRICT OF NEW YORK

UNITED STATES OF AMERICA

- V-

USAMA BIN LADEN,

...2. Al Qaeda opposed the United States for several reasons. First, the United States as regarded as "infidel" because it was not governed in a manner consistent with the group's extremist interpretation of Islam. Second, the United States was viewed as providing essential support for other "infidel" governments and institutions, particularly the governments of Saudi Arabia and Egypt, the nation of Israel and the United Nations, which were regarded as enemies of the group. Third, Al Qaeda opposed the involvement of the United states armed forces in the Gulf War in 1991 and in Operation Restore Hope in Somalia in 1992 and 1993. In particular, Al Qaeda opposed the continued presence of American military forces in Saudi Arabia (and elsewhere on the Saudi Arabian peninsula) following the Gulf war. Fourth, Al Qaeda opposed the United States Government because of the arrest, conviction and imprisonment of persons belonging to Al Qaeda or its affiliated terrorist groups, including Sheik Omar Abdel Rahman.

...In addition, al Qaeda reached an understanding with the government of Iraq that al Qaeda would not work against that government and that on particular projects, specifically including weapons development, al Qaeda would work cooperatively with the Government of Iraq.

...h. At various times from in or about 1992 until the date of the filing of this Indictment, USAMA BIN LADEN and other ranking members of Al Qaeda stated privately to other members of Al Qaeda that Al Qaeda should put aside its differences with Shiite Muslim terrorist organizations, including the Government of Iran and its affiliated terrorist group Hezballah, to cooperate against the perceived common enemy, the United States and its allies;

(http://www.fas.org/irp/news/1998/11/98110602_nlt.html)

The indictment also provides some information that supports the theory that the Saddam regime and al-Qaeda could have worked together directly. The indictment makes mention that al-Qaeda, Sunni extremists, had put aside their differences with the Shi'a terrorists to work against the US. Because the Shi'ites are considered infidels by the Sunni extremists, it provides an indicator that they would be even more disposed to work with the Sunni backed Ba'athists in Iraq.

The indictment states, "Second, the United States was viewed as providing essential support for other "infidel" governments and institutions, particularly the governments of Saudi Arabia and Egypt..." Again, the main common purpose of the leaders of al-Qaeda is to overthrow their own governments so that they can establish an Islamic Caliphate. After 9/11, so many Americans asked 'why do they hate us?'

This is the answer; the U.S. provides an enormous amount of military aid to the governments that they want to overthrow. In their view, U.S. policy is the only thing keeping the Wahhabis of Saudi Arabia and the Islamic Jihad of Egypt out of power.

When Zawahiri and bin Laden use 'US policy' to justify their terrorism, what they are truly talking about is American military assistance to Egypt and Saudi Arabia. This is why Usama bin Laden saw the U.S. as his principle enemy; American troops in Saudi

Arabia propped up the Saudi Arabian government which wanted to depose. The U.S. support of the Saudi Arabian and Egyptian governments is the real war for al-Qaeda leadership, not the U.S. support of Israel.

Toppling the Saddam regime was way down on the al-Qaeda 'to do list'. Until the U.S. took out Saddam, they were happy to sit by and enjoy Saddam's suppression of the Shi'ites. For if Saddam fell, they feared Iraq would fall under the influence of Iranian Shi'ites, a bad situation for al-Qaeda. This is exactly what motivates them to team up with Ba'athist remnants to fight coalition forces in Iraq today—to keep the Sunnis (even if it is in the form of Ba'athists) in power and to reduce American public support for engagement in the Middle East thus end support to Egypt and Saudi Arabia.

The question should also be asked, why would al-Qaeda work with Saddam? Usama bin Laden may have grudgingly accepted Saddam's cause at the urging of the Pakistani 'religious authority' and Ayman al Zawahiri by rationalizing it in the name of the Iraqi people, which in reality meant Sunni Muslim domination in Iraq over Shi'a. Documents indicate the enormous amount of money Saddam provided those who cooperated with him in Afghanistan. Lots of cash would have helped. Toppling Saddam was not a short-term goal of al-Qaeda. It was a long-term goal.

Understanding the true motivations of Islamic terrorists is always difficult because they lie. But a theoretical list of priorities from their perspective helps to understand the decision making process for Sunni extremists:

- Side with those who seek to depose the SA and Egyptian governments if only until those governments are toppled.

- Fight those who provide support to SA and Egyptian governments, chiefly the U.S. to drive them away from SA and Egypt.
- Overthrow SA and Egyptian governments to start a Caliphate in those countries.
- Establish a Caliphate across Northern Africa and the Arabian Peninsula from which launch full-scale war against the Shi'a and secular Arab regimes to secure the entire Middle East and expand in Africa.
- Establish a Caliphate across all of Northern Africa and the Middle East to wage war against Christians and Jews (and all other none Muslims), converting them to Islam.

Their long term goal is to conquer the west but the attacks on America now are meant to drive the U.S. out of the Middle East, not defeat the west immediately. They do not expect terrorist attacks to defeat the U.S. now. They expect it to scare the U.S. out of Muslim lands. They have few rules to achieve their goals. They can be summed up as:

- Any Sunni over a Shi'ite.
- Any Muslim over Christians.
- Use the enemy's resources against them.

By their logic, it is proper, or even desired, to use an infidel (Shi'ite, non-Muslim or secularist) or his resources to defeat that infidel or another infidel as long as it progresses the goal of establishing the Caliphate and defeating the west. That is their ideology instead of refusing aid from the enemy. Even if they truly viewed the Saddam regime as the enemy, Salafi/Sufi extremists would have been happy to take its money to use against them later.

In Afghanistan, Usama bin Laden was happy to take the Saudi government's money to train jihadists to fight the Soviets, even though he considered the SA government the enemy. There is no reason to believe they would reject Iraqi money, especially if it came via a pious third party. Why on earth would they?

How did the Saddam regime fit into al-Qaeda's priorities? Saddam would have helped al-Qaeda against Saudi Arabia, Egypt, and the U.S.—the three main enemies of al-Qaeda. That could do a lot to overcome the secular-Islamic divide. Saddam would have helped al-Qaeda's objectives by maintaining Sunni domination over Iraq and would have been a backstop against the Iranian Shi'ites. Saddam also had the support of the Palestinians, people al Qaeda viewed as a diaspora of fellow jihadists that infused their ranks.

However the sanctimonious leaders of the *global Islamic jihad movement* would surly not want to publicize their ties to the infidel Saddam. So al-Qaeda would reciprocate to governments like the Saddam regime by providing subtle support, like a *fatwa* in the name of the Iraqi people and not to Saddam even though it would have unquestionably strengthened his regime to lift U.N. sanctions. If Usama bin Laden's true goal was to overthrow Saddam he should have demanded tougher action by the UN, not less.

Do these theoretical musings match up with reality? The Jewish Virtual Library has an extensive biography of Ayman al Zawahiri:

Upon reestablishing themselves in Afghanistan in 1996, the two leaders bin Laden and Zawahiri began articulating the position of Al-Qa'ida vis-à-vis the United States. They concluded that America was the Number One enemy of Muslims everywhere and that its support of some Arab regimes, mainly Saudi Arabia and Egypt, has been responsible for the failed efforts to topple those regimes. It was at the end of

1997 that bin Laden and Al-Zawahiri declared war on Americans every-where, after an initial statement of war in 1996 against the American presence in the region only. Afterwards, the objectives were expanded. On 23 February 1998 bin Laden issued a declaration announcing the creation of "The World Islamic Front for Jihad against Jews and the Crusaders [Christians].

[http://www.jewishvirtuallibrary.org/jsource/biography/Zawahiri.html]

As a side note, a section of this biography illuminates a controversial issue. President Bush has been criticized for resorting to simplistic platitudes by claiming the Islamic terrorists hate us because of our freedoms. From the biography:

In his book, Al-Hisad Al-Murr [The Bitter Harvest] Al-Zawahiri articulates his violence-driven and inherently anti-democratic instincts. He sees democracy as a new religion that must be destroyed by war. He accuses the Muslim Brotherhood of sacrificing Allah's ultimate authority by accepting the notion that the people are the ultimate source of authority.

President Bush has made a legitimate argument according to Zawahiri's own writing. While there certainly are other reasons for them to hate us (like U.S. support to Egypt), there is nothing incorrect in stating that the Islamic terrorists hate us because of our freedoms.

The Federation of American Scientists website has an entry on al-Qaeda in which it explains al-Qaeda's motivation:

Al-Qa'ida's goal is to "unite all Muslims and to establish a government which follows the rule of the Caliphs." Bin Laden has stated that the only way to establish the Caliphate is by force. Al-Qa'ida's goal, therefore, is to overthrow nearly all Muslim governments, which are viewed as corrupt, to drive Western influence from those countries, and eventually to abolish state boundaries.

[http://www.fas.org/irp/world/para/ladin.htm]

[Several dozen references listed at the website.]

A Congressional report (RL32759) from January of 2006 entitled *Al Qaeda: Statements and Evolving Strategy,* includes the following statement about Usama bin Laden's beliefs in relation to the war in Iraq:

Politically, he has encouraged Islamist insurgents in Iraq to work with "Socialist" groups (Baathists) and compared cooperation between Islamists and Baathists to Arab and Persian collaboration against the Byzantine Empire in the 7th and 8th centuries.

Study author:

Christopher M. Blanchard

Analyst in Middle Eastern Affairs

Foreign Affairs, Defense, and Trade Division

[http://www.fas.org/irp/crs/RS21973.pdf]

Bin Laden himself has justified cooperation with Ba'athists in order to drive the U.S. from the Middle East. He favors collaboration with Shi'ites over non-Muslims as evidenced by his Byzantine reference. There is no reason to conclude this would not have been his position before the Iraq war. It is also worth noting that his statements reflect the directives of the *Insurgency Plan.*

Yet al-Qaeda clearly favors the Sunni's over the Shi'ites. A CNN report from July2, 2006 entitled Tape: Bin Laden tells Sunnis to fight Shiites in Iraq, demonstrates al-Qaeda prioritization:

Osama bin Laden in a tape posted on the Web encourages Sunnis in Iraq to retaliate against Shiites, deviating from al Qaeda's stand of not promoting sectarian violence. The al Qaeda leader says that Sunnis in Iraq are experiencing annihilation. Bin Laden also says that the only way for them to win freedom is by "holding on to their jihad" and ousting the occupying power from Iraq.

[http://www.cnn.com/2006/WORLD/meast/07/02/binladen.message/index.html]

The hypothetical prioritization of al-Qaeda's goals is well founded in relevant reporting. Understanding the motivation of al-Qaeda can provide insight into its decision making process and help to determine if al-Qaeda would or would not be opposed to coordinating with Iraqi Ba'athists, as bin Laden himself has publicly urged. There is no valid reason to conclude al-Qaeda would not work with the Saddam regime as long as such support was secret.

As for Saddam, there is no reason to believe he would not work with Islamic jihadists to attack U.S. forces in Somalia and elsewhere just as the U.S. government funded Islamic jihadists against the Soviets in Afghanistan. And once he was connected to the EIJ, and to al-Qaeda, and to the NIF, there is no reason to believe he would abandon those relationships. After all, with the seemingly never-ending sanctions which tied his hands in Iraq he might just need these "Arab and Asian Muslim friends" again as they were both in one trench.

We find, based on the documentation and supporting information in the public domain, that while Saddam's direct involvement in 9/11 is not proven, there is sufficient evidence to determine that the Saddam regime was at a minimum a financial supporter of Islamic terrorism specifically for the groups that had a hand in attacking the U.S. on 9/11—al Qaeda, the Taliban, and the Islamic jihad-centric political parties of Pakistan all played central roles. While we cannot find the Saddam regime directly responsible for 9/11 (although it is by no means ruled out), and it is possible the attacks may have happened without the Saddam regime's assistance anyway his culpability is still evident.

* * *

ABOUT THE AUTHORS

Ray Robison, as a former member of the Iraqi Survey Group, is uniquely qualified to speak about these documents and the exploitation process. He worked to analyze, digitize, and archive these documents under subcontract with the Defense Intelligence Agency. He is currently a Military Analyst doing missile research in Huntsville, Alabama. A former army officer with over ten years of military duty, Robison served in the Gulf War and Kosovo. He holds a B.S. in Biology from the University of Tampa. Robison's work has been featured on Fox News, *The American Thinker*, Rush Limbaugh.com, and many other notable political websites.

Richard Dunaway served on active duty in the U.S. Army as an operations officer. He has worked with counterterrorism-homeland security issues as a military intelligence officer. Dunaway was activated for Operation Noble Eagle for three years, and he was awarded two commendation medals for meritorious service. His civilian experience includes service as a consultant to the Marine Corps and Navy for advanced technology, acquisition, operational, and program management issues. He also served as an engineering consultant to the Navy for the design and production of the LPD17 class of amphibious assault ships. He was recently a Military Operations Research Analyst with a major defense contractor in Huntsville, Alabama. Dunaway is a graduate of the U.S. Military Academy at West Point, and he holds a master's degree in international relations from Troy State University.

"Sammi al-Hadir" lived in the Middle East for many years before immigrating to the United States. He loves his adopted home.